Playful Visions

Playful Visions

Optical Toys and the Emergence of Children's Media Culture

Meredith A. Bak

The MIT Press
Cambridge, Massachusetts
London, England

© 2020 Massachusetts Institute of Technology

All rights reserved. No part of this book may be reproduced in any form by any electronic or mechanical means (including photocopying, recording, or information storage and retrieval) without permission in writing from the publisher.

Grateful acknowledgement is given to the Rutgers Research Council for a subvention and grant. A different version of chapter 6 was published in *Early Popular Visual Culture* 10, no. 2 (2012): 147–167. An earlier portion of the introduction was published as "The Ludic Archive: The Work of Playing with Optical Toys" in *Film History* 16, no. 1 (2016): 1–16.

This book was set in Stone Serif and Stone Sans by Westchester Publishing Services. Printed and bound in the United States of America.

Library of Congress Cataloging-in-Publication Data is available.

ISBN: 978-0-262-53871-8

10 9 8 7 6 5 4 3 2 1

For my parents, Pat and Vic Bak,
and for Jordan and Lars

Contents

Acknowledgments ix

Introduction: The Ludic Archive 1

1   Templates, Toys, and Text: Optical Toys in Nineteenth-Century Children's Culture 31

2   Language in Motion: The Thaumatrope Establishes a Multimedia Convention 57

3   Seeing Things: Optical Play at Home 83

4   Movable Toy Books and the Culture of Independent Play 119

5   Color Education: From the Chaotic Kaleidoscope to the Orderly Spectrum 151

6   Democracy and Discipline: Object Lessons and the Stereoscope in American Education, 1870–1920 181

7   Conclusion: Oversized Optics in the Digital Age 209

Notes 227
Index 269

Acknowledgments

This project benefited from many kinds of support from many people. It got underway in the intellectually adventurous context of the graduate program in Film and Media Studies at the University of California, Santa Barbara (UCSB). Thanks to my dear friends and colleagues from that time, including Ryan Bowles Eagle, Hye Jean Chung, Anastasia Hill, Regina Longo, Rahul Mukherjee, Josh Neves, Dan Reynolds, Jeff Schieble, Nicole Starosielski, Athena Tan, and Ethan Tussey. To my wonderful dissertation committee, who supported this project even as it cascaded beyond disciplinary conventions and boundaries: Cristina Venegas, Greg Siegel, Lisa Parks, and Bishnupriya Ghosh. Peter Bloom's belief in this project at the beginning, ongoing mentorship, and friendship have made all the difference. Thanks to him, I understood the importance of approaching this work with curiosity and rigor for as long as it took. I benefited from the vision and support of the film and media studies faculty at UCSB, including Jen Holt, Bhaskar Sarkar, Janet Walker, and Chuck Wolfe. My interests in optical toys were also stoked in Antonia Lant's seminar on Archives, Museums, and Collections at NYU, and working in the Education Department at the Museum of the Moving Image in New York City, where I met lifelong friends (and my spouse).

In the research phase, I am indebted to so many museum and library professionals for showing interest in my work, facilitating access to often challenging objects, and for their patience when I was an inexperienced (but enthusiastic) researcher. The support of a UCSB Dean's Fellowship allowed me to begin my initial research on the East Coast. Thanks to Patricia Hogan, Carol Sandler, and Victoria Gray at the Strong National Museum of Play and Todd Gustavson at the George Eastman House, both in Rochester,

New York. A research grant from Friends of the Princeton Library permitted me to spend a month at the Cotsen Children's Library in Princeton, where I benefited from the guidance and expertise of Andrea Immel and Julie Mellby, whose engagement with my work opened up entirely new possibilities. Thanks also to Aaron Pickett, Ian Dooley, AnnaLee Pauls, and Squirrel Walsh at Princeton.

With support from the Albert and Elaine Borchard Foundation, I traveled to Europe for archival research. Francesco Modolo and Laura Minici Zotti were generous with their time and space at the Museo del Precinema. Many thanks to Raffaella Isoardi at the Museo Nazionale del Cinema in Turin and to Antonella Angelini at the Museo Nazionale's Mario Gromo Library. At the Bill Douglas Cinema Museum at the University of Exeter, Phil Wickham introduced me to many treasures and offered valuable direction. Thanks also to Catherine Howell at the Victoria and Albert Museum of Childhood in Bethnal Green. I spent a month at the American Antiquarian Society in Worcester, Massachusetts, with the support of a Jay and Deborah Last Fellowship, and it was here that many of the pieces of this project began taking shape. Thanks to the intellectual community there, including Laura Wasowicz, curator of children's literature, for sharing her enthusiasm and opening up the world of McLoughlin Brothers to me, Lauren Hewes, Elizabeth Pope, and Marie Lamoureux. Thanks also to Paul Erickson for facilitating such an intellectually rigorous and collegial environment.

Writing and development for this project was supported through numerous fellowships and invitations to engage with intersecting scholarly communities that each informed the book in distinct ways. An Artemis A. W. and Martha Joukowsky Postdoctoral Fellowship at the Pembroke Center for Teaching and Research on Women at Brown University provided a context to gain new perspective on this project. Many thanks to Tim Bewes and Debbie Weinstein, Nadine Boljkovac Berressem, Amber Musser, and the members of the Economies of Perception Pembroke Seminar. At Brown, I was lucky to meet wonderful friends and collaborators, including Michelle Cho and Maggie Hennefeld. Thank you as well to supportive colleagues and friends at Franklin and Marshall College, where I taught in the Department of Theatre, Dance, and Film, including Jeremy Moss, Brian Silberman, Pam Vail, and Dirk Eitzen. My year as a faculty fellow at the Wolf Humanities Center at the University of Pennsylvania during the year themed "Color," resulted in a new chapter for this book. Thanks especially to Jim English

Acknowledgments

and Chi-ming Yang. I was also very fortunate to participate in the 2015 National Endowment for the Humanities Summer Institute in American Material Culture: Nineteenth-Century New York at the Bard Graduate Center led by the late David Jaffee, who was an incredibly generous mentor. During my month at Bard, conversations with David, Catherine Whalen, and Kasey Grier were critical in framing my project. The institute also gave shape to a new chapter of this book. This book also received support from the Rutgers Research Council. Finally, thanks to the collegial community and especially the staff at the New York Society Library, where the draft came together. Special thanks to Susan Buckley, Noah Springer, and Liz Agresta at the MIT Press for their incredible support.

I marvel at my good fortune to work in the Department of Childhood Studies at Rutgers University–Camden with such generous genius colleagues. I am so grateful to work with the faculty, students, and staff at Rutgers, and especially grateful for how we work together. Special thanks to Susan Miller for valuable feedback, Lynne Vallone and Lauren Silver for their advice and support near the completion of this project, and my graduate student research assistants, Katie Fredericks and Heather Reel. Thanks, of course, to my first teachers of film. To Dean Duncan, for introducing me to children's media, and Amy Petersen Jensen, for introducing me to media education—and to both for their mentorship and care. Thanks also to Darl Larsen, Daryl Lee, and Sharon Swenson. My time in your classrooms transformed me.

Thank you, Stephen, for your friendship, which I cherish. Thanks to my parents, Pat and Vic Bak; to my sister Kathryn "Noodles" Weber; and to my brother Nathan "Cho" Bak, whose feedback on every draft allowed me to finish. My greatest joy and all my love to my wife, Jordan, and our son, Lars. I am endlessly thankful for the life that we've built and share together.

Introduction: The Ludic Archive

My introduction to optical toys, like many other scholars of film, was in the first chapters of my introductory film textbooks. There, these nineteenth-century playthings were mentioned as points of origin in a chronological succession culminating in the technology and institution of cinema.[1] The thaumatrope (1825) is a square or round card with part of an image printed on each side (a bird and a cage, for example). When spun on two strings, the two images combine into a single composite. The phenakistoscope (1832) arrayed a sequence of ten or twelve images (a spinning dancer, for instance) around the perimeter of a slotted disk. When the disk is spun and the images' reflections are viewed through the slots, they appear to move as a smooth, animated sequence. The zoetrope (1834) used a slotted drum and changeable paper strips to animate its image sequences, while the praxinoscope (1877) replaced the slotted shutter mechanism with a prismatic mirror (figure 0.1) These toys demonstrated a perceptual phenomenon advanced during the nineteenth century known as *persistence of vision*—a theory that when the eye is exposed to an image, the image remains on the retina for a fraction of a second after the stimulus that produced it is removed.[2] If a series of images depicting incremental phases of movement is presented to the eye rapidly enough, the brain assembles them into a fluid animated sequence. In this way, optical toys contributed to the trajectories of both vision research and media culture that would include motion pictures by the late nineteenth century.

This technological and industrial lineage has largely defined how optical toys are understood in historical context, yoked to the greater invention of cinema. Today, optical toys appear in museums to tell this story. As a member of the Education Department at the Museum of the Moving

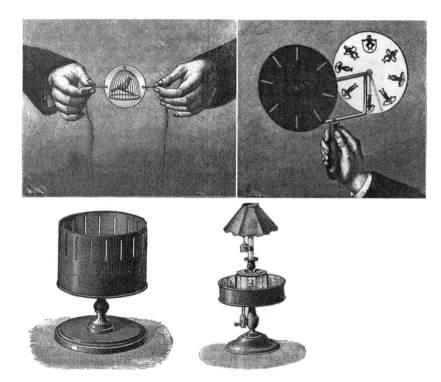

Figure 0.1
Clockwise from top left: thaumatrope, phenakistoscope, zoetrope, praxinoscope. Printed in Gaston Tissandier, *Popular Scientific Recreations* (New York: W. H. Stelle & Co., 1883), 122–126.

Image in New York from 2005 to 2007, I observed thousands of visitors interact with these toys, manipulating them and delighting in their visual effects. I assisted scores of schoolchildren in constructing their own toys—selecting motifs for thaumatropes, carefully aligning the images—creating and consuming personal media experiences. Through these encounters, I came to see that while optical toys play a central role in the history of cinema, they have contributed to a much broader project of shaping children as media audiences and producers. Initially marketed as educational toys, optical devices were part of a wider pedagogical paradigm that stressed the ability to interpret, analyze, and scrutinize visual material.[3] Such skills were thought to prepare the child for modern life: the youth to whom optical toys were targeted would go on to assume a range of occupations both inside and outside the home, destined to become professionals who balance ledgers, oversee factory floors, perform surgeries, tend to needlework, coordinate the colors of household goods, and interpret dynamic traffic patterns.[4] Today, these toys continue to appear in educational toy stores and museums, widely produced and sold under the auspices of STEM/STEAM (science, technology, engineering, art, and math) education. As old media repackaged and reborn, today they address a new set of twenty-first-century needs, encouraging kids to tinker, solve problems, and create (rather than consume) media.

This book tells the story of optical toys as elements of children's media culture. Distinct—but not entirely divorced—from cinema, these toys have endured as educational playthings and played a role in teaching children to see the world and themselves in it. Accordingly, this book examines the earliest encounters children had with the moving image, three-dimensional technologies, and interactive books. It investigates how these optical media both responded to concerns over children's vision and modeled new visual habits at home and at school that came to be regarded as basic perceptual competencies. This historical account thus also helps us understand contemporary children's media culture, where new technologies and the knowledge and habits they cultivate continue to be invested with multiple meanings.

This work is energized by an unlikely set of shared critical commitments in two disparate fields. A vexing question persists at the multidisciplinary heart of childhood studies: "How do we attend to both the physical and imaginary child?"[5] In many ways, there exists an unspoken hierarchy between children as subjects and collaborators in empirical research, who bear the urgent charge of the "real," and the child figure at the center of much humanistic inquiry: the historical child, the literary or cinematic child. This division—seen, for instance, in funding disparities or policy-making priorities—belies assumptions about what questions, archives, and methods are most socially pressing. Yet it is an unfortunate and false division, for actual children's lives are profoundly shaped by powerful (often contradictory) cultural narratives of childhood. This challenge mirrors the work of media archaeologists, who endeavor "to construct alternate histories of suppressed, neglected, and forgotten media" through the study of both actual technologies and those that exist only discursively—the creative, ambitious, or failed media that we imagine at various historical moments.[6] These two strands of inquiry share an abiding belief that subjects, whether children or media, matter not only if they "grow up," or are actualized through markers of success like adulthood or production as consumer products, but are important on their own terms. As this book demonstrates, both largely forgotten media and the historical children who played with them shaped the contours within which children's media culture is still understood today. "The excavation of manifold pasts," Thomas Elsaesser contends, is also an approach to "generating an archaeology of possible futures."[7]

Common to the intellectual projects of childhood studies and media archaeology is a push back against normative developmental frameworks and "chronological history (especially the *infancy-adolescence-maturity-decline* narrative)."[8] "Rejecting biological schema of infancy and maturity," Tom Gunning argues, has enabled researchers to explore historical change as "a jagged rhythm of competing practices."[9] Such a critical orientation often requires turning to new archives and embracing new approaches. These shared investments in uncovering subjects and stories that have slipped through the cracks, in making surprising connections across eclectic constellations of evidence, lead practitioners in these fields to value archives of "the scrap and the scribble," ephemera, "fragments and … traces from the dust and residue of fireplaces, burial grounds, or waste grounds" to illuminate new stories.[10] These overlapping methodological proclivities and philosophical orientations are not coincidental. As this book explores, the constructions of both childhood and media culture in the nineteenth century were mutually supportive.

The archival research at the center of this work reflects the adventurous and playful provocations issued by practitioners in media archaeology and the histories of childhood and material culture. Robin Bernstein's characterization of the archive as "a ghostly discotheque where things of the past leap up to ask scholars to dance" rang true as I spent days with gloved hands in the offsite storage vault of the Museo Nazionale del Cinema in Turin assembling phenakistoscopes and spinning the disks (several of which literally depict dancers in motion).[11] In the basement of the Victoria and Albert Museum in London, I twirled thaumatropes that reanimated nineteenth-century visual puns. At the American Antiquarian Society in Massachusetts and the Cotsen Children's Library at Princeton, I carefully unfolded intricate toy books, which cascaded beyond the confines of their foam supports. At the George Eastman House in Rochester, New York, I watched as a projecting praxinoscope's spinning drum sent a luminous scene onto the wall. Within collections of media, science, and childhood, optical toys appear in a wider historical frame, valued not only for their relation to cinema, but interconnected with a range of visual and material cultures: parlor games and home science experiments, children's periodicals, movable toy books, colorful prints, jigsaw puzzles, valentines, and spinning tops. Optical toys were central to this rich playscape, where new visual vocabularies were established and new spectatorial practices made routine.

The Toy Cupboard as Educational Inventory

Edmund Evans's engraved frontispiece of T. William Erle's 1877 book *Children's Toys, and Some Elementary Lessons in General Knowledge Which They Teach* depicts a dense tableau of children's playthings arranged in a cupboard (figure 0.2). Among familiar nineteenth-century toys such as dolls, kites, spinning tops, model ships, a hoop and stick, and a shuttlecock, a series of optical toys is prominently featured. A zoetrope and its paper picture strips are at the center of the image below a mechanical doll. The zoetrope is flanked by two thaumatropes. A phenakistoscope is displayed below, alongside a kaleidoscope, telescope, and magnifying glass. Many of these toys were commercially introduced in the first third of the nineteenth century. They offered children new ways of seeing the world by extending the scope and scale of the visible, reflecting, and refracting everyday sights in kaleidoscopic arrangements and orienting them to the moving image. Erle's book, also published in at least one other edition as *Science in the Nursery; or, Children's Toys, and What They Teach*,[12] is written in a format common to nineteenth-century juvenile recreational literature. Each chapter is devoted to a particular toy or group of toys, describing its construction and related lessons in optics, physics, or other scientific principles. The prominence of optical toys in the frontispiece mirrors the book's contents, which devotes two of its twelve chapters to such devices. Erle's book and its frontispiece situate optical toys not within other forms of popular visual media or entertainments, but in the nursery as central components of the well-educated child's playscape. These toys both facilitated and responded to changing conceptions of childhood in the nineteenth century as a time of growth and development, which placed new emphasis on play as the child's work. Such optical devices represent a unique link between emerging and uneven conceptions of childhood as a time of innocence and new practices of media

Figure 0.2
Edmund Evans, frontispiece from T. William Erle's *Children's Toys, and Some Elementary Lessons in General Knowledge Which They Teach* (London: C. Kegan Paul, 1877).

spectatorship. The hopes and preoccupations shared by nineteenth-century parents and educators intent on selecting the right media for learning and play bear striking resemblance to contemporary aspirations and concerns. Today, debates surrounding screen time, what constitutes "educational" media, and the commercial imperatives underlying consumer and institutional technology adoption continue to animate public discourse on children and media.[13]

The following chapters chart the interplay of optical toys and related media with other forms of the visual and material culture of childhood throughout the nineteenth century and into the twentieth. In public science demonstrations, the home, and school, optical devices modeled the performance of media spectatorship for children, who were both savvy and aware of how the devices worked, and also taken by the spectacular effects produced. Just as contemporary child consumers are characterized as competent and empowered or seduced by the commercial ills of new technology, nineteenth-century optical play was also a social and commercial practice—largely coded as edifying—that occurred alongside other forms of entertainment and instruction, from parlor games to object lessons. Optical toys participated in manifold educational practices ranging from informal games at home to formal pedagogical exercises in schools.

Unlike many books on juvenile recreational literature, which assumed urban, middle-class readerships, Erle's *Children's Toys*, which so prominently features optical toys, was instead addressed to "gentlefolk" in "country districts," in order "to lighten for them ... the leaden monotony of their lives."[14] Characterizing his imagined readers with a quality of condescension may have been a way to claim the book's transformative potential to enliven "the tiny Reading Room of the Parish, and stir the stagnant atmosphere of the local mind with a few fresh ideas, and the sound of an unfamiliar voice."[15] Similar texts written for urban readers emphasized self-improvement through home recreation as a pathway to success. Inclusive of a rural readership, Erle's book encourages aspirations for middle-class subjectivity without the promise of an accompanying social or economic mobility—a move that at once normalizes a particular class position and simultaneously reinforces the social stratification that makes such positioning possible. With its emphasis on optical toys, Erle's text attaches practices of looking to a democratic, aspirational orientation, as well as to rapidly expanding material and consumer cultures.

Erle's use of the toy cabinet as his central organizing frame aligns with the educational texts and treatises of John Locke (1632–1704) and Jean-Jacques Rousseau (1712–1778) extending back to the seventeenth century, and directly recalls Richard and Maria Edgeworth's landmark 1798 book, *Practical Education*. The Edgeworths advised making a "rational toy-shop" for children, stocked with various carpentry tools, physics and chemistry apparatus, culinary implements, natural history collections, and optical apparatus to encourage learning through play.[16] Throughout the nineteenth century, educational publications and guidebooks such as Erle's reinforced the claim that children learned best through hands-on, sensory engagement rather than rote learning and memorization. Thus, the educational toy, designed for or appropriated by educators, gained traction over the course of the century. Framed as productive playthings, optical toys like the zoetrope, thaumatrope, phenakistoscope, and stereoscope would link the experience of illusionistic media to broader pedagogical aims.

Educational discourses that advocated learning through direct experience with images, objects, and educational playthings centrally addressed white middle-class children, whose daily experiences would increasingly move from the public to the private sphere over the course of the nineteenth century. The separation from the realm of economic production increasingly positioned children as consumers rather than producers.[17] This further justified the need for commercially produced educational materials such as toys, which provided hands-on experiences to which the child may not otherwise have had access. Children were given many things that would prepare them to navigate the social and sensory complexities of modern life, ranging from formal educational materials such as Fröbel's kindergarten gifts, which included wooden geometric shapes and blocks, and educational media like stereoscope slides, to the toys in Evans's engraving. The ideal of the fundamentally innocent child was not universally accepted, but it nevertheless energized education, labor, and religious reform as a standard to which all children should be made to conform. The innocent child is a "mythic" figure that Henry Jenkins has argued helps to anchor and stabilize larger social configurations—the central product of the nuclear family as the basic unit of social and economic reproduction—and is mobilized across the political spectrum still today.[18] The availability of educational playthings and the new notion of play as the child's vocation made the home and school (not the workplace) key sites for learning and linked consumer culture to children's development. Indeed, consumption itself came to be seen as an instructive activity.[19] As optical devices circulated, they helped to shape the parameters within which children's relationships with toys and media would come to be understood, often slung between the poles of possibility and peril.

The tendency to position children as either active participants or vulnerable victims structures much popular discourse on children as consumers and media audiences: a binary that obscures the negotiations and complexities involved in children's engagement with media.[20] Such polarized accounts of children's spectatorship can be observed in response to a range of new technologies over the twentieth century. One might only contrast Hugo Münsterberg's attack of the deleterious effects of the motion picture on children to the discourses of educators who sought to bring film into classrooms or, later, the opposing characterizations of television as variously uniting the family or usurping parental authority.[21] At their most optimistic, these extreme attitudes frame children as empowered, knowledgeable consumers whose needs are heard and met by commercial interests, which provide products and services that will unlock prosperous futures and invite them to create the worlds they wish to inhabit. At their most cynical, these accounts produce conceptions of children as inescapably enslaved by market influence, which reconfigures their physical habits, stifles creativity, and disengages them from social and civic life. Moral panics surrounding children's media and technology usage recur over time.[22] However, the polarized responses to children's media culture familiar to us today are the products of a distinct shift over the nineteenth century informed by the concurrent development and institutionalization of Western childhood and moving-image media. Changing attitudes around children alongside the invention and adoption of optical devices like toys condensed broader ideologies such as the notion of the child as blank slate into discussions of children's vision, thereby making engagement with visual media both a moral and physiological concern.

Recent scholarship on contemporary children's and youth media cultures nuances these polarized accounts, often employing ethnographic methods to frame media culture as participatory and prioritizing young voices in research.[23] Yet voice is subject to its own biases and romantic conceptions, and ethnographic work can be restricted in historical scope.[24] Scholars have identified some historical basis for the dominance of this "effects-based" or "deficit" research approach beginning in the early nineteenth century.[25] "In recent years," this trend has been powerfully countered as "children and media scholars have increasingly challenged both essentialist categories and deficit frameworks in favor of examining the social and cultural conditions by which young people are differentiated."[26] However, alongside such vital social scientific work, it is crucial to unseat and refine the polarizing and exclusionary characterizations of children and media through the excavation of their historical roots, to highlight the perceptual basis for the cultivation of the child as an effects-vulnerable figure. The genesis of this formulation lies in optical toys.

The conception of the innocent, impressionable child came to dominate the cultural imagination concurrently with the development of optical media. The confluence of these two subject positions, the innocent child and the media spectator, found harmony in the characterization of the innocent or impressionable eye, whose surface becomes marked by the visual stimuli it encounters. Erle's book *Children's Toys* (1877) exemplifies how these two institutions mutually reinforced one another. Its first chapter is devoted to the zoetrope and related optical toys.[27] Erle describes persistence of vision—the principle then understood to explain how we perceive motion from the rapid succession of still images—in terms that highlight the eye's materiality. He characterizes the impression of light on the eye as a physical trace, a "scar":

> a local alteration of the structure of the organism of the eye, is induced by the action of light at the spot upon which it falls, and where it brands, as it may almost literally be said to do, its mark. As in the case of other scars, it takes some time for the membrane which has been thus affected to re-establish the original arrangement of its particles, and thus obliterate the traces of the dislocation produced among them through the blow struck by light in its impact on the retina.[28]

Here, as in other nineteenth-century texts, vision is cast as an inscriptive, percussive process in which the eye's surface is struck or marked. To highlight the eye's impressionability in such a way, emphasizing the impact of light on the eye, one may even see the seeds of a nascent "effects" paradigm, a research tradition within communication and psychology that would come to foreground children's exposure to sex and violence.[29] To understand the expenditure of vision and attention as forms of children's consumption and the characterization of persistence of vision as leaving "impressions" on children's retinas, would also presage the twenty-first-century language of online advertising, which relies on the internet user's "impression" as its measurable characteristic. Erle goes on to explain that it is not the eye but the brain that is responsible for sight, making sense of images projected by the eye. He writes that the brain "would be unceasingly misled if it were to suffer itself to be cajoled into accepting the pictures which are brought to it from the retina for correct delineations, as they stand, of the objects whose external characteristics they profess to represent."[30] Vision is therefore understood as a mediated, interpretive process, with the brain actively working to ensure it is not "cajoled" or "misled" by information that the eye furnishes. This is also an essentially defensive or vigilant characterization of vision, suggesting its capacity as a mechanism for information seeking, but one that is open to manipulation. Optical devices, juvenile scientific literature, and movable toy books all initiated children into cultures of spectatorship largely framed in these terms.

Contemporary preoccupations with children's media use—exemplified by concerns about brain development and screen time, waning attention spans, and childhood obesity—are echoes of the discourses surrounding children's vision and attention in the nineteenth century, of which optical toys were a part.[31] From the image on the child's retina characterized as an "exposure" or "impression," to optical play as a "productive" way for children to spend leisure time, these toys and the practices they participated in reveal adult worries over children's time, attention, development, and influences as a longer historical phenomenon. These recurring worries are tied less to specific media technologies than to the concurrent development of modern visual epistemology and the conceptualization of the innocent child during the nineteenth century. As children's earliest encounters with the moving image, such toys thus help illuminate the historical nature of the child media spectator, with its attendant aspirations and anxieties. The aim of this study is not merely to establish this crucial and heretofore underresearched historical continuity. Beyond unearthing the historical origins of children's media spectatorship as it is popularly regarded today is the claim that beginning in the nineteenth century, children became central figures around whom new media culture revolved. This is not only because children and schools represented consumer and institutional markets to support the sale of optical toys, but because children's real and imagined needs and experiences shaped the discourses that animate optical toys (and new media more generally) in the popular imagination.

Vision, Deception, and the Nineteenth-Century Child

Life in the nineteenth century, particularly in the wake of rapid urbanization, was characterized as increasingly perilous, from the velocities of transportation contrivances and the visual and aural overstimulation in city streets to the prevalence of con men and swindlers who took advantage of the weak and naive. Children were introduced into this milieu as subjects-in-the-making, whose genteel sensibilities could be constructed through encounters with the right kinds of commercial influences (rather than corrupting, dishonest ones). The figure of the innocent child, of course, was a raced and classed one, often directly produced by the labor and iconic images of working and enslaved children.[32] Such ethical contradictions could be obscured for white, middle-class children as moral shortcomings came to be shaped in secular as well as religious terms. Popular commercial goods like Milton Bradley's board game the Checkered Game of Life instilled virtues such as charity and industry over corrupting vices like alcoholism. The child as an innocent but socially conscientious subject could thus be established and maintained through consumption and play.

Within this shifting terrain marked by new threats and new opportunities, vision and visuality were central means by which subjectivity was constituted and power consolidated. The expansion of Western empires was predicated on the ability to see and to know racial and cultural "others," which, in turn, were mechanisms for apprehension and possession. Nicholas Mirzoeff refers to "the right to look" as a "claim to a[n] autonomous subjectivity."[33] It is a status that "requires permanent renewal," that is, an ongoing practice rather than a stable position.[34] For much of the nineteenth century, this visual "complex" took shape around the regime of the slave plantation, characterized by the overseers' omnipresent gaze—a position of power that was not reciprocated by the enslaved.[35] Those in relative positions of power thus sought to maintain their "right to look" while denying this visual agency and mode of identification to others. Given this centrality of vision in the nineteenth century, it is little surprise that both formal and informal visual pedagogy flourished at this time.[36]

For instance, abolitionist organizations such as the American Anti-Slavery Society distributed illustrated pamphlets that relied heavily on visual representations of Christian concepts, such as depictions of Christ's light, allowing believers to see the truth of slavery as an un-Christian institution.[37]

The "occularcentric ethos" of abolitionist organizations, Radiclani Clytus argues, was fueled by the belief that sympathies could most effectively be stirred directly through the senses.[38] In such cases, vision functioned as both pedagogical method and religious metaphor. Paradoxically integral to maintaining the social relations undergirding slavery, and simultaneously critical to abolitionist efforts, vision and visuality came to be inextricably tied to self-identification. Learning to see and the conditions of being seen were central to middle-class identity, which crossed lines of race, gender, and, as I argue here, age. The power to visually surveil, discern, or scrutinize the social and material world was one strategy that members of the economically and socially unstable middle class used to fix their own positions. The precariousness of middle-class identity was heightened for the emerging black middle class in the United States. Some black elites may have enjoyed equivalent (or similar) socioeconomic comfort as their white counterparts, but they nevertheless operated within broader white supremacist logics. The adoption of respectable ideals by the black middle class, Erica Ball contends, was not acquiescence to white normativity. Rather, it was a progressive political tactic to link middle-class ideals with antislavery sentiment.[39] This book thus endeavors to be attentive to the multivalent motivations that informed the middle-class experience in the nineteenth century, as well as the varying stakes of asserting middle-class identity. The ascendance of vision as metaphor and core focus of physiological and psychological inquiry during this time offered opportunities to both reinforce and challenge existing social inequalities.

Knowing how to successfully look thus became bound to particular class positions, and the assertion of this "right to look" was a primary mechanism of social posturing. Such connections between seeing and self-identification found parallels in the rising promotion of children's literacy during the nineteenth century. Literacy came to be seen as a kind of "'cultural capital,' with the more or less fantastic capacity to migrate into real property ... Motile yet inalienable," it functioned as "a ballast against the vagaries of new economic relations that tended to dispossess children of traditional modes of inheritance and livelihood."[40] Patricia Crain writes that "the supplanting of property by literacy ... [became] a foundation not only of political and private 'virtue' but of subjectivity itself."[41] The analogous forms of visual literacy that took shape during the nineteenth century added further complexity; the eye's fundamental vulnerability to manipulation required individuals to see from a critical perspective. A discerning observer with the right outlook could both appreciate the visual splendors of modern life and guard against the dangers associated with modernity. Deception and manipulation abounded in the nineteenth century; figures like the con man came to stand in for a broader cluster of hazards that respectable citizens faced.[42] What James Cook called "artful deception" dominated nineteenth-century entertainments, including live variety shows and stage magicians. Exemplified by the work of showmen such as P. T. Barnum, spectacles of artful deception allowed middle-class audiences to revel in the slippage between authenticity and fraud. They delighted in being taken by the illusions and humbugs they saw, yet they were also able to perform the unstable sensibilities of their middle-class positions by practicing discernment and skepticism. Moreover, the public nature of these entertainments ensured that such performances of class identity were also very much on display.[43] These practices of responding to complex and potentially deceptive images would also be adapted for the home in the form of parlor games and play with optical toys—relatively safe or controlled contexts where adults and, especially, children could practice their perceptual competencies and class-based sensibilities.[44]

Wendy Bellion argues that the exhibition of illusionistic art played a pivotal role in the formation and enactment of American identity. Contexts such as Charles Wilson Peale's museum in Philadelphia provided opportunities "to exercise and hone skills of looking. During an era in which the senses were politicized as agents of knowledge and action, public exhibitions of illusions challenged Americans to demonstrate their perceptual aptitude. Thresholds for the practice and performance of discernment, deceptions made exhibition rooms into spaces of citizen formation."[45] Such theorizations of late eighteenth- and nineteenth-century visuality and entertainment understand audiences as active and participatory. Neither complete dupes nor expert observers, they occupied a dynamic position from which their multifaceted identities were in constant negotiation.

These analyses, which tend to foreground public spectacle, concentrate principally on adult audiences. On both sides of the Atlantic, adult members of the precarious and upwardly mobile middle classes uneasily performed in new civic, economic, and cultural roles in response to public displays of illusion. How were these same new middle-class sensibilities instilled and reproduced in children's lives? Changes such as declining infant mortality, mandatory education, and labor policy all facilitated the construction of childhood as a time of innocence and rendered the family a core unit through which national and class identity might be solidified in the form of multigenerational legacy.[46] Many of the entertainments that captivated public audiences were adapted for the home, enabling children to observe and participate in identity work within a comparatively safe and structured environment. New formats such as the movable toy book often thematized public entertainments like zoos, theatrical shows, the three-dimensional scenic peep-show box, and the lantern performance. Optical toys like the thaumatrope, phenakistoscope, and zoetrope reproduced the spectacle of the scientific demonstration made popular in contexts such as London's Royal Institution. The kaleidoscope replicated the dizzying thrill of public life in the defined space of the parlor, while the stereoscope's three-dimensional images permitted children at home and in school to travel the globe and watch industrial processes in action, preparing them for futures where they might engage with these sights firsthand. Focusing on children's first encounters with the moving image beginning in the early nineteenth century shifts critical discussion from the profound anxiety associated with the middle class and instead demonstrates how optical media invited children to conceive of themselves as authenticated and empowered (even if this empowerment sat squarely within the racially and socially stratified cosmology of industrial capitalism).

Optical toys stand out from the broader milieu of "good" children's playthings precisely for their close connection to modern visuality. They came to shape children's worldview not only through their narrative or representational motifs but also at the level of perception, quite literally shaping practices of spectatorship, and indeed vision as a whole, from a particular class-based perspective. As they demonstrated the perceptual phenomenon of persistence of vision, they also suggested how this slippage between sensation and perception (an illusionistic effect) could bring images "to life" in movement. Optical toys and the discourses that surrounded them thus encouraged children to become knowledgeable about their own visual perception as well as invited them to revel in the play between sensation and perception that produced the moving image. These playthings celebrated both the mastery of visual knowledge and the pleasures of running up against its limits. They were thus not simply a class of toys that could be taken up by nineteenth-century educational discourses, but pivotal playthings that showcased optical illusions and established new forms of visual competency.

The child's status as visual subject in training is aptly illustrated in relief against the rube character—a recurring trope across the vaudeville stage, on the early cinema screen, and in cylinder sound recordings, among other media. The rube in cinema, exemplified by Edwin S. Porter's two-minute film *Uncle Josh at the Moving Picture Show* (1902), is an unsophisticated country bumpkin incapable of navigating the increasingly complex, fast, and technologically mediated modern world—particularly the cinema—leading him to behave inappropriately and (for the audience) comically. In Porter's film, Uncle Josh mistakes cinematic illusion for reality and bumbles through a series of encounters: dancing with a woman on the screen, fleeing from an oncoming train, and attempting to intervene in an on-screen romance, thereby pulling the screen down and prompting an altercation with the projectionist. It is not likely that the rube as character type was deployed in early cinema as a way of acculturating audiences to the medium itself; rather, Uncle Josh's humorous misadventures helped reinforce the already standardized norms of cinematic spectatorship and audience decorum. Through humor, Uncle Josh enabled the audience to "flatter itself with a self-image of urban sophistication."[47]

However, the provincial rube stands out not only in contrast to the refined modern urban subject. It also serves as a foil to the figure of the child in the nineteenth century. Children can never be rubes; their lack of lived experience exempts them from the scrutiny to which the adult rube is subject. Throughout the nineteenth century, there are accounts of children misapprehending the effects of media spectacles and making mistakes very similar to the rube's. Yet the rhetorical effect of these stories, while slightly humorous, more centrally includes admiration for the child's imagination and burgeoning sense of optical discernment rather than a condemnation of their backward nature. An 1829 book recounts the exploits of two schoolboys at the cosmorama (an attraction with large-scale landscape pictures that relied on lighting and optical effects to enhance the view). The boys mistake a loose kitten for a tiger on the prowl among the paintings and imagine hoofbeats at the sight of a fly crawling across the scene. Far from being subject to the same ridicule as Uncle Josh's blunders, these moments of confusion are instead seen as possibilities for "the exercise of ingenuity … [and the] occasion of mental excitement the most varied and intense."[48]

What the boys lack in experience they make up for with imagination, described in action-oriented terms such as "exercise," "mental excitement," and "intens[ity]," words that not only position the boys as active audiences but also suggest conditioning and self-improvement. The rube thus represents not only a backward figure out of step with modernity, an object of ridicule for the urban elite, but also a cautionary figure, which the child can avoid becoming through education and practice. In this formulation, the encounter between the child and the mediated image is staged as an exploratory, educational opportunity, and an exciting one at that.

In contrast to the rube, a cautionary figure that the child should work *not* to become, the child's gaze might be more aligned with that of the flaneur, whose patterns of attention and capacity to take in the city rendered them at home in modernity. Baudelaire and Benjamin likened the flaneur to the child, and indeed, the child's marginalized status may have facilitated distinct forms of urban mobility exempt from surveillance and authority.[49] If the middle-class child, increasingly restricted by the mandates of education and confined to sanctioned spaces for learning and play, did not experience the geographic freedom typically associated with the flaneur, they were treated instead to a kind of optical mobility. From the intricate patterns of wallpaper and domestic textiles to enormous mirrors, kerosene then gas lighting, and eventually electricity, the nineteenth-century home was saturated with detailed and dynamic surfaces for the eye to roam.[50] Add to these a host of commercial playthings—movable toy books, puzzles, colorful prints, blocks, and, of course, optical toys—and one can see both the setting and materials that formed the basis of the child's optical education.

Reconfiguring Vision

The ways that media technologies change over time are rarely tidy and one-directional. Historical change is often cyclical and uneven, and "new" media technologies invariably borrow from or respond to earlier prototypes, failed formats, or other apparatus that slip from the popular imagination for a time.[51] Critical concepts such as histories of "screen practice" and the "Cinema of Attractions" have reframed film within larger traditions of performance, exhibition, and reception, countering the tendency to read earlier forms as primitive and later forms as advanced.[52] Similarly, to group optical toys exclusively within the category of precinema is to retroactively wrest them into a coherent and singular historical narrative at the risk of obscuring the other roles they played.[53] There is also a special connection between conventional models of technological development and the study of children's culture. Just as media archaeologists push back on the assumption that technology simply "develops" or "improves" over time, scholars of childhood studies challenge the developmental assumption that children are only rational adults in the making.[54] Studying optical toys and periods in children's culture "on their own terms," rather than as formats and moments in a hurry to become something else, unearths a rich and varied media culture, and occasionally offers the added surprise of revealing powerful continuities and enduring preoccupations that continue to shape how we think about children's media today.

Optical toys permeated many cultural spheres during the nineteenth century: they were used as scientific demonstration apparatus, in the experiments of early experimental psychologists, in the classroom, the middle-class home, and as metaphors reflective of Victorian visuality writ large (as in descriptions of modern urban life as "kaleidoscopic"). Their ubiquity implicates these devices alongside a range of cultural practices in the formation of a new modern observer whose vision is both subjective and subjected to new structures of power related to the emerging industrial order, fixing the terms by which the very act of seeing itself was articulated.[55] As social subjects born into this regime and for whom optical toys and their ways of seeing were always already naturalized, children might represent the prototypical observer par excellence. Yet such formulations privilege dominant or intended ways of seeing over the potential for alternative or oppositional visual strategies that may simultaneously have played out, instead suggesting that such toys exemplified ways that all users might be understood as observers whose vision is subject to modern perceptual paradigm.[56] If understood as ludic devices used to train children's senses, might there be—to evoke Miriam Hansen's work on Walter Benjamin—"room-for-play"?[57]

To an extent, the burgeoning children's media culture to which optical toys belonged *did* reconfigure the value of time for middle-class children in the nineteenth century. Experiments involving persistence of vision sought to determine the thresholds at which observers could perceive fluid motion (a line of thinking that would later shape the standard rate of twenty-four frames per second in the cinema). Optical toys embodied and demonstrated the same concerns over split-second timing that would be at the heart of early inquiries in experimental psychology, labor science, and broader projects to standardize temporal measurement.[58] The fraction-of-a-second intervals required for persistence-of-vision toys like the zoetrope to work were, in turn, juxtaposed with the structure and organization of children's leisure time overall, which could be "spent" productively through the pursuit of recreational activities that were both fun and instructional. This leisure time, which muddled the distinction between education and entertainment, was itself a subset of the child's own developmental time line as they moved to and through adolescence and into adulthood. Likewise, new printing techniques like the chromolithograph and advances in paper engineering after midcentury transformed children's illustrated books into interactive experiences that also experimented with the representation of narrative time, devising novel techniques to explore temporal progression in formats like cautionary tales and fairy tales. During the nineteenth century, new conventions of visual media helped bring these varying temporal scales—the barely perceptible flicker, the youth's leisurely afternoon, the developmental time of childhood, and the one hundred years of Sleeping Beauty's slumber—into relation to one another.

Of course, children frequently refuse to fit within the confines of adult-constructed systems and theories, particularly when such theories presume the normative subject of analysis to be an adult and thus do not attend to the specificity of children's experiences. The ludic dimensions of optical toys, such as the multisensory engagement required for their operation, have the capacity to transform "the player more consciously into a perception maker."[59] Optical toys were not just instruments to demonstrate a perceptual phenomenon. Each toy—the thaumatrope, phenakistoscope, zoetrope, or praxinoscope—has distinct material features that invite different forms of interactivity, manipulation, and social and individual play.[60] Thus, even as these media developed from diverse efforts that coordinated to standardize space, time, and the individual subject's horizon of vision, in play, they also may have initiated transformative ways of thinking.[61] This book traces moments of connection among emerging practices of optical education, new conceptions of childhood in the nineteenth century, and cultural understandings of children's media spectatorship.

Understanding children as new media audiences in the nineteenth century historicizes contemporary discourse on children's media engagement, revealing a rich spectrum of spectator practices that closely parallel many shared preoccupations with the contemporary mediascape. In the century before television, digital devices, and video games were introduced, an array of books, toys, and games concerned with vision, perception, and attention were found in children's homes and hands. These toys explored human perception and also habituated children to interactive visual media as a category overall. Many of these lacked screens and so are excluded from genealogies that privilege screen-based media that often center around cinema. However, toys like the thaumatrope and phenakistoscope taught children how to manipulate a range of interfaces, touching, peering through, and spinning objects to achieve the desired effects, much like young children today "understand that finger taps, pinches, and stretches on touch screen are important new ways of engaging texts."[62] In the nineteenth century, these interactive practices carried over across multiple platforms and drew on multiple signifying systems, from the thaumatrope's composite image and the zoetrope strip to the stereoscopic geography tour and the pop-up book's pull tab. The overlapping desires for both novelty and repetition that fuel the production and marketing of contemporary children's media were instilled and fostered during the nineteenth and early twentieth centuries.

Productivity and Play in the Archive

To trace the history of optical toys through the lens of children's material culture required examining the toys and their related materials across a wide range of archival contexts. I conducted my core research in eight institutions: the Strong National Museum of Play and the George Eastman House in Rochester, New York; the Cotsen Children's Library at Princeton University; the American Antiquarian Society in Worcester, Massachusetts; the Victoria and Albert Museum of Childhood in London; the Bill Douglas Cinema Museum at the University of Exeter; the Museum of Precinema in Padua; and the National Cinema Museum in Turin. Other short excursions to the Getty Research Institute, the New-York Historical Society, Barnard College, and private collections were crucial in assembling and connecting disparate materials. Optical toys, toy books, and related ephemera are situated differently in each of these institutions' collections, variously framed in relation to broader histories of childhood, popular culture, technology, and the history of cinema.

Institutional settings such as the George Eastman House, the Museo del Precinema, and the National Cinema Museum helped contextualize optical devices within histories of cinema and technological development. These apparatuses are also implicated in broader legacies of visual culture, as evidenced by their inclusion in collections such as the Graphic Arts Division at Princeton, which holds numerous devices for viewing and manipulating images, including the stereoscope, zoetrope, praxinoscope, and thaumatrope. Some of the greatest moments of synthesis for this work came when I was examining precinematic objects in relation to paper ephemera such as juvenile popular science and recreational literature, educational materials, advertisements, in their incarnations as do-it-yourself kits, and their adaptations and extensions in the form of movable toy and pop-up books. Yet these are often some of the trickiest moments to broker, bringing paper, metal, wood, and glass together—fragile materials that nevertheless beg to be manipulated. Consulting both physical artifacts and paper ephemera often means working with materials governed by different access policies and procedures under different conditions.

The collections at the Strong National Museum of Play and the Victoria and Albert Museum of Childhood enabled me to locate optical toys within the visual and material cultures of childhood specifically. In these settings, optical toys stood out not as technologies, but as playthings that were taken up alongside other amusements like puzzles, paper dolls, and spinning tops, forming constellations that "make ... new sense" of these objects.[63] Such contexts prioritize their role in play. During my month at the Cotsen Children's Library at Princeton and another spent at the American Antiquarian Society, I was introduced to rich collections of movable toy books, which represent another area of children's culture that played with vision, reinforced new conventions of storytelling, and further demonstrated the link between optical toys and print culture. Home versions of public amusements such as peep shows and panoramas gave insight into how children's books borrowed from, adapted, and sustained a culture of optical entertainment in the domestic context. The collection amassed at Exeter by the late filmmaker Bill Douglas and Peter Jewell has resulted in a unique set of artifacts such as promotional toys and cardboard novelties, referred to by curator Phil Wickham as "bits and bobs," which may not have been deemed worthy of preservation in other institutional contexts, but are of great value in characterizing the role of optical toys in the world of nineteenth- and twentieth-century childhoods.

By the time I finished the research for this book, many of these media and devices had been photographed, scanned, and digitized. Such developments have been hugely important in facilitating broader access to reference materials. Yet the prevalent discourses asserting optical toys' near-perfect alignment with digital surrogacy also threaten to erase the specificity of each of these devices.[64] The digitization of the late Richard Balzer's collection, for instance, was accompanied by enthusiastic (and inaccurate) proclamations that "These Incredible Animated GIFs Are More than 150 Years Old."[65] Digital reference copies engage the tactile imagination very differently from the artifacts in person. Although the following chapters do identify a number of striking continuities between historical and contemporary children's media cultures, they do so not on the basis that historic media formats and apparatus conveniently conform to the logics of digital media. Rather, I have identified the shared currents of optimism or anxiety that seem to run through time on the basis of close examination.

Robin Bernstein's foundational method for material culture analysis integrally informed my interpretation of archival materials and helped clarify the range of claims possible to make from such material. In her book *Racial Innocence*, Bernstein outlined the field-changing theory of "scriptive things"—the belief that material things furnish "otherwise inaccessible evidence of past behaviors. The method entails," she explains, "using archival knowledge and historical context to determine the documented, probable, and possible uses of a category of object." This range of actions is encoded within particular artifacts and found in constellations of contextualizing primary evidence.[66] This spectrum, between what children were *supposed* to do with optical toys and what was *possible* to do with them, provides a pivotal analytic for rethinking the often binary discourses surrounding children's media. Media neither enrich nor corrupt, but instead offer manifold possibilities for engagement. Thus, even as my research conditions differed from those in the nineteenth century—for instance, sitting under the cool fluorescent lights of a large art storage facility instead of a dim, intimate parlor—in handling these artifacts, in taking the time to play, I attempted an empathetic connection to their original contexts and users. In this spirit, each chapter is anchored by a brief narrative of archival or observational experience that highlights challenges or moments of discovery and endeavors to model the unique insights gleaned from the materials themselves.

Opportunities for archival play became key ways to speculate how children may have learned through, derived pleasure from, and experimented with optical toys—experiences that I replicated in researching these objects. Play, which surfaced in Benjamin's mechanical reproduction essay, functions as a perceptual and aesthetic category that does not simply perpetuate prevailing ideological conditions but a practice capable of facilitating political change.[67] Not exclusively disciplinary or liberating, these toys instead helped articulate those positions as the parameters inside of which children's media use would be understood. Within this range, children had the capacity to be consumers, experimenters, and makers, exercising multiple forms of agency in relation to this new visual media culture.

Children's visual education in the nineteenth century played out across a wide network of literature, picture books, printed ephemera, toys, and other optical experiences. Optical toys were thus not only physical playthings brought home at Christmastime, but ways of thinking about vision that surfaced in advertising, play culture, the school, the psychology laboratory.[68] These new media were almost at once considered "timeless" or "old" in a culture of perpetual technological change. Yet they persist even today in a range of forms, commonly allied with a wave of new playthings meant to stimulate interest in STEM/STEAM fields. To reconstruct this historical media culture framed from the perspective of children required examining a broad archive of diverse, sometimes fragmented evidence. Putting diverse objects and documents into conversation with one another invoked in some small way the broad conditions under which these toys were used and revealed the cultures of visual media spectatorship to which children were introduced. This investigation afforded opportunities to understand the negotiation of power and agency among various actors and agents rather than a top-down, unidirectional flow.

Within this framework, it is possible to identify not only the ideological forces that shaped the design and dissemination of optical toys but also to recognize the children who used them as agents. I articulate the patterns of looking, engagement, and interactions that optical toys were designed to elicit from young users, while also acknowledging the multiplicity of children's experiences and the possibility that they used these toys in transgressive and creative ways. This project is less about following particular figures, inventions, or institutions (all of this has been extensively documented in previous accounts) and more focused on how these toys factored into children's media culture more broadly. What connotations framed their use? What were the attributes of the ideal spectator that they helped to cultivate and naturalize? By the end of the nineteenth century, these toys had laid the groundwork for a growing culture and industry of children's media. Many of them also continue to live robust afterlives in multiple forms and contexts.

Scope

My investigation encompasses the introduction of the kaleidoscope in the 1810s through the early decades of the twentieth century as American educators reappropriated the stereoscope for use in schools. Some of the pedagogical theories that provided a rationale for the inclusion of these toys into children's education and play were developed earlier. Educational playthings like alphabet blocks, known as "Locke's blocks" extend back to the seventeenth century, and approaches to learning that incorporated hands-on exploration were popularized in the late eighteenth century by publications such as Richard and Maria Edgeworth's *Practical Education* (1798), which built on concepts established by Locke and Rousseau. The development of Friedrich Fröbel's kindergarten approach in the early and mid-nineteenth century provides educational context during the time that optical toys were in circulation. The first kindergartens in the United States were established in the 1850s and 1860s; Milton Bradley (1836–1911), who manufactured the zoetrope in America, would also manufacture and distribute kindergarten supplies. Optical amusements for children circulate not only within histories of media but also within the broader framework of education, which disclose the kinds of sensory experiences they were meant to facilitate and how they established the idea of vision as a site of agency and amusement as well as vulnerability. Such an approach necessarily follows optical toys across different cultural contexts, from their introduction to their perceived replacement by newer devices, tracing their trajectory from scientific communities to family recreation and into the realm of childhood.

While most of these toys are originally attributed to European inventors, the toys themselves and the ideas associated with them developed rapidly and concurrently across the industrial world. John Ayrton Paris (1785–1856) introduced the thaumatrope in the United Kingdom, which almost immediately appeared in American texts thereafter. Scottish scientist David Brewster (1781–1868) had earlier debuted the kaleidoscope and would later unveil his model of the stereoscope, which gained fame at the Great Exhibition of 1851. Brewster's stereoscope was soon adapted by Boston-based Oliver Wendell Holmes, who developed but did not patent his own variation in 1861. Independent of one another, and almost simultaneously in late 1832, Joseph Plateau (1801–1883) and Simon Von Stampfer (ca. 1792–1864) developed the phenakistoscope in Brussels and Vienna, respectively. William George Horner of Britain invented the zoetrope in 1834, calling it the daedaleum; he died a few years later. The device was later patented by Rhode Island–based inventor William F. Lincoln in the 1860s and manufactured as the zoetrope by lithographer Milton Bradley.

These devices were ubiquitous on both sides of the Atlantic, their production and distribution facilitated by a range of technological and commercial factors. The chromolithograph, which gained traction in the second half of the nineteenth century, enabled the inexpensive mass manufacturing of colored illustrations such as colored pictures in movable books. The two primary producers of stereo views in the United States examined in chapter 6—Keystone View Company and Underwood & Underwood—both relied on recycling images taken across the globe and marketed their boxed sets of stereo views within and beyond the United States. In the absence of strong international copyright policy, picture books manufactured by the New York–based children's publisher McLoughlin Brothers were often modeled after nearly identical British versions and, conversely, McLoughlin books were copied by other firms.

Certainly, optical toys and the discursive forms that accompanied them existed within particular regional, national, and cultural contexts—especially with regard to cultural and regional specificity of some of their iconography. However, the optical principles that they actualized and disseminated were meant to universalize vision by breaking it down into a measurable and predictable sensory system. Common to the nineteenth-century scientific study of vision across national boundaries was a shared concern to understand the limits of vision's reliability.[69] This understanding of human vision as subjective and subject to manipulation correlated with the rise of scientific objectivity as an "epistemic virtue."[70] Optical toys promoted an attitude toward vision within the industrialized Western world that sought to standardize and level it, establishing a measurable norm. This universal conception of vision was inextricably tied to a Western "technoscientific ideal" that marked the rational and educated seeing subject as belonging to the middle class, extolling the same values of respectability, efficiency, self-improvement, and industry.[71]

A diffuse, racially, and ethnically heterogeneous group, the middle class is broadly understood in the context of this book as distinguished by participation in nonmanual forms of labor and for their possibilities—however tenuous and uneven—for upward mobility. Middle-class ideology tended to perpetuate itself in nineteenth-century America: "Small entrepreneurs, clerks, wholesalers, jobbers, and agents—all non-manual workers—frequently earned enough income to enjoy a variety of other 'patterns of experience' that, in turn, contributed to and reinforced their class status."[72] Foundational to this social position was a degree of disposable income and leisure time to enjoy it, along with a degree of economic and social precariousness—specters that came to be embodied for some in fears like deception and virtues such as sincerity. Yet class, as Karen Sánchez-Eppler argues, is "an identity to be grown into, and childhood [is] a powerful site for such growth."[73] Indeed, the dominant notion of childhood itself as a vulnerable time characterized by leisure rather than work presumes middle-class norms.[74]

Chapter Summaries

How did optical toys circulate within the contexts of children's visual, print, and material cultures? Who purchased them, and why? Chapter 1 addresses these questions and charts the movement of optical toys from the context of the public science demonstration to the family parlor, where they eventually came to be seen as children's toys. I argue that in addition to their distribution as material playthings, optical toys enjoyed much wider visibility as printed templates and as textual descriptions found in books of home recreation for juvenile readers. As templates, toys, and text, optical devices were staples of informal home education practices. Their perceptual effects thus became common knowledge alongside other playthings and practices, such as parlor games, magic tricks, and popular-science facts, establishing optical play as a key component in the formation of modern middle-class childhood.

Having established the ways that optical toys were introduced and distributed over the course of the nineteenth century, chapter 2 provides a close analysis of the thaumatrope (1825) in the lives of children and youth. Like other media formats, such as the rebus and jigsaw puzzle, the thaumatrope engaged in a complex interplay between language and image, part and whole. Through a detailed look at the toy's form and motifs, I demonstrate its role in expanding conceptions of children's literacy to include visual acuity and the capacity to play with, rather than to simply understand, language. The thaumatrope's linguistic and perceptual play formed a set of cultural competencies that young users drew on to understand and negotiate their social positions. From playfully manipulating images of birds in cages to using the toy in courtship games, children and youth growing up with the thaumatrope understood its perceptual effects within a social matrix that valued language's subtleties and drew analogies between visual veracity and the moral intentions of one's social circle. Imagining the social contexts in which optical toys were used reveals their part in positioning children as active and engaged spectators capable of optical discernment.

Chapter 3 investigates what it was like to play with toys like the phenakistoscope and zoetrope and hypothesizes how children may have understood and participated in such play. Counter to scholarly accounts positing that optical toys provoked anxiety as they revealed the limitations and fallibility of the eye, I argue that their pedagogical framing invited children to exercise a sense of visual mastery, understanding optical principles but simultaneously reveling in the perceptual experience of optical deception. This set of attitudes was commensurate with tenets of psychology and labor science that framed mental and manual labor as analogous exercises. It was thematized in recurring mechanical motifs in optical media that commonly maintained racial hierarchies and valorized children's visual and cognitive work while distancing them from manual labor.

Over the course of the nineteenth century, new media formats like the movable toy book gained traction, while the purveyors of other media, such as the stereoscope, continually sought new markets and applications. The final three chapters consider the expanding industries that produced children's visual experiences and explore attempts at institutionalizing optical play within new disciplinary and educational paradigms. Chapter 4 examines the ascendance of movable toy books in the second half of the nineteenth century, tracing how their remediations of both traditions of home rational recreation and of public amusements established a leisure culture for children to experience independent of adult oversight. While this culture was lauded for promoting literacy-related play and celebrated in certain mothers' advice literature for keeping children busy, it was also met with a cautionary counterdiscourse that critiqued movable toy books for replacing active outdoor play and warned that their bright, garish colors damaged children's aesthetic sensibilities and even their moral outlook. In this way, movable toy books inaugurated a media culture framed in familiarly polarized terms.

By the late nineteenth century, children's visual experiences increasingly came to be organized according to commercially constituted aesthetic conventions, including the vibrant colors of chromolithographed media like movable toy books, puzzles, and tin toys. In chapter 5, I explore the burgeoning industry and pedagogical theories of color education to demonstrate how commercial interests shaped discourses about color perception and framed children's vision in dichotomous terms: as a site of both great potential and of potential risk. The beginning of the nineteenth century was dominated by the kaleidoscope's chromatic delights, but by the 1880s, color splashed across all commercial media was regarded as an aesthetic experience run out of control, with little order or reason. This chromophobic orientation analogized the velocity of new technologies like the locomotive, capable of exhilarating new experiences of time and space but also of catastrophe. In response to concerns about color, several systems of color education were developed and popularized in the late nineteenth century in order to tame and order children's chromatic experiences.

Chapter 6 examines another site where sensory training was formally adopted in schools—the stereoscope's second life as an educational medium in the late nineteenth and early twentieth centuries. Nineteenth-century educators widely adopted the pedagogical method of the object lesson. They believed that students' senses were awakened by learning directly from physical objects and that sensory encounters helped cultivate both reasoning and communication skills. Objects, they believed, helped make sense of the world in a way that rote memorization did not. Following the heyday of the stereoscope as a parlor amusement at midcentury, the stereoscope industry capitalized on the object lesson's philosophy to repackage the device as another such sensory aid. From the 1880s through the 1920s, companies such as Underwood & Underwood and Keystone View repackaged stereo views into sets for institutional markets like churches and schools, accompanied by guidebooks, patented maps, and other materials to assist with classroom implementation. Bolstered by work in experimental psychology—itself an emerging field—which certified the stereoscope's vivid imagery as a "real" mental experience of travel, the stereoscope industry promised the device's ability to deliver vivid object lessons. However, the views and the discourses surrounding them reveal the paradoxical role that the stereoscope played in schools, both imagining children's freedom and subjecting them to rigid disciplinary standards.

In conclusion, chapter 7 studies contemporary optical toys from large-scale public installations to children's STEM/STEAM toys. Stroboscopic sculptures by fine artists and commissioned for ad campaigns by companies including Sony, Coca-Cola, and Stella Artois indicate a continued fascination with the ways of looking that optical toys encourage. As both children's toys and large-scale installations, contemporary three-dimensional zeotropic sculptures are today aligned with the tenets of STEAM education, seen as critical to preparing children for the twenty-first-century workplace. These toys' physical attributes mitigate anxieties about the digital image's ontology and ground optical play within contemporary creative industries that appear inclusive and thriving. The ongoing lives of optical toys within children's play cultures and public spectacle frame them within the purview of STEAM education and foreground children as creators, whose romanticized natural inclinations for tinkering and curiosity prime them for future success. The coda of the book is a survey of the contemporary landscape of these devices as advertising vehicles, children's science toys and public art, exploring ways that these visual paradigms have adapted and endured since the nineteenth century.

Nearly two centuries after optical toys organized children's visual fields in alignment with the interests and concerns of a distinct class position, commentators on new media would proclaim young people "digital natives," whose facility with new technology was radically different from that of previous generations, disregarding (among other factors) the socioeconomic conditions undergirding both children's access to and orientation toward new media formats.[75] The figure of the digital native can "subsume orientations to both utopian and dystopian visions of young people," yet in its all-encompassing and leveling capacity, the notion of the digital native also "conceal[s]—and reproduce[s]—digital inequalities and uneven distribution of Internet access and digital skills among adolescents."[76] Foregrounding how nineteenth-century discourses of vision encouraged the formation of a spectatorial identity built around work and play, education and diversion, reveals the establishment of a visual episteme that cast the prototypical or ideal observer within a clear class matrix. Drawing these comparisons, this book is thus both a historical study and a contemporary intervention that considers how conceptions of children continue to shape our understandings of media.

1 Templates, Toys, and Text: Optical Toys in Nineteenth-Century Children's Culture

An article in the 1881 Christmas edition of the British weekly magazine the *Boy's Own Paper* outlined "the near and far limits of a vast optical playground" and introduced a series of optical toys—the thaumatrope, the phenakistoscope, and colored spinning tops. A special chromolithographed supplement accompanied the article with four preprinted thaumatropes and two phenakistoscope disks that boys could cut out and assemble (figure 1.1) The paper toys depicted familiar motifs: a rat in a cage, a horse bucking its rider, a dancer, and a boy eating an orange.[1] The article asserts that "optical toy sport was the first sport of baby life to most of us," suggesting widespread familiarity with these toys and their optical effects.[2] The toys' inclusion in the magazine, moreover, highlights print culture as a core way that optical knowledge circulated. Located at the interstices of print, visual, and material cultures, the colorful paper toys were meant to be assembled and manipulated and to inspire original creations. The supplement's production was enabled by the technology of the chromolithograph, its distribution facilitated by the established network of the periodical's circulation—a form and industry that flourished over the course of the century. The toys and the optical effects they generated made exceptional subject matter for such supplements.

Working with this full-color supplement exemplifies some of the challenges of reconstructing the role of optical toys within nineteenth-century childhood from archival materials. I first encountered this object preserved under a glossy protective cover at the Bill Douglas Cinema Museum at the University of Exeter, which holds the extraordinary collection of precinema material collected by Bill Douglas and Peter Jewell. This colorful object tells only half the story.[3] It is classified as an "optical toy/metamorphosis"

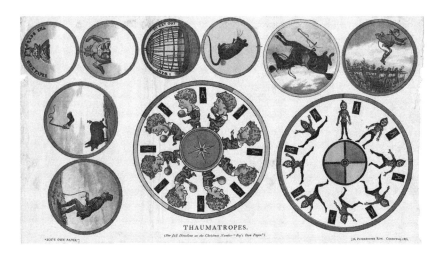

Figure 1.1
Optical toy supplement to a December 1881 issue of the *Boy's Own Paper*. Courtesy of the Bill Douglas Cinema Museum, University of Exeter.

(item 69430), while the accompanying article in the *Boy's Own Paper* is held separately as a "press cutting" (item 78083). Like all historical material, which either implicitly or explicitly cannot help but gesture to the network of images and artifacts that formed its original context, the colorful supplement and the article point to one another. Considering the two in relation to one another, as well as to other related materials, helps coax them into articulating their meaning in the lives of nineteenth-century children.[4] The accompanying article on optical sport in the *Boy's Own Paper* furnishes instructions for assembling the colorful templates and describes the construction and the effects of the two phenakistoscope disks. In action, users will see the boy "speedily demolish the orange"—perhaps a Christmas delicacy—and the man will dance frantically. Yet in explaining the thaumatrope, the article playfully withholds the answer. In the spinning thaumatrope, the text says, "You will see—what? Try for yourselves."[5] This provocation models the experiential pedagogy that characterized nineteenth-century popular science recreation, which demanded young people discover rather than simply absorb information.

In many institutions, graphic and textual materials like these are organized separately, often divided as prints and manuscripts. I was fortunate to encounter these materials at Exeter, where all of the pieces are there, carefully cataloged so that they are easy to find and link and where they can be accessed together. Yet the archival encounter differs dramatically from how the toys were originally used. The supplement was meant to be cut out, mounted onto card, and twirled around. Finished, child-made versions are less likely to survive. The uncut template points to possibilities and intentions rather than the resulting play. Together, the article and the supplement indicate the extent to which optical education permeated boys' lives and document the efforts that the magazine's publisher made to provide its young subscribers with a colorful Christmas treat in the form of popular science play.

In circulation until 1967, the *Boy's Own Paper* enjoyed enormous success. "By the late 1880s," Kirsten Drotner writes, the *Paper* and its counterpart for girls "were deemed by far the most popular magazines for adolescents."[6] Such publications were principally aimed at children in middle-class families, whose ranks swelled on both sides of the Atlantic in the nineteenth century. Adult members of this growing middle class worked white-collar jobs largely outside the home. They navigated complex social and professional networks, their lives structured around work and leisure, with the disposable income earned from the former sustaining the latter.[7] While their parents enjoyed new-found material comforts—coupled, paradoxically, with economic precariousness—children were introduced to the sensibilities and concerns of their social tier through consumer products such as books, toys, and magazines like the *Boy's Own Paper*. Children increasingly occupied a new status, not as economically valuable but of sentimental importance—a position that Viviana Zelizer asserts was solidified in first decades of the twentieth century.[8] Throughout the nineteenth century, social and educational reforms would endeavor to make some form of education accessible to racially diverse children from across the socioeconomic spectrum, but for white middle-class children, the home remained a key site where moral and intellectual development would be overseen and cultivated. As children's lives were increasingly structured around the institutional demands of schools, productive use of leisure time held special importance, particularly as an opportunity to instill a love of learning thought to be the natural vocation of children and cultivate the sensibilities of middle-class gentility in youth.

Accordingly, the nineteenth century saw a boom in juvenile print culture, with periodicals and guidebooks that suggested appropriate and productive leisure pursuits for young readers. Books of parlor games and popular pastimes gathered under the rubric of rational recreation, as well as periodicals such as the *Boy's Own Paper*, encouraged learning through play in wide-ranging forms, from social and physical games to magic tricks, scientific experiments, and home toymaking. As the descriptive article and supplement from the *Boy's Own Paper* attest, this print culture provided a key context for the dissemination of optical toys. While the inclusion of optical toys in juvenile literature is widely known within contemporary media studies scholarship, the attendant significance of children as core users of these toys and the specificity of their class positioning have received comparatively little critical theorization. Optical devices were sold as physical toys, but they also appeared as textual descriptions in innumerable juvenile books and periodicals and as colorful premade templates for children to assemble at home. As templates, toys, and text, optical toys proliferated across print media. Understood from such a perspective, these toys were not merely precursors to the cinema, but widely varying configurations of the moving image that linked specific ideas about visual perception to a distinct social position. In their many forms, they were so broadly disseminated that they reached generations of children and youth from the 1830s into the twentieth century. Although the visual effects these toys generated would eventually link them with the cinema and other screen-based entertainments, tracing their various forms and circuits of distribution highlights their equal prominence in the history of commercial playthings.

This chapter explores the ways that expanding print cultures and the juvenile literature market made optical toys available to children during the nineteenth century. It traces how these toys were taken up in popular informal educational discourses and, by the end of the century, had come to be understood primarily as children's playthings. As physical toys, they were sold through booksellers, opticians, toy shops, and children's publishing companies. For decades, they appeared as descriptions and illustrations in home recreation texts spanning the categories of science, magic, and parlor game. Finally, they were mass-produced as ready-made templates awaiting assembly, sold cheaply, given away as promotional items, and appearing in newspapers and magazines.[9] In these three forms, optical toys participated in a growing culture of rational recreation, characterized by family-oriented educational play that usually relied on sensory and experiential learning (such as experiments in chemistry and optics). Although particular technological changes facilitated how these toys could be reproduced, such as the chromolithograph enabling the production of full-color templates after midcentury, these three forms do not represent successive changes. Rather, by the end of the nineteenth century and into the twentieth, optical toys simultaneously circulated as textual schematics, printed templates, and both commercially produced and homemade toys. Charting these toys across various media forms excavates their place not only in moving-image media history, but connects them to a set of cultural practices that shaped the contemporary construction of childhood itself. In their various iterations, these toys help characterize the interests and concerns of their young users and reveal their integral role in shaping how middle-class children envisioned vision.

From Public Curiosities to Educational Toys at Home

The thaumatrope (1825) and, later, the phenakistoscope (1832) and zoetrope (1834), were the first commercially produced toys that showcased persistence of vision. These new media drew on a longer tradition of public visual entertainment and spectacles, such as lantern performances given by traveling showmen and visits to peep shows set up in public squares. Box-like peep shows contained three-dimensional scenes viewed through a hole or lens, often with added effects, such as day-to-night transitions. Children commonly appear alongside adults in eighteenth-century prints depicting public peep shows. While children likely would have attended these shows, their prominence in such iconography, Richard Balzer contends, may have functioned "to conjure up a sense innocence and wonderment."[10] It is also likely that some of these traveling performers were children.[11] Eighteenth-century lantern shows performed by traveling showmen often included scary or supernatural content, which cast the lantern as a medium known for frightening and deceiving audiences.[12] Because of their association with the lantern, these itinerant showmen were regarded as bogey figures who populated children's folk stories about abduction.[13] This tradition of the lantern as projector of ghosts, spirits, and other frightening things would take its most institutionalized form in the late eighteenth-century phantasmagoria staged in Paris by the lanternist and balloonist Etienne-Gaspard Robert (known also as Robertson).[14] Robertson's supernaturally themed performances involved lanterns that projected onto the screen from behind, the lantern thus concealed from the audience. Lanterns were often mounted on wheels, which, when moved, gave the impression that ghosts, Medusa's heads, skeletons, and other frightening images were moving toward the terrified spectators. The elaborate shows involved trick lantern projections onto glass that gave the illusion of ghostly apparitions, smoke effects, and music supplied by the eerie glass harmonica.

Neither Robertson nor the itinerant lantern operators before him sought to enlighten or inform audiences, but to control and manipulate optical effects to elicit surprise and fear. Not only did the spectacle and wonder associated with early optical entertainments frame them as entertaining rather than educational, the centrality of children in the iconography and lore surrounding them helped advance a conception of child spectators as figures filled with "wondrous innocence," frightened and delighted by the optical marvels they beheld.[15] When, in the nineteenth century, optical devices and spectacles acquired reputations as more respectable entertainments associated with scientific inquiry, child spectators came to be seen as beneficiaries of the optical education these toys and experiences afforded.

Over the course of the nineteenth century, technological advancements such as improved illumination sources and glass lenses enhanced the capacities of apparatuses like microscopes, telescopes, and projecting lanterns. Such apparatuses extended the scope and scale of human vision, rendering visual phenomena identifiable and measurable. The higher-quality, industrially produced magic lanterns of the nineteenth century were used to showcase not only the hazy, luminous monsters of prior generations, but educational content and religious stories as well. Combined with photographic technology, lantern images ranged in scale from world sites to magnified microscope slides. Industrially produced and commercially distributed optical devices thus came to function as tools for scientific inquiry and educational demonstration rather than spectacle alone, transforming a deceptive medium into an instructive one.[16] The scientific lantern found application in a range of institutional settings, such as museums, religious organizations, schools, and scientific societies. These some of these venues would be the initial sites where persistence-of-vision toys were exhibited and sold.

It was within the context of one such scientific establishment that the thaumatrope was introduced to the public. The commercial thaumatrope (which translates from the Greek as "wonder-turner"), attributed to physician John Ayrton Paris, was published by William Phillips in London in April 1825 and sold at the Royal Institution. The institution was founded in 1799 with "the aim of introducing new technologies and teaching science to the general public."[17] Paris's original set of thaumatropes depicted a variety of subjects, from the bird-and-cage and horse-and-rider motifs that have become the toy's archetypal forms to images of Harlequin and Columbine and flowers in a pot. The content was not scientific, but in optically uniting two images on opposite sides of the disk, the toy's operation itself was a kind of scientific demonstration—one that was quite amusing. The thaumatrope's introduction coincided with the institution's move to more directly cater to young audiences. Just months after the thaumatrope's publication, in December 1825, the institution inaugurated the Christmas Lectures series for juvenile and family audiences on topics in natural philosophy, astronomy, chemistry, electricity, and geology. Scheduled around school holidays, the Christmas Lectures offered foundational scientific knowledge to young audiences and inspired youth by showcasing the advancements achieved by the institution's members. The institution's original auditorium could accommodate over a thousand spectators, who were treated to spectacular large-scale demonstrations of scientific phenomena. Central to the Royal Institution's pedagogical approach was the ability for the audience to experience and observe phenomena for themselves.[18] This philosophy emphasized the child spectator's role as an active interpreter and evaluator of scientific information, much like the sensory emphases of other educational methods, such as the object lesson, which also gained popularity in the United Kingdom beginning in the 1820s.

As a consumer product, the thaumatrope extended the Royal Institution's tradition of firsthand scientific spectacle. Illustrations chosen for the toy commonly engaged social or political humor, thus uniting scientific phenomena and consumer culture all in a small set of disks neatly packaged in a cardboard box for home use.[19] The phenakistoscope (whose Greek name alludes to the notion of optical deception), developed simultaneously by Joseph Plateau and Simon von Stampfer in 1832, would similarly introduce scientific experimentation and demonstration into the realm of consumer culture, linking the science institution to the home.[20] The contrast in scale between public and domestic exhibition was at times imaginatively rendered in the phenakistoscope's packaging. Boxes commonly featured vivid tableaux of the toy's subject matter as larger than life, dramatizing the toy's optical and psychological effects. One box marketing the phenakistoscope as Wallis's Wheel of Wonders (ca. 1834), for example, arrays a busy round tableau of life-sized versions of the animated figures—dancers and jugglers—in a circle around a seated woman, who occupies a prominent position at the bottom center of the image.[21] She holds the spinning phenakistoscope before a large mirror steadied by a young boy, while a young woman looks on. Behind her, an oversized phenakistoscope disk features a series of images representative of the set's contents: a dancer, a juggler, an acrobat, and a musician. Representing these images as oversized figures not only evoked the rich sensory experiences that the device purported to offer but also gestured to the traditions of public spectacle and demonstrations from which these toys derived. Such iconographic motifs point to the device's intended family audiences and indicate how these toys popularized and reproduced scientific demonstrations in the home.

Like the Christmas Lectures and the thaumatrope, which framed scientific inquiry as family entertainment, early phenakistoscopes were aimed at adult buyers at least in part for family use. Plateau's device was marketed as the Fantascope and sold at Rudolph Ackermann's, a fine bookseller, in 1833.[22] Ackermann had been in operation as a book and print seller since the late eighteenth century. In the early nineteenth, he began producing his own illustrated books and prints, as well as a monthly periodical, the *Repository of Arts*. He moved his shop to 96 Strand in 1827, where the Fantascope would be sold.[23] We can infer from both iconography and sales contexts that children and families represented at least one intended market for Plateau's original Fantascope. Ackermann sold three series of images for the toy. The first was inspired by an early sample device, commissioned from the painter Jean-Baptiste Madou, and included leaping frogs, twirling dancers, slithering snakes, and abstract designs, among other motifs.[24] The second series, drawn by Thomas Talbot Bury, and the third by Thomas Mann Baynes, were all available in a folio for fourteen, twelve, or ten shillings, respectively. Children at play were depicted in some of the disks' iconography, such as one in the third series by Thomas Mann Baynes, which features images of a boy riding a rocking horse and a child skipping rope.[25] A mirror and box could be purchased separately for three shillings. The Fantascope was advertised alongside Ackermann's *Forget Me Not* books of prints and engravings, available in both adult and juvenile versions, designed to be a fine birthday or Christmas gift.

Optical toys continued to be sold by booksellers like Ackermann, as well as purveyors of scientific apparatus, such as the shops of Philadelphia opticians James Queen and William McAllister, where zoetropes sold alongside eyeglasses, stereoscopes, and other "chemical and philosophical apparatus and toys" for the 1867 Christmas season.[26] Such circuits of distribution positioned the toys as curiosities for the whole family to enjoy. However, the thaumatrope, phenakistoscope, zoetrope, and related toys would also come to find a particular foothold in the burgeoning worlds of children's literary and consumer culture, increasingly manufactured and sold by children's publishers and makers of toys and games. Within children's consumer culture, these toys retained the status as educational playthings with connections to scientific inquiry and were thus distinguished on the market from other commercial goods for children considered mere frivolous diversions.

Milton Bradley's zoetrope (Greek for "wheel of life"), patented in April 1867, is representative of this orientation of optical toys toward children's culture. The zoetrope consists of a spinning slotted drum (instead of the phenakistoscope's disk), inside of which a paper strip printed with a sequence of pictures depicting motion is placed. Viewing the spinning drum through the slots makes the pictures appear to be moving. The device initially appeared in early 1834 as the Daedaleum, produced by an Englishman named William George Horner. Horner died in 1837, and the zoetrope did not become commercially available until the 1860s, when various iterations of the toy were patented in the United States and France.[27] The toy was available widely in disparate parts of the United States even before Milton Bradley's 1867 patent, found in 1866 Christmas advertisements in Columbus, Ohio, and in *Colman's Rural World*, a St. Louis–based publication that targeted farm and agricultural populations.[28] Bradley also licensed the zoetrope and many of its paper strips that showcased people, animals, machines, and abstract images in motion to the London Stereoscopic and Photographic Company in 1867.[29] In the United States, the zoetrope's production and distribution by Milton Bradley situated it more squarely within children's and family markets. The Springfield, Massachusetts–based Bradley had begun his career as a lithographer whose business had taken off after his Checkered Game of Life gained popularity, particularly in a travel-sized version made available for soldiers during the Civil War. The Checkered Game of Life offered a secular take on earlier games such as The Mansion of Happiness, which oriented winning around virtues and vices aligned with religious ideals.[30]

Advertisements in publishing trade journals such as the *American Stationer* feature The Game of Life alongside the zoetrope, which was available in large "parlor"-sized models and in smaller "toy" versions. The products' pairing in the ad illuminates the broader social orientation of the zoetrope's intended users. Both playthings were at home in the well-appointed middle-class parlor. Although The Game of Life's ideological aims are more immediately discerned, both the game and the zoetrope share similar cultural commitments. Where the game explicitly championed aspirations like gaining professional influence, the pursuit of love and marriage, and the desire for political office, the zoetrope was meant to instill in users a scientifically grounded understanding of their visual perception that more broadly aided them in distinguishing truth from deception. This discerning perspective was perceived as an essential skill for navigating modern life. In this way, both products encouraged the same social and moral outlook associated with middle-class identity.

By the end of the nineteenth century, Milton Bradley had created a robust business in books, games, and toys for the home, as well as in educational toys, such as materials associated with the growing US kindergarten movement and theories of color education. The company had offices in Springfield (where the manufacturing headquarters were based), New York City, Atlanta, and Kansas City. Newspaper ads from the 1860s through the turn of the twentieth century indicate the zoetrope's availability from booksellers, stationers, and toy sellers across the United States, including Kansas City; Sacramento; St. Paul; Burlington, Vermont; Wheeling, West Virginia (where it was available from at least two retailers); and Topeka.[31] Meanwhile, other companies began positioning optical toys more specifically as children's fare within their inventories. In the catalog for the 1865 semiannual New York City trade book sale, the phenakistoscope is listed by Philadelphia-based publisher Davis, Porter, & Co., grouped with picture books, toy books, fairy tales, nursery rhymes, puzzles, and alphabet blocks.[32] The New York–based children's publisher McLoughlin Brothers also sold its own version of Emile Reynaud's praxinoscope under the name "whirligig of life"—a term reminiscent of the zoetrope—in the late 1870s, alongside its extensive inventory of children's books, games, and puzzles. These commercial contexts reveal these toys' role not only in scientific and technological inquiry but also as children's playthings. Their placement among dolls, building blocks, tabletop games, and toy vehicles demonstrates the integral relationship between toys and emergent cultures of the moving image.[33]

Optical toys became ubiquitous not only as playthings fashioned from cardboard, metal, and wood sold through book and toy shops but were also reproduced in inexpensive paper templates, like the example from the *Boy's Own Paper*. In the 1860s, London publisher John Neal distributed at least nine series of zoetrope strips sold in sets of three as Neal's Penny Games, complete with instructions for constructing the zoetrope at home (figure 1.2).[34] The *Boston Herald* included a zoetrope template with its April 5, 1896, Sunday edition. If the *Herald*'s average Sunday circulation of 64,851 in 1877 is any indication, its "Wheel of Life" was likely seen by hundreds of thousands.[35] The instructions accompanying such sets also outline the kinds of manual competencies children required in order to assemble optical toys. They assumed the ability to glue the premeasured slotted drum to a pasteboard backing, cut out the slots, find a round base of cardboard or wood, and accurately measure its center. As cheap or promotional templates, as well as toys, optical devices reached children and families from broad socioeconomic backgrounds.

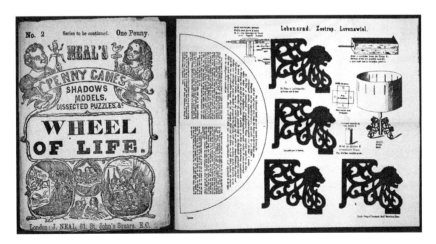

Figure 1.2
Paper zoetrope templates. Left: *Neal's Penny Games: Shadows, Models, Dissected Puzzles &c: Wheel of Life* (London). Right: Lebensrad Zootrop (Germany, ca. 1890). Princeton University Library.

Optical toys enjoyed circulation across multiple markets, from high-end booksellers and opticians' shops to purveyors of children's print, visual, and material cultures, where they were sold with board games, alphabet blocks, and picture books. Their production shared many material affinities with other forms of children's print matter and toys, and they enjoyed distribution through the same networks established by these industries. They reproduced and domesticated the engaging form of education associated with public demonstration in scientific institutions. This growing tradition sought to democratize the understanding of scientific phenomena by allowing audiences to observe them firsthand. Much can be learned from observing the markets that these templates and toys traversed, but optical toys also gained popularity through their inclusion in juvenile rational recreation literature as textual descriptions and illustrations. Literary sources demonstrate the extent to which optical toys and their perceptual phenomena were introduced to children on both sides of the Atlantic. The volumes of this literature, and the degree to which content was borrowed, stolen, and reprinted, suggests that optical toys would have been as familiar to children as other playthings and pastimes like spinning tops, hoops, ball games, parlor games, and kites. Furthermore, these toys' textual incarnations clarify their part in advancing a distinct construction of middle-class childhood characterized by a preoccupation with the prudent expenditure of time and the acquisition of popular or vernacular knowledge in contrast to the elitism of the classics.

Productive Playtime and the Construction of Contemporary Childhood

Optical toys gradually moved from public exhibition into the home as industrialization and urbanization "led to a radical restructuring of the temporal and spatial patterns of economic and social life."[36] For the middle and, increasingly, working classes, whose time was largely structured between work and play, leisure came to be institutionalized in parks and museums. These institutions were unified by "the belief that leisure time should be spent in some improvement of self and society"—a set of cultural ideals known as rational recreation.[37] For children and youth, the increased separation of public and private spheres and the formalization of mandatory schooling all rendered the middle-class home an important site for informal educational play—a kind of domesticated version of the public entertainments that was rational recreation for adults. Treatises, manuals, and books of parlor games, amusements, indoor and outdoor sports, science, and magic tricks proliferated on the juvenile market, all proffering advice for how to occupy children during their free time outside school.

Home recreation literature of the nineteenth century was a diverse genre that broadly assumed childhood as a developmental time when leisure pursuits helped shape children's character. Like the Royal Institution's Christmas Lectures, these texts encouraged learning through immediate sensory encounters. Rather than teaching specific content, this literature modeled a distinct conception of childhood itself, using toys, games, and experiments to awaken children's "natural" curiosity and inquisitiveness. Pursuing such edifying past times, John Henry Anderson's 1855 book, *The Fashionable Science of Parlor Magic*, contended, "causes the mind to fall into inductive trains of reasoning" and to sharpen the senses.[38] Subjects ranged from physics and chemistry experiments and magic tricks to social games such as blind man's bluff and thread the needle, which provided outlets for physical play and invited competition, cooperation, and free movement, in contrast with the stationary, disciplined positions children occupied in schools.[39] The toys, games, and experiments these books described encouraged youth to think about and engage with the social world. This literature stressed the idea that middling sensibilities included not only the tasteful forms of consumption and display but also the prudent expenditure and organization of leisure time, which gained new importance as an opportunity to strengthen one's character, round out one's education, and forge social bonds.

This widely reproduced set of social practices had deeper roots in seventeenth- and eighteenth-century educational treatises, whose readerships were largely restricted to the upper classes. While their thinking diverged on many issues, both Locke and, later, Rousseau contended that education occurred best not in the schoolroom but in the natural environment or the home. Both advocated child-motivated learning driven by experiential encounters. Locke believed that young children learned well from physical implements, such as encouraging literacy with alphabet blocks, while Rousseau stressed learning through exploration of the natural world, objects, and games.[40] Rational recreation in upper-class homes became popular during the eighteenth century, with books such as William Hooper's *Rational Recreations* (1774) and apparatuses that sought to direct the child's leisure time to productive pursuits.[41] Hooper's text, for instance, described optical instruments and games but maintained a clear hierarchy through narrative strategies such as making servants the butt of optical tricks and deceptions (in much the same way that Robertson's phantasmagoria was calculated to frighten rather than educate).[42] By the time that the first American edition of Locke's *Some Thoughts Concerning Education* was published in 1830, his advice—originally aimed at the parents and private tutors of a few elites—enjoyed broader reception among both professional educators and a more socially and economically diverse group of parents. Of course, the heterogeneous middle class who took up this literature was still constituted through the assumption of social tiers below them.[43] However, the economic and technological conditions that made the wide dissemination of this literature possible also rendered previously more defined social strata considerably more flexible. The figure of the child was perhaps the most emblematic of the promise of this kind of mobility.

Like later nineteenth-century rational recreation literature, Locke's pedagogical approach was framed around children's aspirations. He advised parents to pretend that young children's literacy materials were for older children and "that it was the privilege and advantage of heirs and elder brothers, to be scholars."[44] Locke argued that a child's motivations would be stoked if parents "let him think [literary education] is a game belonging to those above him."[45] Such aspirations for younger children to enjoy the same opportunities as their older siblings were analogous to the appeals in nineteenth-century publications that stressed middling children's potentials to elevate their social and economic status through rational recreation. One text referred to its young readers as "embryo statesmen and unfledged poets" and "young ladies who are anxious to become housekeepers."[46] These texts helped children cultivate the interests that would later serve them in their parents' dynamic social worlds and linked the trajectory of children's development to later aspirations of upward mobility. They espoused a kind of democratic potential in line with Paul Ringel's conception of "American gentility … constructed upon the belief that individuals, even if they lacked substantial income or prestigious lineage, could improve their status by constructing a public persona that balanced polite manners, Protestant morality, and tasteful display of consumer goods."[47]

Building on the work of Locke and Rousseau, Richard and Maria Edgeworth (respectively, 1744–1817 and 1768–1849), whose educational writings included *Practical Education* (1798), also positioned early childhood as a critical time and advocated home learning with everyday objects. Children's attention was of particular concern to the Edgeworths as an attribute to be cultivated and refined, and they believed the child's attention could be captured through interest in the subject matter.[48] *Practical Education* derided brightly painted expensive toys, which had few affordances beyond their specified use. Instead, the book argued that children should "have things which exercise their senses or their imagination, their imitative, and inventive powers."[49] In early education, children need little more than objects that "invite comparison" and enable them to explore a world of material relations related to shape, size, form, texture, and material.[50] When the child succumbs to the tastes associated with fancy toys, the Edgeworths warned, "instead of attending to his own sensation, and learning from his own experience, he acquires the habit of estimating his pleasures by the taste and judgment of those who happen to be near him."[51]

This approach to tastemaking aligned with the pedagogical philosophy of the public science demonstration, which allowed onlookers to see scientific phenomena for themselves and reach their own conclusions accordingly rather than looking to adults or peers for validation or explanation. Such an individually oriented position may have been especially appealing for middle-class children, whose social worlds were not simply inherited, but for whom the project of identity formation was actively undertaken in social practice and who were assumed to possess the "ability to shape his or her own success."[52] In the tradition of the Edgeworths, later titles like Ebenezer Landells's *The Boy's Own Toy-Maker* (1859), *The Girl's Own Toy-Maker* (with Alice Landells, 1863), and Thomas William Erle's *Children's Toys, and Some Elementary Lessons in General Knowledge Which They Teach* (1877) urged children to learn through play with toys like the top, the kite, and blown soap bubbles. These authors argued that educational toys equipped children with unique tactile and sensory competencies that shared equal importance with traditional forms of literacy. "Toys," Erle stressed, "speak a language of their own which is Greek to the ignorant, and requires construing into simple English, but which, when it is thus rendered intelligible, is found to be rich in instruction, and to teem with suggestiveness."[53]

Optical toys were a staple of home recreation, and literary texts were responsible for both the wide dissemination of optical principles and framing their use by children. Shortly after the thaumatrope's initial sale, Dr. Paris capitalized on the trend toward home recreation with his juvenile literary work *Philosophy in Sport Made Science in Earnest*, first published in the 1827. Paris dedicated *Philosophy in Sport* to Maria Edgeworth, and in keeping with her approach, the book is written in conversational style. It orients home education in progressive terms, deriding corporal punishment in favor of child-based inquiry and exploration. "Imagine not … that I shall recommend the dismissal of the cane, or the whip," Paris proclaimed in his preface. "On the contrary, I shall insist upon them as necessary and indispensable instruments for the accomplishment of my design. But the method of applying them will be changed; with the one I shall construct the bow of the kite, with the other I shall spin the top."[54] Representative in tone of much home recreational literature, Paris's repurposed cane and whip evince a belief in the malleability of material objects and, by extension, children themselves, capable of flourishing if given proper toys and training.

Philosophy in Sport chronicles a series of home lessons given by the character Mr. Seymour to his four children while his son Tom is home on a school vacation. Mr. Seymour furnishes lessons in science using toys and everyday objects as demonstration apparatus. During his lessons, the family is joined by a number of others, including Mrs. Seymour (who, in some versions, offers modifications and improvements to the experimental devices), and Mr. Twaddleton, the village's antiquarian vicar. The three-volume work features a range of homemade and commercial toys, including an extended episode detailing the thaumatrope's principles and uses. Though Edgeworth herself may not have approved of the thaumatrope—a commercial toy with a single use—Paris's decision to frame his text in relation to Edgeworth's philosophy justified the commercialization of educational play.[55] Indeed, as children came to occupy a new status as highly cherished, highly visible, sentimental members of the family, their position as such was sustained through the acquisition and use of commercial goods seen to facilitate their healthy growth.[56]

The home lessons described in *Philosophy in Sport* take place over a school vacation period. Like many other home recreation texts, Paris's book positioned this important social and scientific education expressly outside formal schooling and, in fact, regarded school pejoratively—an attitude that solidified in response to the growth of mandatory schooling in Europe and America. In the United States, figures like Horace Mann (1796–1859), who served as secretary of the Massachusetts Board of Education from 1837 to

1848, proposed the reorganization of locally and regionally run schools into larger state- and federally controlled systems. Within thirty years of Mann's initial reforms, American public schools had become increasingly standardized and more widely available to urban and rural populations.[57] Yet the mandates to provide adequate education for all were unsurprisingly uneven in their application, subject to cultural, regional, racial, and economic disparities. In the North, schools' racial integration was determined on a state-by-state or even city-by-city basis. For instance, "Rhode Island, for the purposes of school taxes, counted black children as five-fourteenths of a white child," whereas Indiana and Illinois denied entry to black students and in the 1850s issued refunds to black taxpayers.[58] Some cities, such as New Haven, Boston, and New York, supported separate black schools.[59] The New York African Free School joined the city's public school system in 1835.[60] The equity that was at least conceptually at the heart of public education did not always play out in practice. Nevertheless, even the notion of a public education to which all children had access inspired concerns about the upending of a social order predicated on cultural and economic stratification.

For middling Americans, the association between common schools and older models of "charity schools" for the poor stigmatized public education, rendering it "a highly contested development."[61] Mann's reforms that sought to make education available to all meant that "not only the methods but the very meaning of education would have to change," for example, by addressing health and hygiene needs and focusing curricula more on projects of national assimilation.[62] Similarly in the United Kingdom, the Elementary Education Acts of 1870 and 1880 mandated schooling for all children from ages five to ten, but universal education raised concerns that empowering the laboring classes would threaten the social order. In the United States, public education attempted to assimilate and unify increasingly diverse and growing populations and provide the basic knowledge requisite for civic participation. Within this context, members of the upwardly mobile middle class found in-home education an opportunity to teach their children the habits of mind and social orientation that they would not get in school. Home education did not necessarily stress particular content, but worked to naturalize an individual and collective habitus that included particular ideas about race and gender, along with social and economic opportunity.[63]

Rational recreation standardized the child's waking hours into forms of study and play to mirror the spatially and temporally demarcated rhythms of modern life. This literature imagined a family "magic hour," as one book described in this way: "There is no time in the day when home is so pleasant as at twilight, or in the early evening hour. Then all are gathered (or should be) together at home. In the country it is after tea; in cities, particularly New York, it is after dinner."[64] Books such as Paris's, set during school holidays, or others, aimed at "relieving the tediousness of a long winter's, or a wet summer's evening," all distinguished rational recreation from formal education.[65] Middle-class mothers were advised to take an active role in child rearing. Fathers, whose responsibilities were increasingly outside the home at regular times each workday, were encouraged to consider their roles as both economic providers and attentive patriarchs. In the preface to her book *Popular Pastimes for Field and Fireside* (Milton Bradley, 1867), Caroline Smith inquired of fathers: "Is it not better to devote at least an hour a day to your children, than to spend every moment earning money for them, which, unless you rightly direct and train them, will surely prove their ruin?"[66]

Whereas fathers were encouraged not to imagine their time exclusively in economic terms, children were conversely advised to consider their time a precious resource to be wasted or well spent. The notion of time as a finite resource to be used judiciously was not new. However, the increasing standardization and quantification of time in the nineteenth century further defined time in economic and developmental terms.[67] Within this frame, childhood gained enormous significance as a period during which children had the greatest potential to establish a trajectory for later success. From the 1840s onward, most editions of Paris's *Philosophy in Sport* were prefaced by an eight-line segment of William Cowper's 1784 poem "Tirocinium":

> 'Tis not enough that Greek and Roman page
> At stated hours the sprightly boy engage;
> E'en in his pastimes he requires a friend,
> To warn, and teach him safely to unbend;
> And levying thus, and with an easy sway,
> A tax of profit from his very play,
> To impress a value, not to be erased,
> On moments squander'd else, and running all to waste.

Cowper's poem, a critique of formal education, crucially orients the project of home recreation as an opportunity for development and self-improvement, positioning play within broader temporal and sensory economies. Juvenile recreation literature's concern for children's "squander'd" moments anticipates with surprising clarity twentieth- and twenty-first-century preoccupations with children's media consumption, commonly embodied in the concept of screen time, which has sparked a profusion of parenting advice manuals advocating caution and balance.[68] In the nineteenth century, the conception of childhood as a time of carefree innocence was thus not without its demands. Children were asked to think strategically about how to use their time; rational recreation literature offered both a new method of learning and a new corpus of knowledge.

New Knowledge, New Media

Home recreation texts assumed that children learned differently than adults do and, reflecting their broader middle-class readership, gained privileged knowledge directly from experience over more traditional content like the classics. The introduction to Ebenezer Landells's *The Boy's Own Toy-Maker* positions home recreation as a distinctly youth-oriented practice, drawing a generational divide in learning methods and subject matter: "Grown men who could talk with Virgil or Homer in their own tongues, are ignorant of many things of every-day life, which very little children are now taught in play and learn with scarcely an effort."[69] Landells entreats readers to imagine the better companion with whom to be stranded on a desert island: Someone who knows only Greek and Latin or someone who can build a toy boat?[70] Landells's belief in 1859 that children not only learned differently but should learn different material than their parents did would anticipate the distinction between "legacy" and "future" content that Marc Prensky identified in his 2001 article describing what he called "digital natives." Like nineteenth-century progressive educators, Prensky argued that teachers should move away from traditional academic subjects (reading writing, arithmetic, and history) toward teaching technological competencies and socially relevant content like "*ethics, politics, sociology,* [and] *language.*"[71] Home recreation literature similarly framed everyday knowledge and new technologies like optical devices as important contemporary media to which children were naturally drawn. Simultaneously, despite this literature's broad middle-class appeal, it commonly linked optical toys to knowledge possessed primarily by more privileged children. In so doing, it cast visual education largely as the domain of youth, while defining youth within particular social and economic parameters.

Home recreation literature tended to deride the classics through humor. Ambivalence toward the esoteric and elitist Greek and Latin terms was evident in discussions of optical toys, with Greek names that were perpetually misspelled, used interchangeably, and otherwise adapted. The phenakistoscope, for example, was variously known as the stroboscope, stoboscope, phantascope, phantasmascope, fantascope, phenakistoscope, the magic wheel, the magic circle, the magic disk, and the wheel of life. Publications lampooned scientific terms as "frequently atrocious hybrids of Greek and Latin."[72] Names may have varied to avoid sounding complex, or they reflected publishers' concerns to appear original in a competitive market. One text's reference to a phenakistoscope (identified as a "phenatascope") defends the toy by saying it is "not nearly as bad as it sounds."[73] A French book of scientific experiments refers to the thaumatrope as a "barbaric" word, though the author acknowledges that its Greek roots—"wonder" and "to turn"—aptly describe the toy's function.[74] Optical toys thus embodied a peculiar combination of tradition and modernity. Their Greek names provided a sense of authority, while the toys themselves offered a modern kind of play.

A similar tension between older traditions and youthful play is observed in Mr. Twaddleton—the antagonistic vicar in *Philosophy in Sport*, who humorously embodies classical or traditional learning. Set up as comical straw man against rational recreation, the vicar proclaims, "Amusement and instruction ... are not synonymous in my vocabulary."[75] When shown the thaumatrope, he says, "I like your toy, but cannot discover the advantage of alloying amusement with such spurious wit, and of associating science with buffoonery."[76] Mr. Twaddleton eventually acquiesces to the allure of the thaumatrope, not for its scientific merit but for its potential applications in showcasing classical illustrations such as Greek myths and the works of Virgil. Significantly, he is also persuaded when shown a model that, when twirled, superimposes a bishop's vestments onto his own image, projecting his personal aspirations of upward mobility.[77] The ambivalence toward the classics that this literature claimed was thus complex.[78] To interpret the vicar as a tiresome, satirical character, readers needed to recognize his allusions to Greek myths and to interpret short Latin mottoes such as the thaumatrope's packaging bearing Virgil's caution: *Timeo danaos et dona ferentes*—Beware of Greeks bearing gifts. These texts assumed familiarity with classical content even as they stressed the acquisition of more popular or vernacular knowledge. Middle-class youth reading this literature and engaging in optical play thus paradoxically leaned on but also distanced themselves from the classical knowledge of prior generations.

Philosophy in Sport's humorous contest between the "old" ways of learning and the new tenets of home recreation, set against a scenario of family leisure time, demonstrates the role that this literature played in reproducing narratives of both upward mobility and childhood. Home recreation texts were often compiled and published in the form of gift books and annuals, which represented "the chief literary fare of children" for much of the nineteenth century.[79] These volumes with gilt and embossed covers were copiously illustrated and reflect the aspirations that adult gift givers had for the children in their lives, materially signifying their young owners' social positions and educational aspirations.[80] Bookplates and inscriptions in spidery nineteenth-century script tell us that they were given for school prizes, birthdays, Christmases, and New Year's gifts by parents, grandparents, uncles, sisters, friends, and school officials. Books given as "A New Year's token," "with a Father's Love," and one to a little girl named Virginia "with many wishes that she may have a Merry Christmas" evince a sentimental attitude toward children that was both reflected in and reinforced by the circulation of this literature.[81] These texts' wide production and distribution attest to the depth and breadth of their cultural reach, while singular copies indicate their intended roles in the lives of individual children.

Such publications also provided suitable alternatives to objectionable media like penny dreadfuls and kept children safe and occupied at home.[82] Most editions of *The Boy's Own Book*, for example, lamented the availability of "publications of an objectionable character, [purchased] mainly because their low price placed them within … reach." Directed at "those, who had the guardianship of youth," *The Boy's Own Book*'s prelude praised its careful editorial selection and billed it as "much more amusing and instructive to the juvenile mind than the cheap trash on which the hoarded shilling is usually expended."[83] Pastimes like parlor magic promised "instructive as well as recreative entertainment, without having recourse to any of the vulgar modes of killing time."[84] These books helped establish a cultural discourse around children's leisure time and consumption understood in terms of quality and benefits, heightening the importance of selecting the best products for children's development.

Indeed, adult buyers of this literature had to navigate a competitive market. While these texts differed in style and organization, they often included virtually identical content. Many volumes, like the gift book and annual, were compiled and repackaged material that had appeared as stand-alone periodical articles. Some were written in narrative prose style, as Paris's text was, some directly addressed the reader with an instructional tone, and still others were more encyclopedic and descriptive in style. Nearly all were structured as compendia—promising a comprehensive overview of games and activities and the instructions to carry them out at home. The same verbatim descriptions of optical toys, their perceptual effects, and suggestions for home construction are found in both European and American books—evidence of alliances between British and American publishers and a reflection of absent or lax copyright laws.

These books' introductions and prefaces often framed content as new and improved, updated, expanded, or otherwise superior in an oversaturated market. They appealed to concerns over quality with apologies for any content that may seem "borrowed … by an accidental and unrecognised waif of memory."[85] Aware of the proliferation of recycled material, introductions frequently promised no "padding," which served only "to swell the bulk of the whole publication to a size which may appear to justify its price," providing quality assurances and reflecting buyer concerns over the book's value.[86] Rampant plagiarism, absent authorial attribution, or attribution under pseudonym all make it difficult to trace the origins of this content or to consider these texts as individually authored in the traditional sense.[87] Instead, the discussion of optical toys in this literature was widely distributed, common knowledge that permeated the popular imagination.

The inclusion of optical toys in this literature demonstrates how broadly they were disseminated in textual form. Paris's *Philosophy in Sport*, where the thaumatrope made its literary debut for children, was published and reprinted in numerous editions throughout the century by multiple publishers, including Sherwood, Gilbert, and Piper; Harvey and Darton; George Routledge and Sons; and John Murray, who reprinted the book in at least nine editions. British editions were readily available in the United States, and the book was also published by several American publishers, including

Philadelphia-based Lea and Blanchard (1847) and New York–based Clark, Austin, and Smith (1853). The book's passage on the thaumatrope quickly became a fixture in other books of juvenile recreational literature on both sides of the Atlantic, found in such varied titles as *The Boy's Own Book* (Boston: Monroe and Francis, 1829), *Book of Sports* (Boston: Lilly, Wait, Colman, and Holden, 1834), *The Boy's Book of Science 3rd Edition* (London: Thomas Tegg, 1842), *Every Boy's Book of Games, Sports, and Diversions* (London: John Kendrick, 1852), and *The Young Ladies' Treasure Book* (London: Ward, Lock, and Company, 1884). Publications from the 1830s onward often included descriptions of the thaumatrope alongside the newer phenakistoscope and zoetrope. Optical toys were standard playthings with which children practiced and performed as playful learners. Ubiquitous in the nineteenth-century playscape, these toys appeared in titles as varied as *Parlor Magic*, *The Magician's Own Book*, and *Scientific Amusements for Young People*.

As these diverse titles suggest, categories such as branches of science and the distinction between toy, sport, game, science, and magic were permeable within this literary tradition. Optical toys in particular transcended classification; the thaumatrope's placement within several such titles exemplifies its movement across categories. In the first American edition of *The Boy's Own Book* (1829), the thaumatrope is included in a section on "minor sports," preceded by entries on the peashooter and kite and followed by an entry on battledore and shuttlecock—variants of badminton.[88] Curiously, the thaumatrope is not found in the book's separate section dedicated to optical amusements, unlike in Robin Carver's *Book of Sports* (1835), where it appears alongside other optical demonstrations and devices such as the "invisible wafer" (an experiment in binocular vision) and the camera obscura.[89] A late nineteenth-century encyclopedia of games and sports is organized alphabetically; there, the thaumatrope is sandwiched among tennis, tent pegging (a version of the knife-throwing game mumblety-peg), and "three-faced pictures" (a homemade lenticular image). It is followed by the outdoor game called thread the needle, which invites young people to hold hands in a long line and pass under one another.[90] These contextual clues foreground the multidisciplinary and interactive qualities of optical toys as they were found alongside other playthings and activities and incorporated the eye into a broader social and corporeal education.

It is difficult to determine whether authors and editors considered optical toys filler or padding in these texts or whether such toys were regarded as indispensable elements of home recreation. In some instances, their inclusion represented the financial interests of the author or publisher. It is unsurprising, for instance, that Paris's *Philosophy in Sport* extolled the thaumatrope's virtues, or that Milton Bradley's publications featured the zoetrope with special enthusiasm. In other cases, the thaumatrope, phenakistoscope, and zoetrope appear as stock childhood pastimes along with kite flying, blowing soap bubbles, and card tricks. Yet over the course of the nineteenth century, visual perception—and particularly its relationship to knowledge and truth—would come to hold increased importance. In their ubiquity, these toys exemplify the ocularcentrism that now characterizes the nineteenth century.[91] Vision became a privileged mode of learning within the context of formal education as well. Horace Mann imagined that visual instruction would "increase tenfold the efficiency of our Common Schools."[92] He argued that visual acquisition of knowledge with visual aids such as images and objects would permit pupils to clearly "see" ideas as though they were physical forms. Such disciplined forms of looking, Mann contended, would cultivate "the materials of philosophers, statesmen and chief-justices."[93]

Although educators like Mann saw great potential for visual learning, especially in the education of students from broad social and cultural backgrounds, his conception of vision concentrated principally on seeing as a means of knowledge acquisition. Mann described the eye as a "thoroughfare" between exterior reality and one's mental impressions, but simultaneously maintained that "seeing is believing" and that vision was the most effective means of knowledge transmission.[94] The optical toys and experiments in home recreation literature conversely encouraged children to think of vision and sight as complex, even problematic processes. As will be seen, optical toys, illusions, and effects played with the senses and encouraged children to identify visual "deceptions." This informal visual education was congruent with other forms of home recreation, such as parlor games like blind man's bluff, which took vision, judgment, and the negotiation of social codes as their central features.[95]

Conclusion

From their introduction in the 1820s and 1830s to and through the turn of the twentieth century, optical toys appeared relentlessly and repetitively in multiple incarnations. As they moved from the contexts of the science institution and public demonstration to the white middle-class parlor, they popularized and domesticated new forms of knowledge and learning that privileged immediate sensory encounters, child-driven exploration, and the child's individual role in his or her education over passive forms of learning like rote memorization. As these toys encouraged the curious, inquisitive child to engage in optical play alongside science experiments, magic tricks, and parlor games, they played a role in the construction and maintenance of modern childhood itself. Concentrating on these toys exclusively as commercially produced playthings may imply their short "life spans" as they were replaced and eclipsed by newer media: the thaumatrope for the phenakistoscope, the phenakistoscope for the zoetrope. Considering their instantiations in print form challenges this linear narrative and tells another story altogether, in which optical toys circulated widely among one another for decades and were ubiquitous across virtually all facets of middle-class childhood. Indeed, while the perceptual effect of persistence of vision would come to place optical devices within a trajectory that includes cinema, video games, and other screen-based media, an examination of where and how they were sold and used aligns them as much with the top, kite, bubbles, and ball. The mass production of paper templates, illustrations, and textual descriptions of optical toys likely resulted in innumerable homemade devices, and still more children internalized the operative optical principles by reading and watching. The distribution of optical toys in these forms was facilitated by a rapidly expanding market for children's literature and the surging popularity of children's magazines. Authors and editors clamored for content to fill pages, and paper templates of optical toys, which could be fashioned into playthings that demonstrated immediate effects, struck the perfect balance between recreation and education befitting respectable children's periodicals.

This alternate genealogy of optical toys offers insight into the kinds of children who played with them, how their play was organized, and what values may have been reinforced, challenged, or otherwise negotiated during play. Commercially produced optical toys and home recreation literature perpetuated the ideology of the nuclear family by unifying parents and children in edifying home play. Home recreation demanded that activities be both instructional and entertaining, solidifying the importance of childhood as a time of innocence and development. Spared from the factory, middle-class children instead found their time structured between school and home, the latter of which became an informal laboratory for learning. This conception of leisure time appeared to hold great democratic potential by rewarding those youth willing to "invest" their time wisely with the greatest set of potentials. In practice, however, rational recreation was a "resource-intensive educational regime" that demanded not only time but space, materials, and a participatory social circle of family and friends.[96]

Even as home recreation—of which optical play was a part—was framed in opposition to formal schooling, the literary guidebooks that outlined best practices assumed knowledge from traditional learning environments. These texts purported to sever the linearity and exclusivity of aristocratic heritage by mocking Greek and Latin and speaking to the upwardly mobile and dynamic middle classes. Simultaneously, however, the popular scientific knowledge that this literature imparted assumed familiarity with the classics, resulting in a kind of hybrid, intergenerational pedagogy where old knowledge unlocked the gateway to new and supported the construction of future citizens. With their antiquated Greek names and new modes of image visualization, optical toys straddled the old and the new in distinct ways. As "new media," they advanced contemporary modes of understanding vision as subjective, individual, and a process of active interpretation. Their inclusion in home recreation literature—held in esteem by adults but aimed largely at children—suggests their part in the making of future generations of educated subjects. As such, this literary tradition and the optical play associated with it advanced an essentially liberal imagination of childhood: forward thinking and expansive rather than protectionist, as later discourses of media would turn. Now that the integral place of optical toys within the domain of nineteenth-century childhood is firmly established, the subsequent chapters will consider the kinds of knowledge and skills associated with these toys, the experiences of play, and the various aspirations and anxieties that they generated and resolved.

2 Language in Motion: The Thaumatrope Establishes a Multimedia Convention

A set of twelve thaumatropes in the collection of the Cotsen Children's Library at Princeton University forms the basis of a flirtation game for young men and women.[1] Dating from the late nineteenth century, the thaumatropes are fashioned from rectangular cards and packaged neatly in a box. Six of the cards, with blue strings tied on either end, were to be wielded by young ladies; the remaining six, designated with red strings, to be operated by the gentlemen. A series of unintelligible letters is printed on each side of the card, and directions instruct the user to "take the Strings between the finger and thumb of each hand and twist the Card rapidly round." Doing so combines the letters into a legible question or response, such as, "Are you engaged? Can I refuse? Oh dear! No. Do you love me? Yes, to be sure" (figure 2.1).

I discovered these fascinating flirtatious devices during my month-long research trip to Princeton by channeling nineteenth-century commentators, who used multiple spelling variations in their discussion of optical toys. Searching the standard "thaumatrope" retrieves numerous relevant examples, which I also consulted. However, searching for "thaumotrope," also retrieves this hidden gem. These examples are unusual because of their primarily textual rather than illustrated content, and they speak volumes to the rhetorical and interpersonal work that the thaumatrope (or thaumotrope) may have performed in the nineteenth century. Although these thaumatropes demonstrate persistence of vision, their main purpose was not scientific demonstration. Instead, they exploit the optical principle to facilitate playful flirtatious exchange, their content inextricably tied to the toy's formal attributes. The thaumatrope's common linguistic and visual motifs, and the punny epigrams that often accompanied it, demonstrate its

Figure 2.1
Flirtation thaumatropes, late nineteenth century. "Are you engaged?" "Can I refuse?" Princeton University Library.

central feature as a device that "enacts an intense intertwining of the verbal and the visual, and the literary and the technological."[2]

The thaumatrope was both constitutive of and a contribution to a changing visual culture in the nineteenth century that integrated language and image in novel ways. It reinforced a fluid relationship between word and picture, between perceptual illusion and literary allusion. The thaumatrope, and toys like it, allowed users to participate in a growing set of cultural practices that drew on written and visual literacy as interchangeable modes of expression. The ability to interpret messages using this distinct combination was a key component in the making and maintenance of an educated middle class in the nineteenth century. The flirtation thaumatropes were not meant to be used by children but by youth approaching marrying age. They courted in a time when commercial valentines were widely available. Elizabeth Nelson notes that "valentines were often [designed as] puzzles in the form of love knots, rebuses, acrostics, and riddles" and that "the pleasures of decoding that these valentines offered contributed to the lighthearted nature of the holiday's celebration."[3] Yet they also functioned as "vehicle[s] through which authenticity could be captured, making the act of consumption of a particular kind of card an indicator of taste and authenticity."[4] In this way, such flirtatious commodities linked visual perception to the moral orientation of middle-class gentility.

Like puzzle valentines, the flirtation thaumatropes were commercial products that enabled sentimental and romantic exchange. Their operation required knowledge not only of the complex social codes governing courtship but also of how the thaumatrope itself worked. With the toy, users could express their romantic intentions, but such expressions were embedded within a network of ideas about vision, truth, and sincerity. No longer a new medium, by the late nineteenth century, the thaumatrope had been in circulation for nearly seventy-five years. Youth users were likely familiar with the toy and could call on its associations with childhood to imbue courtship with a sense of innocence and play. Yet the thaumatrope's reliance on a perceptual trick also allowed users to play with visual veracity as a way of examining their prospective partner's moral intentions and sincerity.

The thaumatrope's engagement of language and image connect it with many nineteenth-century media forms for children and youth. This chapter considers the thaumatrope in relation to a range of print and visual media. It explores the toy's contribution to a broader project of multimedia literacy, which connected visual interpretation with reading instruction and foregrounded the eye as an interpretive organ. The thaumatrope's commercial development was informed by a desire to use persistence of vision to tell jokes, express puns, and deliver social commentary. From its earliest days, the thaumatrope's visual effects thus became tied to middle-class concerns over notions of truth, deception, sincerity, and humor. It entered the market alongside other children's media that similarly relied on the interplay between the visual and the textual, fragmentation and assembly. Early reading primers used text and image together to reinforce iconographic and linguistic concepts. Such books commonly broke words down into their component parts: letters and syllables. Images of all kinds were made into jigsaw puzzles, which fragmented a unified whole and demanded that children engage in reassembly. Rebus puzzles conveyed content like Bible passages, poetry, and nursery rhymes in paragraphs where pictorial symbols and words and letters alternated. The sense of empowerment gained from being able to "read" words and images together was thematized in the thaumatrope's common motifs, like the bird in the cage, which similarly addressed power dynamics. The thaumatrope's prototypical bird-and-cage design enabled children to playfully transgress behavioral expectations (such as those surrounding conduct toward animals) through visual manipulation. Older youth exercised the same kinds of perceptual competencies in social games in the exchange of romantic calling cards, conversation cards, and valentines. In such contexts, the thaumatrope's perceptual play allowed users to broach sensitive topics like moral intention, contrasting the deception of optical illusion with the sincere expression of romantic affection.

This chapter recontextualizes the thaumatrope, considering its role not within a history of cinema but among the materials and paper ephemera that engaged children and youth in literacy and social instruction—valentines, jigsaw puzzles, early readers. During the nineteenth century, these media forms mandated the exercise of a unique interplay among written, visual, and tactile modes of interpretation. Scholars of visual culture rightly caution against the limitations of "reading" as a metaphor for all interpretive processes.[5] Indeed, "literacy," so-named as a coherent idea, did not emerge until the 1880s.[6] Yet the work of rendering content intelligible across disparate media forms was, for the children who used them, a diverse set of skills thought requisite for modern life that might be understood as "literacies" in the contemporary meaning of the term. Alongside traditional reading instruction, the practice of reading across multiple surfaces—paper, wood, glass, cardboard—manipulating the surfaces of book and toy objects, and alternating between word and image all transformed reading into a multisensory process meant to engage and delight as much as to instruct. These patterns of education and entertainment were themselves a kind of class-based instruction. To this complex set of processes the thaumatrope introduced the added element of visual illusion as its operation engaged language and image through the demonstration of optical phenomena.

From Fiery Circle to Commercial Toy

Although John Ayrton Paris's introduction of the thaumatrope in 1825 and its sale by London publisher William Phillips marked the toy's commercial introduction, the precise intellectual origins of the device are considerably more complex.[7] Commercially associated with Paris, its invention has variously been attributed to several other figures involved in nineteenth-century scientific experimentation and practice. For example, during a dinner party in the 1820s, astronomer John Herschel is said to have challenged colleagues to consider ways to make both sides of a coin visible simultaneously. In response to the challenge, according to the memoirs of Charles Babbage, geologist William Henry Fitton later produced a card with strings featuring a hand-painted bird on one side and a cage on the other as an answer to Herschel's initial provocation. The thaumatrope's invention has thus variously been attributed to both Fitton and to Herschel himself alongside Paris.

These histories of the thaumatrope's origins have been reproduced in many accounts.[8] However, the device's attribution to a single inventor is perhaps less significant than two key factors related to its eventual dissemination as a commercial plaything. First, the toy in commercially produced form consolidated a line of inquiry inspired by optical phenomena and bodily sensations commonly experienced in everyday nineteenth-century life. From the blurred spokes of a wagon wheel observed in an 1820 issue of the *Quarterly Journal of Science* and explained by Peter Mark Roget in 1824, to the later sensation of a train moving when stationary, the nineteenth century was marked by increasing velocity and competing visual stimuli in both public and private settings.[9] The commercially produced thaumatrope singled out, packaged, and marketed an optical phenomenon, providing "a scientific explanation *and* a device ... to be sold as a popular entertainment."[10] Second, and closely related, the commercial form that Paris's thaumatrope took emphasized not only perceptual play, but linguistic play as well. Paris's decision to combine optical effects with written epigrams, iconographic puns, and other verbal and visual motifs aligned the thaumatrope with broader trends in print, visual, and material cultures in operation in the first half of the nineteenth century.

While the thaumatrope's commercial form eventually took shape as a circular or rectangular disk with a pair of strings, children were taught about persistence of vision in other ways both before and after the thaumatrope's introduction. The perceptual phenomenon can be demonstrated by virtually any rapidly moving object: a spinning coin, swinging rope, or optical toy. Indeed, home recreation texts commonly reference a persistence-of-vision experiment known as the "fiery circle." This activity involved "whirling round [the end of] a lighted stick" or attaching a burning stick to the end of a rope and swinging it. In rapid motion, the burning wood "will exhibit not a fiery point but a fiery circle in the air."[11] The demonstration—aside from being potentially dangerous—was not one that could easily be commodified. As one juvenile periodical wryly pointed out, though "philosophically adequate, bits of burning string, as gifts, have not yet received the sanction of Santa Claus."[12] Thus, even as a variety of objects and activities could conjure the phenomenon of persistence of vision, the thaumatrope notably made the optical effect marketable. Paris's original set of eighteen sold for the considerable price of just over seven shillings. The cost was justifiable, David Brewster lamented from his personal experience inventing the kaleidoscope, because pirated copies would surely follow. Brewster wrote, "It is quite fair that the inventor should be remunerated for his invention and to be so he must sell the Thaumatrope while it is new for the construction of the toy is so easy that it will soon be copied by everyone capable of drawing and become as common as another philosophical and beautiful invention the Kaleidoscope."[13] As the previous chapter demonstrates, soon the thaumatrope was everywhere, including reproduced in home recreation literature.

Alternate versions of the device also point to other ways that it might have developed, privileging its ability to simulate motion rather than produce a still composite image. An alternate design, frequently described in recreational literature but less commonly seen in archival collections, featured three sets of strings rather than one. To operate the six-string model, the user could select different combinations of strings, thereby altering the disk's axis of rotation (rather than the single horizontally positioned axis of the standard design). In some cases, one set of strings was described as elastic cords, enabling the user to quickly change the slack and tautness in rotation to better manipulate the images. Changing the disk's axis in turn changed the position of the two images in relation to one another, often resulting in figures in slightly different attitudes or in the middle of different actions. In one example, one side featured a juggler in the process of tossing two balls in the air. The other side featured additional juggling balls in space. Manipulating different sets of strings could variously give the impression of the juggler throwing three, four, or five balls at once, depending on how the images overlapped. A skilled operator could even manipulate the strings so that the juggler appeared to introduce additional balls before the observer's eyes.[14] Another variant depicted a man with an open mouth on one side and a disembodied hand holding a bottle on the other. Depending on how the strings are pulled, the man may be seen either holding the bottle or tipping it back to drink. Because this version of the thaumatrope seems to evoke motion, it privileges a linear account of optical toy development moving toward devices that showcased moving images like the phenakistoscope and zoetrope. However, the thaumatrope's most popular two-string form charts another historical trajectory that instead foregrounds the dynamic relationship between word and image.[15]

From the start, the thaumatrope's perceptual trick was deployed in the service of social commentary. Drawing on the collections of Richard Balzer and Lester Smith, Stephen Herbert offers the most in-depth explication of the social allusions made in Paris's first set of thaumatropes.[16] Early motifs exploited word play for political jabs (using *wig* for *Whig*, for example), and satirized social figures, such as the incompetent watchman ejected from his post. Textual mottoes often accompanied the thaumatrope or, as Herbert indicates, were sometimes manually written onto the disks. Persistence of vision was not simply instrumental to the novel production and display of the thaumatrope's images. Rather, the perceptual phenomenon was integral to the conveyance of each disk's message. Drawing vision and social commentary together, it functioned as a way of seeing and understanding perception itself that was linked to a specific set of social interests.

The visual and textual literacies that the device's operation required suggested forms of reading and looking not only for utility but also as an opportunity for play. The political satire and puns that the original thaumatropes expressed may have been more squarely aimed at adults. However, as the previous chapter indicates, such optical playthings quickly became the purview of children and found use among a range of related new media. Media combining visual and verbal modes of communication gained popularity as educational tools at home and in schools. After midcentury, as Barbara Finkelstein and Kathy Vandell assert, the wide availability of colorful media such as "alphabet blocks and wooden blocks, manufactured toys, and attractive pictures and puzzles attest to a growing taste for objects rather than books for very young children."[17] Among these myriad forms, rebuses and jigsaw puzzles stand out as exemplifying a conception of "reading" as involving play with both language and image as they imparted moral, religious, patriotic, or sentimental messages that children worked to decipher.

Fragmentation and Assembly

The thaumatrope circulated within broader print and visual cultures where many media formats similarly organized visual and textual material in novel ways. The thaumatrope contained two distinct sides whose relationship was apparent only when the toy was in motion. Other media, such as jigsaw puzzles and rebuses—puzzles that combined text with iconographic representations of words to form short rhymes, songs, and passages—engaged a similar dynamic between language and image, fragmentation and assembly. These playthings did not simply teach children how to read and write to impart didactic content. Instead, they required a more complex negotiation between looking and reading, assembling and deciphering—all forms of literacy tied to new media formats and interfaces. The interpretive and perceptual skills that such playthings stressed were available most readily to the children whose parents could afford them, and thus, these new cultural practices of spectatorship were linked to particular race and class positions. Simultaneously, however, as the previous chapter indicates, optical toys likely circulated across a broad socioeconomic spectrum as physical playthings, paper templates, and do-it-yourself instructions. As they infiltrated children's playtime in the middle-class parlor or within the homes of the laboring classes, these forms of perceptual play helped reinforce new notions of what it meant to "read" and "see," attaching social value to these processes.

The pedagogical approaches espoused by these new visual and textual media in the nineteenth century were more progressive than those of earlier didactic forms such as the hornbook and primer. Hornbooks were flat wooden paddles with handles with alphabets and prayer texts on them "laminated" by a thin piece of horn overlaying the text. Like hornbooks, eighteenth-century educational texts like primers "were permeated with religion, duty, and rules of civility."[18] Such learning implements combined "a complex intermeshing of texts and strategies for teaching reading and for teaching the construction of particular modes of being."[19] Religious morals and cultural mores were not, of course, absent from nineteenth-century children's media. However, the didacticism of earlier texts would be replaced by approaches that more critically considered the child's motivation in the educational process and could be implemented in increasingly crowded and culturally and linguistically diverse classrooms.

This pedagogical orientation also shaped reading instruction. Proponents of phonics and spelling were pitted against advocates of the whole-word approach, such as Horace Mann and Josiah Bumstead, the latter a Boston merchant whose interest in children's reading led him to write a series of primary school textbooks on the subject. Whole-word advocates believed that pupils were engaged by the word as a full concept rather than as composed of abstract letters. Using an optical metaphor, Mann argued that words "should be looked at as a medium, and not as an end ... the page should only be as the mirror, or picture, through which objects are beheld."[20] Much like the child-centered tenets of home recreation, this approach characterized the child as an active, curious learner. The whole-word philosophy, Bumstead wrote in one of his textbooks, "presumes that the scholar is a thinking being, and not a mere piece of mechanism."[21] Yet even as whole-word advocates appealed to children's interests, their strategies were also calculated "to arrest and fix [students'] attention," thereby creating orderly, manageable classrooms.[22]

Rebus puzzles, which combined images with letters and words to form phrases, exemplify this conception of active learning. Rebuses and children's "hieroglyphic" bibles had been common since the mid-eighteenth century, but enjoyed enormous success in the nineteenth when many eighteenth-century texts were reprinted. Riddle columns and sections became staples of children's magazines, such as "The Riddle Box" page in *St. Nicholas*, which featured "charades, rebus, double crostics, anagrams, decapitations, and hidden words."[23] Their graphic format made them easy filler content for books and magazines, and their merits were easily framed within new notions of child-led learning. The preface of McLoughlin Brothers's *Rebus ABC* (New York, ca. 1875) suggested the puzzle form's ability to "help arouse the minds of children to action." It continues, promising that "rebuses will beget a habit in children of independent thinking, and of seeing and judging of things readily and correctly. It is object-teaching in the best style."[24] Emphasizing the importance of the learning method as much as the content of the encoded message, the rebus reflected broader trends in nineteenth-century education toward training the senses and habits of mind over simply memorizing facts. The rebus exchanges words for pictures or alternates between picture and text, requiring the reader to navigate written and pictorial symbols. Whole words, letters, and pictures might be displayed in jumbled groups, for example: a prominent "V," a block of ice, the letter "B," two conjoined rings, and the word "ruin," translating to "Vice brings ruin," or the letter "F" alongside an illustrated ear, followed by the word "God," meaning "Fear God."[25] Such combinations of pictorial symbols, along with phonetic cues (such as U U = "use") encouraged young readers to make meaning through word and image recognition and experiments sounding things out.

Like the rebus, the thaumatrope emphasizes not only the result of the interpretive process (content comprehension) but the process itself as a form of knowledge. "To solve a rebus," Tom Getton asserts, "various sorts of looking must be deployed; here the pleasures of sight are closely connected to the pleasure of mastery."[26] The rebus's combination of image and text made a game of deciphering coded messages, inclining children to internalize the puzzle's moral content through the pleasure and investment of solving it. These media reinforced a kind of multimedia literacy that presumed a reading subject capable of coordinating his or her senses and intellect. The thaumatrope's fun is linked to committing oneself to a perceptual conundrum, as some packaging prominently declared its ability "to illustrate the seeming Paradox of Seeing an Object which is OUT OF SIGHT."[27] The toy's composite picture is ephemeral, belonging to a category that Tom Gunning calls "the technological image." These images "owe their existence to a device and are optically *produced* by it rather than simply reproduced," meaning that they are visible only while the toy is in motion. To "master" the thaumatrope, then, is to acknowledge the eye's complicity in this form of image production through a perceptual phenomenon.[28]

These media rely on the eye's ability to read text and images interchangeably and push the eye to its perceptual threshold. The conception of the eye as active and "muscular" was advanced in physiological optics from the middle of the nineteenth century onward by practitioners such as Hermann von Helmholtz, whose first treatise on the subject was published in 1856.[29] The eye's central role as an engaged perceptual organ connected to the larger nervous system also rendered it a powerful symbol of the individual self—a connection made explicit in the rebus puzzle's substitution of the word *I* with the image of an eye. The thaumatrope's production of the "technological image" demonstrates the eye's critical role as an intermediary between the internal self and external world. Psychologist Herbert Spencer would describe the retina as the part of the eye "brought more directly into contact with the external agent acting on it than … any other peripheral expansion of the nervous system."[30] Because the thaumatrope's image is produced only in action, appearing as a series of stimuli hit the retina, the eye is the site at which the composite image is inscribed (although it is the brain that makes sense of that image). Without the seeing subject, the thaumatropic image cannot be perceived.[31]

Because the image literally materializes on the eye, vision is personal and subjective, emphasizing the individual as independent observer. To understand vision in this way attributed individuals with the capacity to read and interpret the world around them. The eye thus became central to an individual's outlook or perspective (these terms themselves laden with visual valences). If properly trained and disciplined, the child's eye could discern right from wrong, truth from falsity—all attributes essential for youth learning to navigate increasingly complex social and technological worlds. This dynamic between the self and the collective has been explored in relation to other cultural forms, such as adults' home entertainment literature, which—like children's rational recreation—staged physical and mental contests among members of the middling classes, enabling players to perform and examine their social positions.[32]

Yet to privilege the eye is in keeping with nineteenth-century psychologists and physiologists such as Spencer, who would posit that the eye was a central gateway between the self and the external world. In this capacity, it was, as Lynda Nead contends, always active, even when the rest of the body appeared in stasis.[33] Such an understanding of the active eye helped to draw equivalencies between the manually laboring body and the mental labor of the managerial class. The eye's connection to the nervous system, moreover, promoted an atomized way of thinking that would distinguish the self from the wider social body, the home from the workplace. As industrialists imagined workers' bodies as energy-producing arms and legs responsible for ever-more-specific tasks, scientists drew more precise divisions among their fields and specialties, and newly professionalized teachers broke sentences down into words and letters. The body, broken into component parts, could be understood as labor potential and as a series of features that socially located the individual. Proponents of physiognomy, for instance, practiced "reading" the body "as a way to turn visual observation into a source of information and power." As Sharrona Pearl writes, "People became pictures, objects, and analytical units—analyzing and to be analyzed."[34]

This preoccupation with the relationship between part and whole, fragmentation and unification, manifested in the formal attributes of a range of media. Invented in England in the 1760s, the jigsaw puzzle (with its hallmark interlocking pieces) saw tremendous popularity in the nineteenth century. Along with other "dissected" puzzles, jigsaw puzzles fragmented all genres of text and image into smaller parts.[35] Early dissected maps, meant to aid in geography instruction, most explicitly helped to normalize notions of imperial expansion—their survey of land and water suggesting a totality to be divided up and possessed by different entities. As jigsaw subjects expanded to encompass illustrated prints, stories, and virtually all other forms of children's visual culture, the form of the puzzle demanded a play pattern that favored coherence and unity and "provide[d] a model for self-recognition in praxis in which the only direction available to participants is that of recomposition."[36]

Still other new media stressed not the satisfaction of putting pieces into their singular correct places, instead exploiting possibilities for endless recombination. In 1819, Ackermann and Co., the same London printmaker and bookseller that went on to sell Plateau's phenakistoscope, produced two games, the Changeable Ladies and Changeable Gentlemen, boxed card sets featuring portraits "dissected into three, just below and above the nose[;] the pieces can be combined in various ways to make different faces."[37] The composite portraits with universally compatible facial features allowed for playful combinations that arranged the features of different social types "for the mirth of a party round a table, or the more serious study of physiognomy," as well as served as artists' models.[38] These figures—many of whom were recognizable individuals—were broken down by individual features like headwear indicating position or ethnic identity and nose shapes: bulbous, hooked, rounded, and so on.

Examples of this fragmented, physiognomic view of the body abound in children's consumer and do-it-yourself cultures throughout the nineteenth century. The American Antiquarian Society, for instance, has a small boxed set, Modern Transformations for Boys, which contained thirty-six cards—twelve heads, twelve bodies, and twelve sets of legs—that could be arranged at random to form combination figures related to military iconography, musicians, a rabbit, and Asian and African caricatures. A book of "Funny Transformations" for children published after 1860 similarly includes pages of chromolithographed human and animal figures split into head, body, and legs that could be turned into various combinations. *The American Girl's Handy Book* (1898) provided instructions to make a "transformation scrapbook" with pages cut into thirds onto which girls glued images of heads, torsos, and legs cut from old picture books and advertisements. Careful alignment of similarly scaled images enabled men's and women's bodies, fat and thin, to be humorously remixed. The book's description of a similar activity hints at the violence of the remixed body: "Heads may be ruthlessly torn from bodies to which they belong, and as ruthlessly clapped upon strange shoulders."[39] The atomized, transformable bodies in these toys and games reified existing social and racial hierarchies in their conventions of caricature and stereotype. Yet the interchangeability of these features at least implied a fluidity or mobility among these types, acknowledging the rapid changes wrought by industrialization and urbanization that served as mechanisms for individual transformation.

The rebus puzzle similarly broke down the human body, using images of body parts interchangeably with text. One of the rhymes reproduced in Sherman and Co.'s *Mother Goose in Hieroglyphics* (New York, 1855), for example, dissects the body of a thief for observation by a market seller (figure 2.2):

> As I was going to sell my eggs
> I met a thief with bandy legs.
> Bandy legs and crooked toes,
> I tripped him up, and he fell on his nose.[40]

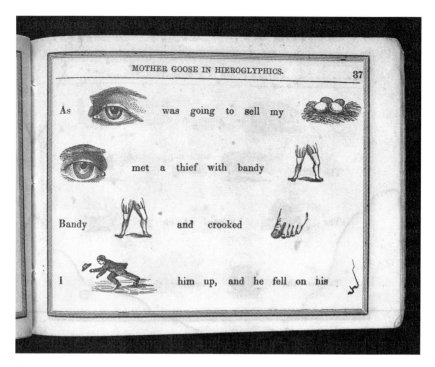

Figure 2.2
Rebus puzzle in *Mother [Goose] in Hieroglyphics* (New York: Sherman and Co., 1855), 37. Princeton University Library.

Of the puzzle's eight images, the "eye" is featured twice. It stands in for the speaker of the rhyme, in the marketplace to conduct legitimate business. Five of the remaining six images depict the thief's body, in whole or in part—his "bandy" legs and "crooked" toes, and an image of the thief's full body falling. The rebus thus pictorially emphasizes the speaker's surveillance of the thief (the latter perhaps identified because of his physiognomic traits or general appearance), while the satisfying meter and rhyme validate the speaker's violent enactment of justice. In this way, the individual parts of the body, the body as a whole, and the individual's place within a larger social order are all represented and naturalized as a coherent system.

Thaumatropes fragment their visual material by arranging it on either side of the card. The toy's single side in stasis often appears incomplete. Examples abound of a bucked rider, thrown from an unseen horse, a hanged man dangling from invisible gallows. In other instances, the individual body is fragmented—ladies' fancy hats and dresses suspended in place but subjectless or, conversely, disembodied arms, legs, and heads float on the card, waiting to be united with a body and clothing. Unlike the rebus, where body parts might stand in for other concepts (eye for *I* or nose for *knows*, for example), the thaumatrope's disembodied images required spinning the toy to make their meaning known. For example, the following verse accompanied an early disk that depicted a floating head, arms, and legs on one side and a king's regalia on the other, so that when turned, the man transformed into a king:

> Legs, arms, and head, alone appear,
> Observe that *no-body* is here,
> Napoleon-like, I undertake
> Of *nobody* a King to make.

An 1825 article discussing this thaumatrope in the *Cincinnati Literary Gazette* just months after the thaumatrope's initial sale in London points out the design's ability to exploit the multiple uses of the word *revolution*. The author notes that while a (political) revolution typically overthrows a king, the thaumatrope's physical revolution conjures the king's image.[41]

This use of the word *revolutionize* is an opportunity to capitalize on the homonym linking political upheaval with the literal turning of the thaumatrope. Like the example in Paris's *Philosophy in Sport*, in which the vicar sees a thaumatrope that overlays the vestments of a bishop, the thaumatrope's "revolutionary" expression emerges from the relationship between the toy's physical motion and the transformations of social status represented in its motifs. Whether the linear career progression from vicar to bishop or the radical upending of social order in the case of political revolutions, the thaumatrope invited users to exercise verbal and visual competencies to play with social power relations. These features made the toy an apt vehicle for political satire, alongside other forms and genres, such as the political sketch, which gained popularity from the 1830s on and similarly commented on the attributes of various social types and figures.[42] Yet as a *toy*, the thaumatrope's engagement with questions of power was particularly salient for children—many of whom, in the nineteenth century, enjoyed new positions as innocent, cherished family members and were simultaneously dispossessed of other forms of agency. Their separation from the economic sphere and relegation to the home bestowed on them both sentimentalized and marginalized status.

Birds and Cages

The thaumatrope helped to establish a sense of perceptual mastery that was linked to a particular imagination of the social world as increasingly atomized, where individuals occupied shifting positions of power relative to one another. Such notions of control are most explicitly thematized by the thaumatrope's most common motif: the bird in the cage. Like many other thaumatrope subjects, the bird-and-cage motif registered on both literal and figurative levels. It referenced the common practice of bird keeping in the nineteenth century (which included both domestic and exotic birds), and it drew on the bird's image as a symbol of freedom, liberty, and even morality. In some early instances, the bird's association with freedom functioned as political allusion. Herbert points to the motto accompanying the bird-and-cage disk in the original Paris set: "Why is this bird like an Opposition member, who gives over to the Ministers? Because, by TURNING ROUND HE GAINS A BIRTH [BERTH], and CEASES TO BE FREE!!!" Herbert hypothesizes that it references a "member of the Opposition ... who turned from Whig to Tory (thus supposedly gaining a position, while losing his 'freedom')."[43] In other instances, the bird's freedom and captivity serve as metaphors for virtues and vices. In Paris's original set of thaumatropes with mottos printed directly onto the card, one endorsed temperance: "'Why is this Parrot like a drunken Man?' ran the legend beneath the bird. 'Because he is often in the Cage.'"[44]

What might the thaumatrope's bird-and-cage imagery have meant to children playing with the toy? Kasey Grier explains that during the nineteenth century, "Birds ... occupied a special place in popular sentiments toward animals because of their apparent monogamy and devoted parenting. These qualities meant that birds were natural models for middle-class family life, and some people may have kept pet birds as living examples for their children."[45] Birds not only modeled appropriate moral and family sentiments but also provided occasion for children to exercise benevolence over creatures less powerful than themselves. Children were thought to need moral guidance in the proper care of animals: "Higher than animals, yet lower than adults, children required education as a means of controlling their natural cruelty."[46] Broader discourses of animal conduct stressed proper pet care as a moral imperative and a reflection of good manners. In some cases, this took the form of children's activism. A welfare group, "the

Army of Bird-Defenders," for instance, was organized through *St. Nicholas* magazine beginning in 1873. Its members pledged to protect and not abuse wild birds.[47] The recurrence of caged birds in children's cautionary tales also reflects these sentiments.

The child's capacity for cruelty is illustrated in a book titled *Lessons for Children: or, Rudiments of Good Manners, Morals, and Humanity* (1828), published in its first edition prior to the thaumatrope's commercial introduction. The book features a story, "The Brown Linnet," detailing the fate of a bird that a boy captured for a pet. Thus imprisoned, the bird is unable to care for its babies, who are blown to the ground and die of starvation. The boy loses interest in the linnet and stops cleaning its cage. A tabby cat scratches the linnet through its cage and the bird eventually succumbs to its injuries. The story condemns the boy, at whose hands the bird "was made to suff-er more pain and tor-ment than we know how to de-scribe."[48] Commonly seen in many texts for early readers, complex words are broken down by syllable, and a set of vocabulary words precedes the story. This story's vocabulary, like the narrative itself, foregrounds questions of agency and control with words such as *cages, cleaned, secure, provide,* and *destroy*.

Similarly, Lydia Maria Child's story "Gertrude and Her Birds" (1854) chronicles the eponymous protagonist's mishandling of a series of exotic birds brought to her by her sailor uncle. Alas, the narration informs the reader, "Poor Gertrude did not have good luck with her birds." Her paroquet is accidentally poisoned by berries; her Java sparrow dies of unknown causes. Gertrude's only success is a yellow-breasted bird, which she releases at the end of winter. She concludes (and so the reader is meant to agree) that birds are not meant to be caged; rather, they should be allowed to fly freely in their native habitats. Shortly after her revelation, Gertrude's affections are redirected to a new object to torment and admire: her baby brother, Frank, about whom she remarks, "I don't have to keep him shut up in a cage. That is a good thing."[49] The rationalist logic of such tales extends back to Locke and Rousseau, who stressed that children's empathy for animals was founded through an acknowledgment not of mastery but of their shared defenseless state—often both considered dumb and "speechless."[50] Stories like Child's reveal layers to the social hierarchies within which children found themselves. In the case of "Gertrude and Her Birds," baby Frank appears as helpless and vulnerable as Gertrude's ill-fated pets, even as Gertrude's own treatment of her birds reflected her own efforts at asserting control.

The thaumatrope's prototypical motif likely reminded children of the lessons encountered in these literary contexts. The example of Gertrude, whose focus shifts from the bird to her baby brother, particularly suggests the way that the bird-and-cage iconography may have allowed the child to play at exercising control over those with less power in the social order. The thaumatrope reinforced the symbols of liberty and constraint, extending their meanings to other social situations. A French example from the late nineteenth century simply refers to the bird as "the prisoner," added in a handwritten title (figure 2.3), while another textual example from an Italian text suggests that it's humanity's tyrannical nature to put the bird in the cage.[51] Broadly, comparisons between children and animals rendered both equivalently helpless, as Susan Pearson writes: "Associated with middle-class domestic ideals, the regime of kindness consigned both beasts and babes to a similar position in the household's affective economy, assigning them a mutual role as objects of sentimental investment."[52] This association helped solidify the conception of childhood innocence, making the child confined to the gilded parlor an apt simile for the caged bird. To conceive of the child as innocent is to divest him or her of power. This may have made the temptation to spin the thaumatrope and capture the bird all the more alluring for children as an occasion to transgress conventional moral guidance, imposing their will on someone below them in the social hierarchy.[53]

The bird-and-cage thaumatrope's visual paradox to show something "which is OUT OF SIGHT" parallels the moral conundrum that it presents to its users, inviting them to entrap the bird within a broader cultural discourse that discouraged such treatment. The colorful thaumatrope depicting a rat and a cage distributed with the *Boy's Own Paper* discussed in the previous chapter illustrates this quandary clearly. Printed around the edge of the disk is an epigram written from the rat's point of view, declaring, "I want to get out." The text, written in first person, bestows the rat with subjecthood, capable of addressing the child and making its demand known. However, the toy's overall form asks the child to disregard the rat's plea. The thaumatrope's "determined" scripts, which Robin Bernstein describes as "actions that are necessary for a thing to function," that articulate the set of uses to which it is to be put, thus place the young user in a complicated position. To operate the thaumatrope as intended is to violate an assumed

Figure 2.3
"Le prisonnier" bird-and-cage thaumatrope. Princeton University Library.

ethical principle.⁵⁴ Such toys that encouraged children to "play" at moral transgressions thus worked to naturalize the operative power relations they thematized.

A similar tension played out in many nineteenth-century children's texts and toys, used in particular to transform racially motivated violence into play. Bernstein examines E. W. Kemble's 1898 book *A Coon Alphabet*, which subjected black characters to violence and ridicule on the introduction of each letter. Bernstein notes how the book's form and content in concert naturalized reading practices that "conflate [the page-turning] action with the perpetration of violence against African American child characters, [and] … substitute satisfaction at a completed rhyme for any other emotion one might feel while participating in violence—and [asked readers] to repeat that sequence twenty-four times."⁵⁵ Other examples include mechanical banks with racial motifs, or a toy gun described by Gary Cross, with a figure of a Chinese man on top and the phrase, "The Chinese must go," printed along its handle. When the trigger is pulled, a metal boot kicks the Chinese figure, who pitches forward.⁵⁶ Attention to broader social repertoires as well as to the interaction between representation and materiality thus reveals how playthings including optical toys worked to choreograph children's actions in line with prevailing social formations.

The thaumatrope's prevalent bird-and-cage motif and other animal iconography made routine a set of nested logics of anthropocentrism that, by extension, ordered raced, classed, and gendered people into stratified relations. In play, the thaumatrope situated the child user within a social matrix governed by expectations of benevolence and stewardship as well as those of leisure and play. Bird-and-cage thaumatropes and related examples—such as

Figure 2.4
Cat out of the Bag thaumatrope. H. G. Clark, London, ca. 1860s. Victoria and Albert Museum, London.

one that, when twirled, features a dog who appears to leap out of its house toward a boy tormenting it with a whip—tempted—even authorized—children to transgress the moral codes to which they were meant to subscribe. In so doing, the toy linked visual mastery to social mastery. Another thaumatrope, produced by the London firm H. G. Clarke, ties animal imagery to more explicit social relations, as turning the toy "lets the cat out of the bag" (figure 2.4). But the thaumatrope's caged bird, tormented dog, and confined cat were manifest in the spirit of fun, only illusory, ephemeral. They appeared only as the toy was in motion, allowing children to play at domination as they played with vision without any impact on actual animals. These forms of visual play that waffled with but ultimately reified a position of moral sincerity would accompany children through their youth and into adulthood, where optical discernment and the toy's association with childhood would authenticate yet other social interactions.

From Birds to Bodies: Flirting with the Thaumatrope

Young adults who had played with rebuses, jigsaw puzzles, and the thaumatrope in childhood and youth would be well acquainted with a range of literary and perceptual competencies, which formed an intertwining moral and optical education. Young men and women who encountered the flirtation thaumatropes in the late nineteenth century likely found in them a familiar childhood pastime. The thaumatrope's status as a toy lent it an air of innocence and play—a sentiment that presided over courtship and kept more overt sexual overtones at bay. The thaumatrope's use in courtship is described in detail in *Children's Toys, and Some Elementary Lessons in General Knowledge Which They Teach* (1877):

> [Imagine a] Pretty young lady, unmarried, but with no intention to remain so. Eligible young gentleman, a warm admirer of the young lady, but perhaps bashful, perhaps irresolute; at any rate he does not come quite to the point of saying what he ought to say, and what the young lady desires that he should express in the shape of a formal and distinct proposition. After a long and somewhat embarrassing silence, young lady takes up, with seeming inadvertence, a card with two strings attached to it, and begins to twirl it. It is but a mere child's toy, quite innocent and unmeaning, since it has only a few letters, spelling apparently nothing, on its face. The letters are these S A A. When the card is spun, the coincidence is disclosed that it is inscribed with some other equally unmeaning letters on its back, namely A K P P. These latter, when the motion becomes rapid,

combine, through the persistence of vision, with the other letters on the retina of the young gentleman's eye, and they form together the words, "Ask papa." The two assemblages of letters, when thus conjoined, are fraught with obvious significance and suggestiveness.[57]

The text stresses child's play as an alibi, "quite innocent and unmeaning," but it also points to the thaumatrope's ability to move the courtship along to its next phase. The thaumatrope plays a role in advancing courtship when the young man in question fails to act and, interestingly, provides the young woman an opportunity to take an active role moving an engagement forward (albeit within a context requiring a suitor to "Ask Papa" for approval).

Although in this example, the young woman takes control of the courtship's development, the flirtation thaumatropes in the Princeton collection unsurprisingly tend to put young men in a dominant role, furnishing questions like, "Do you Love Me?" "Are you engaged?" "Will you be mine?" and "Name the day?" The young women's cards, conversely, position them more as responders than instigators, with answers like, "Can I refuse?" "Oh dear! No." "Yes to be sure." and "With pleasure." Despite the infinite compatibility of the thaumatropes' questions and answers, the set still determines what sentiments are appropriate to express and by whom. Such commercially produced flirtation aids toed the line between romantic pursuit and social propriety and also reinforced the verbal and visual education advanced across so many forms of juvenile print media. Although the library catalog record refers to this set of thaumatropes as a flirtation game, the accompanying instructions offer no information on the sequencing of play. Instead they specify how to use the thaumatrope itself, instructing users how to hold the toy and operate it. It is hard to know whether players strategically selected their thaumatropes to express a particular feeling or whether the fun was in the spontaneous revelation of randomly selected messages. The focus on the thaumatrope's form in the instructions, however, suggests that its optical effects brought something distinct to flirtation.

Indeed, the flirtation thaumatrope's question-and-answer format resembled other forms of nineteenth-century parlor amusements, such as conversation cards—themed card sets with printed questions and responses meant to aid discussion through the endless combination of universally compatible inquiries and answers (figure 2.5). An 1882–1883 catalog page from New York–based children's publisher McLoughlin Brothers features a range of courtship-related card sets, boasting their universal appeal, suitable

Figure 2.5
Advertisement for conversation card sets. McLoughlin Brothers, *Catalogue of McLoughlin Bros. Toy Books, Games, ABC Blocks, &c.* (New York: McLoughlin Brothers, 1882). Courtesy of the American Antiquarian Society.

not only "for people of small conversational powers" but for "pleasure-seekers of all classes." The description further asserted the cards' short- and long-term potentials: "To bashful people they are a great blessing, not only furnishing an hour's amusement, but sometimes leading them to the gates of matrimony."[58] Related to the more formal practice of visiting or calling cards, conversation cards were another form of ephemera exchanged in private settings. Their themes and designs varied widely, and their sentiments ranged from reserved to aggressive. They used humor to establish a rapport between potential romantic interests and helped both givers and receivers navigate the complexities of courtship.[59] Each card's unique style and address, from the fonts, colors, and embossing to the written text and selection of images, reflected the giver's character and social orientation.[60]

Such cards were instrumental in forging new social connections. Unlike predetermined aristocratic marriages that formed powerful economic or political alliances between families, members of the heterogeneous and diffuse middle class, particularly in cities, would not necessarily know their future spouses from childhood but would meet later. When seeking romantic partnership, youth already engaged in active projects of identity formation would also have to weigh romantic feelings against financial stability and were cautioned against dishonest or disreputable prospective mates.[61] Commercial products like valentines, calling cards, and conversation cards were important ways to express genuine sentiment while emphasizing romance over finance.[62] Some such forms, like "vinegar valentines," which used cruel, mocking humor, were sent to enforce social norms through harassment and, as Annabella Pollen claims, functioned as instantiations of the carnivalesque in a social context otherwise governed by restraint and propriety.[63] Yet in other cases, commercial flirtation products both furnished appropriate romantic sentiments and served as a means of verifying the same.

The generic, mass-produced quality of stock conversation cards and commercial valentines meant that recipients of such tokens of affection had to be assured of their givers' intentions.[64] Indeed, as Elizabeth Nelson notes, even popular fiction thematized the potential mismatch between a prospective lover's sincerity and "the [commercial] conditions of [a valentine's] production."[65] To this complex playing field, the flirtation thaumatropes contributed the added dimension of visual perception, which both contributed a playful tone to flirtation and, critically, helped authenticate the sincerity of the romantic advances. The thaumatropes' content shared a broader preoccupation with the question of intention, with examples like the question, "Are you sincere?" (asked by a young man) and the response, "My love is true" (delivered by a young woman). Importantly, the flirtatious messages that the thaumatropes broadcast were only conjured in the fleeting act of spinning the card and were thus visible only to the eye (and in the brain) of the beholder, making the message just for that person in that moment.

The description of the thaumatrope in Paris's *Philosophy in Sport* many years earlier would further validate its use in social situations that required reading another's intentions by characterizing it as a neutral instrument. In one of the earliest editions of Paris's book, the toy is introduced as "a small machine, which is calculated to deluge us with puns," gesturing to both an understanding of the device as mechanical in nature, as well as evoking pleasurable excess of a deluge.[66] In an 1833 edition, the thaumatrope is billed in a punny passage as "a hand mill by which puns and epigrams may be turned with as much ease as tunes are played on the hand organ and old jokes so rounded and changed as to assume all the airs of originality."[67] Although commercially produced and distributed, the toy's direct engagement with the senses and its capacity to "produce" the image in practice may have exempted it from the same kinds of criticisms that befell conventional valentines. Its affiliation with rational recreation thus transformed its deceptive qualities into scientific curiosities. As youth navigated the complex terrain of romance and courtship, then, media like the thaumatrope offered assurances that potential mates possessed the sensibilities worthy of partnership. The playful quality of the toy's ephemeral images and its association with childhood allowed users to broach sensitive subjects with caution and levity, while the perceptual play that it required assumed a form of visual competence that suggested a distinguished observer.

Conclusion

The thaumatrope was not just a perceptual toy. It allowed users to negotiate word and image, to encode and decode various kinds of content. In addition to falling within a sequence of later moving-image devices, it was also embedded in children's literary and visual cultures. There it circulated alongside a range of other media formats, such as the jigsaw puzzle and rebus. From its beginnings, its perceptual effects became inseparably connected to forms of social and political expression, uniquely drawing language and image together. This link between the written and the visual, the part and the whole, aligned with changing educational practices that expanded the conception of literacy that encompassed not only the written word, but the playful interplay between graphic and text. These educational practices positioned children less as recipients of knowledge and more as active participants in learning, who were best engaged by sensory and contextual encounters.

Children growing up with the thaumatrope and related media formats thus internalized habits of visual perception as an expanded form of literacy, and this visual education was commonly thematized in ways that reinforced existing social hierarchies. The power dynamics at play in the thaumatrope's rotation are clearly demonstrated by its most common motif of the bird in the cage, which at once reaffirmed middle-class standards of animal welfare and invited children to playfully disregard them. In the bird and the cage, the thaumatrope thus managed to provide an outlet for children to act on their "natural" inclinations toward cruelty while simultaneously producing a well-behaved child, whose hands were occupied and whose gaze was attentively trained on the device. These currents of benevolence and mischievousness also located the child more broadly within a complex social system in which markers of affinity and difference registered across race, class, and gender. Engaging the senses, the thaumatrope endeavored to make the child see from a particular moral and ideological perspective within this matrix. As children grew, they faced new challenges and opportunities brokering social relations, including seeking out a future spouse. Media that exploited visual perception like the thaumatrope highlighted the blurry relationship between vision and truth, which made courtship playful and mitigated anxieties about authenticity and sincere expression.

Just as the rebus puzzle substituted an eye for "an I," the thaumatrope's composite image was personal and subjective, drawing an analogy between visual perception and the self. In repeated uses, the process of anticipating the thaumatrope's visual illusion became a naturalized practice, and the kinds of images depicted were familiar tropes. Young users came to expect that spinning the card would put the bird in the cage, combine letters into words, place the rider atop the horse, or otherwise complete the circuit through persistence of vision. As it became a familiar device, it paved the way for additional toys that further articulated the conditions of modern media spectatorship according to the same visual paradigm. Because the thaumatrope uses persistence of vision like later optical toys such as the phenakistoscope, zoetrope, and praxinoscope, it has most commonly found a place at the beginning of long technological series culminating in the cinema. Yet it also has a powerful alternate legacy in its complex interplay between word and image, which, in their distinct combination, produced layers of socially embedded knowledge. This knowledge would come into play in the use of a wide range of optical toys set into motion for groups of people, young and old, offering opportunities to both revel in and distinguish oneself from illusionistic displays.

3   Seeing Things: Optical Play at Home

The beginning of the Behind the Screen exhibition at the Museum of the Moving Image in New York features historical examples of a phenakistoscope, thaumatrope, praxinoscope, and zoetrope disks displayed in a glass case. Directly below, working replicas are accessible to museum visitors. The encased artifacts attest to these toys' historical status, but the curators place equal weight on the contemporary models that are durable enough to handle and manipulate, stressing the importance of direct engagement. When museum visitors approach these replicas, they often initially use the toys the "wrong" way: they peer over the top of the zoetrope or stare at the phenakistoscope's reflection outside its slots. It is only through experimentation that visitors discover how each toy works and experience its optical effects. This trial-and-error process instills in the museum visitor a sense of mastery, both of the operation of the toy and, by extension, the perceptual principle behind it. In groups, this optical play has a significant social dimension. Visitors watch one another as much as they watch the toys. They ask, "Can you see it?" They exclaim when they see the effects themselves.

The sequential pedagogy of this interactive display—experiment, discuss, comprehend—is consistent with this part of the exhibition's linear design, which goes on to demonstrate other applications of persistence of vision: Muybridge and Marey's motion experiments, contemporary stroboscopic sculpture, stop-motion animation. Although working optical toys do not replicate optical play as children would have experienced it in the nineteenth century, museum visitors' interactions with contemporary reproductions can illuminate the range of agencies that historical children may have exercised when encountering such toys. Such engagement can "re-sensitize [users] to the sensorial and performative dimensions" of optical devices more than reading about them alone could accomplish.[1] Even play with digital surrogates, John Plunkett argues, is "able to recuperate something of the curiosity and wonder that previous moving image technologies initially aroused."[2] Similarly, considerations of optical play today highlight the kinds of questions and observations that might be made of historical practices of spectatorship in order to better understand them. A study examining children's processes of scientific thinking involved a similar analysis of children's interactions with zoetropes in museum contexts. The researchers developed four possible categories of interaction, which focused on how the child manipulated the zoetrope (either stationary or moving), and on how the child looked at the zoetrope (either over the top of the drum, producing a blurred image, or through the slots on the side, producing a clear illusion of motion). Perhaps unsurprising, the researchers found that children were more likely to enter all four experiential categories (that is, to experiment with the toy moving and stationary, and look at it over the top and through the sides) when accompanied by a parent who facilitated the interaction.[3] Such findings mirror the device's implementation in the nineteenth century, when children's play was guided by instructions in recreational literature and by adult modeling, all calculated to help them understand and internalize persistence of vision.

In the nineteenth century, optical play was similarly characterized as a process of mastery—a set of skills unconsciously practiced by the trained eye. An 1877 book described the visual experiences of everyday life as a kind of optical education:

> You thus find that the eye is a credulous greenhorn of easy gullibility in respect of the facility with which it may be duped. It is so often mistaken about what it supposes itself to see, that hereafter if any one should asseverate some unlikely thing which you may not be prepared to accept as a fact, and should say, "Must I not believe my own eyes?" you, remembering the zoetrope, will be emboldened to reply, "Certainly not in all cases."[4]

While the author of the book admits that the eye is a "greenhorn" that "may be duped," he highlights the zoetrope's role in producing an observer who is an informed, discerning subject, "emboldened" by his or her optical knowledge. This quality of optical discernment was both a sensibility and an ongoing practice achieved through experiment and experience, and exercised in social context.[5] Exploring where children played and what kind of content they saw in these devices reveals an early home media culture in which young people reveled in surprising animated effects and forged an understanding of their place within a broader social matrix beginning at the level of perception.

The cognitive and physiological labor required to perceive moving images has long factored into critical formulations of cinematic spectatorship. Despite the advancement of theories involving other perceptual phenomena, such as beta movement and phi phenomenon, persistence of vision recurs as a dominant perceptual model, perpetuated, for instance, in introductory textbooks.[6] Within studies of psychology and the moving image, persistence of vision has long been inextricably yoked to the conception of the spectator as not being agential, implying "a passive viewer upon whose sluggish retina images pile up," rather than the active and muscular eye implied by mid-nineteenth-century physiological optics.[7] This formulation of the eye as either "sluggish" or muscularly engaged reifies the familiar limiting dichotomy of active and passive spectatorship. Moreover, because persistence of vision fundamentally suggests that vision is subject to manipulation, it has led scholars to consider how nineteenth-century observers responded to objects and experiences that questioned the association between vision and truth. On one hand, these forms of visual manipulation and deception have led to assumptions that optical toys made viewers anxious and unstable. On the other, these toys' capacity to play with perception has been celebrated for surprising and delighting viewers. Still other critical formulations, such as Jonathan Crary's foundational account, subsume other explanations, demonstrating how persistence of vision's production of spectacle and subjectivity renders it commensurate with capitalist logic.[8]

These positions of belief and doubt, credulity and incredulity, indoctrination or liberation, cannot always be neatly applied to children, to whom these toys were introduced within an informal educational framework, as the previous chapters detail. The visual, material, and literary traditions where optical devices circulated offer little evidence that such toys produced anxiety for young users. Optical play was profoundly social and likely produced a range of responses. Like museumgoers nearly two hundred years later, nineteenth-century children had opportunities to play with these toys the "wrong" way, to both discover and disavow the lessons they sought to impart. The stakes of optical play for children were paradoxically both urgent and inconsequential. These toys directly endeavored to train developing bodies and minds, yet as mere child's play, their lessons were flexibly constructed. This conceptual space between importance and triviality offers critical space to imagine children's play as complex and multifaceted. Much like Benjamin's notion of *spielraum*, or "room-for-play," which Miriam Hansen described as "an aesthetics that could counteract, at the level of sense perception, the political consequences of the failed—capitalist and imperialist, destructive and self-destructed—reception of technology," optical play was invested with multiple potentials.[9] This chapter considers where and how optical toys were used, the social configurations that formed around their use, and the content represented in optical media to explore how children may have come to see themselves and their social worlds through optical play. Investigating the toys themselves, their material environments, and images of their use, the chapter articulates how these toys issued "a set of invitations that necessarily remain open to resistance, interpretation, and improvisation" within complex social environments.[10] The speculative reconstruction of optical play and its domestic contexts in turn reveals both the intended spectatorial disposition of young, white, middle-class players, as well as the potentials available to them to refuse or negotiate the ideological orientation that optical devices sought to ingrain.

As the previous chapters have explored, optical play was embedded within children's broader visual and moral educations. Optical toys circulated among texts and lessons about vision that intertwined moral and scientific sentiments. Examining optical toys within this culture nuances prior accounts of how users may have responded to perceptual play. These toys played a significant part in a program of visual literacy that assumed a connection between optical discernment and social mobility.[11] Changing ideas in the vision sciences led to new analogies to describe the eye as both inferior to scientific instruments and as a servant to the intellect. This conception of the senses as unreliable allegorizes a range of middle-class anxieties that were not only social and economic but also gendered and raced to varying degrees. For instance, as Erica Armstrong Dunbar contends, middle-class African Americans experienced heightened precariousness as "the weight of racism and disenfranchisement as well as the concern for millions of blacks held in bondage compounded fears regarding the stability of their own financial and social status."[12]

Developments in vision science and visual education thus produced parallel preoccupations. The limited reliability of the eye mirrored the increasingly abstract marketplace, growing urban contexts where deception ran rampant, and a range of social inequalities that could be maintained through practices of visual surveillance and classification. As "the space for psychological refuge from the rigors of economic life as well as the proper site for expression of familial love and guidance," the home was a safe context for children to experiment with the limitations of vision.[13] There, optical toys tested and refined the child's gaze and instilled a sense of optical discernment linked to future political autonomy and financial possibility. The contours of this visual education take shape in representations of optical toys in use. Images on packaging and advertisements imagined idealized scenes of optical play. This iconography visualizes not the instability of middle-class life but complex social exchanges wherein persistence of vision was demonstrated, observed, and understood as a form of cultural transmission. In this respect, optical toys endeavored to habituate children to new ways of seeing and responding to the moving image that prepared them for modern social life and future encounters with new media.

The spectatorial positions that optical toys invited children to adopt were active and engaged, in contrast to later cultural tropes such as the couch potato, the video game–addicted child, or the child glued to a screen. Optical play involved flexible arrangements in which children's attention shifted between the illusionistic display and the social environment around them. This form of divided attention allowed children to exercise the visual agency to look or not to look, and prepared them for life in an increasingly media-saturated and simulating world, where there would be many demands for their attention. The images that children saw through optical toys, moreover, naturalized both the flexible position of the viewing subject as well as the leisure time necessary to enjoy optical play. The prevalence of industrial motifs and recreational activities made the daily cycle of work and play a familiar routine and romanticized the efficiency of mass production. For children who were more likely to see industrial machinery represented in a toy than firsthand on the factory floor, optical toys synchronized the rhythms of work and play in a way that drew analogies between mental and manual labor, helping to justify and reinforce a division of labor in those terms.

Envisioning Control

Scientific understanding of vision underwent a substantial epistemological reworking during the nineteenth century—a change aided by and reflected in an array of cultural and technological forms, including optical devices. Changes in illumination and optical technologies enabled the widespread production and proliferation of devices like microscopes and telescopes, which expanded the scope and scale of the perceivable world. These configurations opened up both new possibilities and new threats by extending the realm of the visual at both micro- and macroscopic scales, producing "a radically ungrounded world, with an extraordinary, exhilarated skepticism."[14] Simultaneously, the proliferation of lens-based technologies helped define instrumental vision as a standard against which human vision might be measured.

Unsurprisingly, technologies that permitted observers to parse the visible world (and beyond) at ever finer scales were variously put to work in cultural projects that sought to both maintain and contest existing social and racial stratification. For instance, Britt Rusert details how the wide adoption of optical instrumentation metaphorically reinforced African Americans' ongoing challenges to evade what Nicholas Mirzoeff calls "the plantation complex."[15] Rusert writes, "African American and abolitionist periodicals [like the *Liberator*] routinely ran treatises on optical instruments and also reprinted philosophical meditations on the cultural—and existential—significance of instruments like the telescope and the microscope." These visual technologies evoked both "conditions of invisibility and a cruel 'diminishment of corporeality' under slavery and forms of spectacular hyper-visibility and surveillance under liberal 'freedom' in the North."[16] The "objective" qualities of optical instruments were wielded in the imagination of multiple conflicting futures. In his 1857 *America and Europe*, Count Adam Von Gurowski intimated the radically different racial conclusions derived from the purportedly empirical gaze of optical instruments: "The pro-slavery microscope distorts or changes the form of the cellular tissues, the epidermis of the blacks, while the truly scientific instrument shows that black and white tissues are alike."[17] The practical and metaphorical deployment of optical technologies meant to fix and stabilize the world in objective terms thus always already reflected (to use another optical metaphor) profoundly different social realities and priorities.[18] Persistence-of-vision toys organized the social world by inviting viewers to acknowledge the eyes as mediating agents that required the disciplined practice of discernment. To submit to the optical toy's logic was to interrogate the self as a seeing subject and bear the responsibility of the validity and voracity of one's own perspective. This interrogation began with comparisons between the eye and its instrumental counterpart.

Unlike the microscope, telescope, and optical lantern, which extended and expanded the scope of human vision, optical toys demonstrated a disjuncture between external reality—sensation—and the observer's subjective, interpretive process of seeing—perception. They revealed to the viewer that unmediated vision was subject to exploitation and deception. The nineteenth-century faith in vision was thus accompanied by a sense of limitation, often expressed through comparisons between the human eye and the objective optical instrument. Gaston Tissandier, editor of the science magazine *La Nature*, for instance, remarked that "the eye is generally regarded as a perfect instrument, but it is not yet so by any means. One of our great philosophers remarked that if an instrument were sent home to him so full of errors he would feel justified in returning it to the optician."[19]

The vulnerability of sight, and the attendant fear of visual deception, underpins many scholarly accounts of nineteenth-century visuality. Describing human vision with "an insistent vocabulary of deception and failure," Mary Ann Doane claims, resulted in the "inevitable production of anxiety linked with the revelation of a body that cannot even trust its own senses, when vision is uprooted from the world and destabilized."[20] Similarly, Susan Horton suggests that Victorians had to work "to justify a happy spectatorship and ... come to terms with the unreliability of vision."[21] Many forms that this work took were recreational. The middle class had abundant occasions to confront the notion that their eyes could be tricked, such as public exhibitions of trompe l'oeil paintings, lantern and phantasmagoria shows, and panoramas. These opportunities to play with perception helped them practice and perform acts of reasoning and discernment, both submitting to and challenging the illusions they encountered.

The prevailing conception of unreliable vision paralleled the precariousness of middle-class status itself, often bound to shifting, unpredictable financial fortunes.[22] While economic stability was not guaranteed, middling white families modeled and sustained their aspirational sensibilities not only through practices like conspicuous consumption but by performing middle-class ways of seeing—a kind of fake-it-'til-you-make it strategy.[23] Optical discernment was a key element of this strategy, central to the development of a middle-class habitus, a system of dispositions designed to be self-perpetuating, which took shape, in part, through the circular notions of *being seen as* but also *of seeing as* a successful, sincere, and civically engaged subject.[24] This position was commonly enforced during optical play, when, as Helen Groth asserts, "the consummate test of character becomes the capacity to control and mediate the seemingly perplexing phenomena that inundate one's senses."[25] Children are especially important subjects through which habitus proliferates, given Bourdieu's assertion that "early experiences have particular weight because the habitus tends to ensure its own constancy and its defence against change through the selection it makes within new information by rejecting information capable of calling into question its accumulated information, if exposed to it accidentally or by force, and especially by avoiding exposure to such information."[26] In this way, the new forms of seeing that optical toys engendered were tied to the interests of a distinct racial and class position.

Participating in both public and private displays of optical spectacles was a significant way that the nineteenth-century middle class inhabited and negotiated the tenuousness of their social and economic position. As formats like public panoramas and peep shows were adapted and scaled for children's use in the home alongside optical toys like the thaumatrope, phenakistoscope, and zoetrope, such exercises came to be associated with the tradition of rational recreation. Rational recreation itself had undergone a significant expansion since the late eighteenth century, largely due to the production and distribution of more affordable books, as explored in chapter 1. Within the relative security of the domestic sphere, children could practice and exercise their senses in play. Thus, although optical toys are often considered emblematic of a perceptual regime of untrustworthy vision, their use was part of an informal education that sought not to dismantle vision, but to position its training as a developmental skill. Children's popular science and morality literature further framed this visual pedagogy within class-based terms, linking visual perception to a particular social orientation.

For children, vision and the other senses were framed within the context of the authoritative ethos of pedagogical, scientific, and recreational literature. As the previous chapters suggest, optical toys circulated alongside a range of print and visual media forms, broadly contributing to what might now be understood as a kind of media literacy. Children were framed as active learners who not only mastered specific content, but more important, interpretive methods that could be applied to a range of situations. Considering optical play within this broader frame refutes claims that understanding vision as unstable was widely anxiety inducing. Within parlor play and home recreation, this notion of subjective perception was at the root of a sensory education premised on self-governance and discipline. Optical toys were central in the introduction and practice of this sensibility. They also, of course, formed the prerequisite perceptual skills necessary to participate in the alluring practices of what would come to be known as media spectatorship.

Instructional literature commonly used metaphors and analogies to frame physiological concepts in moral terms, positioning the relationship between the senses and the brain as a hierarchical one in which the senses were overseen and evaluated by the intellect. This frequently took the form of analogies of familiar social stratification. Author and educator Elizabeth Prentiss's book *Little Susy's Little Servants* (1856) typifies such a corporeal education that links the body to both moral precepts and social hierarchies. New England writer Prentiss came from a devout religious family and married a Presbyterian pastor. Her service to God and community permeated her "Little Susy" stories, which were published in the United States and United Kingdom at least through the 1880s. Written in the first person from the perspective of a growing infant who gradually comes to learn about the world through her developing sensory skills, *Little Susy's Little Servants* discusses the sense organs (the eyes, hands, feet, ears, and tongue) as unruly forces that must be trained in order to perform correctly and function in the service of the unified whole. The book implores young readers to play along by consulting a mirror to see their own set of servants with which God has equipped them.[27]

Susy's sensory education is positioned primarily in relation to her duties to God, and she is reminded that she must develop and control her servants in order to serve him and, by extension, others. Danger abounds for Little Susy. Her untrained body threatens to injure itself, while her eyes in particular are responsible for keeping her mind morally pure. Her senses are naughty and destructive, such as when her "two truant feet" carry her into a busy street or when she tries to climb out the window.[28] Likewise, while at church, although Susy manages to get her hands and feet to behave, her eyes could not sit still and "looked round a good deal."[29] Susy is an archetypal child, whose inexperience is coded as a kind of innocence, her naughtiness a result of a natural lack of discipline (rather than, say, the malice of original sin). Her disobedient hands, feet, and eyes recall the unruly disembodied limbs on either side of the thaumatrope or a dissected figure game, as described in chapter 2. Susy, unlike the thaumatrope or character-type puzzles, does not require assembly or visual synthesis, but mental and moral coordination to bring her body into disciplined alignment.

When Susy attempts to string beads in inadequate light, her father and nurse accuse her of abusing her eyes, likening the harm of eyestrain to chopping off a finger.[30] After seeing a fight through an open door, Susy's mother cautions her to "teach your little eyes not to look at things they ought not to see." She chastises Susy, saying, "Didn't you feel, all the time, that it was not quite proper for you to stop and watch in that way? Always make it a rule never to look at *any* thing, no matter what, if you have even a little bit of a feeling that you ought not. Your eyes are your own, and you must teach them."[31] This multifaceted notion of protection—against strain and fatigue and against exposure to unsavory sights—exemplifies how nineteenth-century visual epistemology helped shape conceptions of the modern Western child as vulnerable to both physical and moral corruption. Prentiss emphasizes Susy's ownership of her eyes, and implores readers to preserve *their* own eyes, guarding them against both physical wear and inappropriate impressions. These analogies brought visual perception into a kind of economy, understood as a resource to be strategically deployed. Such analogies also positioned children's vision as a special faculty in need of training, care, and protection.

Published much later, Cecil Bullivant's *Home Fun* (1910) maintained the servant analogy, referring to the eyes as "faithful servants, fit to be trusted in ninety-nine cases out of a hundred, but like all good and faithful servants there is that hundredth case when their judgment goes wandering, and when they leap to rash conclusions, carried away by deceptive appearances."[32] Such texts both reinforce a model of subjective vision and equate this physiological relationship with familiar forms of social stratification. The servant analogy is of particular interest, given the volume of child-rearing literature in the latter nineteenth century advocating that mothers, not nurses or servants, bear responsibility for their children's home education and upbringing.³³ Children were similarly instructed to "use" the labor of their sensory organs, even if that work could not fully be "trusted" and required oversight and supervision by the intellect. Such texts thus deftly explained to children that their senses were helpful (if not wholly reliable) and framed the child in a position of authority and control that could not be delegated to others. The servant analogy distinguished between manual and mental labor, placing social and moral weight on the latter. The model of vision that these texts perpetuated (indeed, the entire bodily schematic they mapped for young readers) flexibly aligned with both religious sentiments and the terms of popular science, locating consciousness as the seat of moral agency and reason.

The broader cultural and technological developments that framed vision as unreliable coincided with new educational methods that privileged sensory learning over rote memorization. This pedagogical orientation was reflected in a range of approaches, from Fröbel's kindergarten to the ascendance of the object lesson and color education. Appealing to the senses was one way to coordinate learning in the increasingly large and diverse classrooms that progressive educators found themselves in front of in the second half of the nineteenth century. Yet color education and the object lesson (discussed in chapters 5 and 6, respectively), stressed sensory training to get students to conform to a distinct sensory paradigm without problematizing the senses. By contrast, optical play was tied to the acceptance of a perceptual order that required continuous vigilance. It was, in a sense, training in Mirzoeff's "right to look" that requires continual "renewal."³⁴ For middle-class children, opportunities for home play would become important means by which they could distinguish themselves, available to them as their daily lives were increasingly oriented apart from the perceived threats of urban life.³⁵

Alongside texts that personified the senses and learning aids that stressed the acquisition of visual knowledge, optical toys taught young people about vision through hands-on, experiential engagement. Home recreation was a key context for sensory training and the parlor "ha[d] a special role to play as a material and social ensemble."³⁶ Nineteenth-century authors' accounts of their childhood homes frequently emphasize sensorial experiences, recalling, for instance, sensations of mobile perception and feelings that seemed to move through the body.³⁷ Removed from the perceived perils of the public sphere and the rigors of school, the home offered a safe space to develop scientific knowledge and visual acumen, and it provided a social context to practice and perform these skills. As such, home optical play with books and toys positioned this visual education as a set of spectatorial practices available to the leisure class outside of formal educational contexts.

Bound up in this sensory education was a belief in the political efficacy of discerning spectatorship.[38] Books of parlor magic, which frequently included optical toys, explained the amateur magic show to young conjurers in terms of the concealment and revelation of information.[39] These texts framed the observation of spectacles with a critical eye as an essential component of social and political autonomy, as one article on scientific deceptions noted:

> Deception by means of scientific experiment now serves only the two ends of instruction and amusement.... In early times, however, deception by means of scientific experiment served only one purpose: it was a powerful instrument employed by the rulers to awe the people, and, to this end, prince, priest, and sage were leagued together to impose on the masses, who at times could not be impressed unless by some appeal to what they, in their ignorance, considered to be supernatural.[40]

Recalling eighteenth-century traditions like the phantasmagoria, discussion of optical illusions and deception cautioned children against being "led astray by others whose knowledge of the laws of optics is greater than our own" in order to safeguard against those "capable of amusing us or imposing on us, according to our ignorance of natural laws."[41] Unlike later media literacy discourses that would frame deception largely in relation to the messages of commercial enterprises, nineteenth-century texts are primarily concerned with deception's capacity for political oppression. This association suggests the social and civic importance of visual discernment and positions commercial media as an aid to strengthen these skills rather than a force threatening to corrupt the child.

At Play in the Parlor

What was it like to play with these toys? How did they allow children to practice optical discernment? Unlike optical trickery writ large, which included magic tricks and the lantern projection of ghosts and phantoms, persistence-of-vision toys deceive the eye at the level of the perceptual threshold. It is impossible to recreate in full the original contexts where these toys would have been used, and harder still to imagine the experiences and assumptions that the nineteenth-century observer brought to optical play. However, representations of children at play and the toys' formal attributes provide rich insight into how groups may have gathered around them, handled them, and viewed their optical effects. In use, each optical toy invited particular audience configurations. Members of the household and social circle participated in distinct ways as operators and onlookers. These were fluid positions that individuals occupied and abandoned at will. Players and observers were alternately absorbed by and removed from the illusions these toys produced, their engagement variously approaching and retreating from what Oliver Grau defines as immersion, "characterized by a diminishing critical distance to what is shown and increasing emotional involvement in what is happening."[42] Such a critical distance was spatialized in the parlor, as children sometimes peered intently through these devices' spinning slots and sometimes shifted their attention elsewhere in the room. Rather than giving themselves over completely to the visual experiences that optical toys produced, users engaged in optical play likely oscillated between affective investment and rational distancing. This movement itself was as much a part of the play as the devices' dazzling effects.

These toys' instructional nature comes into sharp relief in images of their use. Parents and adults are frequently seen demonstrating toys for children or observing children at play. Attention to these configurations of viewers and operators enables us to imagine how persistence of vision was demonstrated as a perceptual model. This imagery provides a better understanding of how nineteenth-century children may have both actively delighted in and dismissed the optical effects they observed, following much the same pattern of attention that museum visitors still exhibit today when they encounter these devices. Many images of optical toys in use are promotional, and thus present the idealized rather than the actual circumstances of optical play. Nevertheless, they convey the values invested in these toys and an idea of how they were meant to be used. Moreover, even in their idealism, these images disclose the range of bodily attitudes children likely took toward optical toys, which encompassed multiple modes of attention and visual mastery. Closely considering such imagery differs from simply recounting how each toy works by factoring in the toy's physical details alongside broader contextual elements—the lighting, the furniture, the time of day—to better understand the role that these toys played in cultivating children's vision.

Optical play was commonly staged at home in the parlor—a hybrid space that negotiated "domesticity ('comfort') and [its occupants'] cosmopolitan character ('culture')." These two notions, writes Kasey Grier, "designate two complex collations of ideas, attitudes, and assumptions that together represent a critical tension in Victorian culture" where the broader social world and the sacred family converge.[43] Among the parlor's many significant roles was its disclosure of the social and moral orientations of its occupants through furnishings, objects, and other details. The selection, arrangement, and display of such elements, Thad Logan argues, is itself a kind of "play."[44] Uncle Tom–themed material culture, or "Tomitudes," for instance, or statuary like John Rogers's *The Slave Auction* conveyed to visitors a family's abolitionist sentiments, activating complex networks of ideas about race and Christian sentiment.[45] The middle-class interior was thus densely populated by images and objects that implicitly or explicitly communicated a wealth of social information and competed for occupants' attention.

Optical instruments were enjoyed within the already busily patterned parlor, adding a further dimension of visual complexity.[46] The small size of the commercial thaumatrope indicates its intended use in relatively intimate or personal settings like the parlor rather than larger-scale demonstrations. If shown to someone facing the toy, the image will appear upside down to the operator. Viewing the thaumatrope in action thus likely took three main forms. A single user might operate it in front of a mirror, or an operator might demonstrate the device for a small group gathered in very close proximity. It is also possible for a small group to congregate around the operator on the same side of the device for all to view the thaumatrope simultaneously. The flirtation thaumatropes discussed in the previous chapter offer an excellent example of subject matter that likely drew users together to observe it in motion. One can imagine the toy in the parlor—the close, personal nature of its content reinforced by seating configurations expressly designed for romantic encounters, such as the "courting chair" or loveseat, which, by the nineteenth century, was manufactured in a variety of styles such as the tête-à-tête or S-shaped arrangements.[47] The thaumatrope's more intimate appeal also reflects its conversational nature, given the frequency of iconographic and textual jokes and puns reproduced in thaumatropic form. Much like a whispered in-joke, the toy's illusion appears in an ephemeral flicker, caught only by those immediately nearby.

A few years later, the phenakistoscope maintained a similarly intimate connection between apparatus and viewer. It allows only one user at a time to view its motion sequence by peering through the slotted disk into a mirror, or, in some models, two disks are mounted parallel to one another—one with the slots and one with the image sequence. Those nearby the operator/viewer cannot simultaneously see the moving image. This one-on-one relationship might suggest solitary play, but the phenakistoscope is seldom depicted in use by a single person in isolation. Rather, the boxes and folios in which phenakistoscopes were packaged imagine optical play as a social experience involving the entire family. Often women are shown viewing the animation in front of a looking glass or instructing children to do the same. In many instances, men and more children look on at the spectacle, suggesting that the phenakistoscope was not restricted by users' age or gender. This presumption is corroborated by the toy's inclusion in a variety of rational recreation titles for boys, girls, and wide audiences, and its promotional production for publications like *The Boy's Own Book* and the French young ladies' magazine *Journal des Demoiselles*. Within the context of the home, optical play and the modes of informal scientific engagement it afforded appeared more inclusive than later toys would be.

A German example from around 1835 from the collection of Richard Balzer depicts a spacious domestic interior. A woman views a phenakistoscope in a mirror, while a quartet of children play behind her. On the other side of the room, women and children appear to be consulting prints at a table.[48] In another example, advertised as the Magic Disk in French- and English-speaking markets, the device's box features the image of a broad, spacious interior. On the far right, a woman stands before a mirror peering into the disk, while a boy next to her holds a second phenakistoscope and is being instructed by a man leaning over him. Across the room, a woman seated at a table holds a third phenakistoscope handle aloft, surrounded by an abundance of extra disks, while four eager children clamor around the table for their turn (figure 3.1). The recurrence of group scenes—even on the packaging of a toy that only one person could use at a time—suggests a context where participants exhibited different models of attention toward the device. These images connect optical play to general visual culture practices, such as looking at colorful prints, and suggest how its use was more

Figure 3.1
The top of a phenakistoscope box depicting a busy social scene. Courtesy of the Bill Douglas Cinema Museum, University of Exeter.

broadly construed as a pastime. One can imagine children gleefully sorting through the colorful, grotesque, and humorous disks and waiting their turn to animate them before the looking glass. When the phenakistoscope was in use by one person, others may have observed its blurred images, listening to narration of what the observer saw or waiting to see it for themselves. The ability to alternate perspectives between the smooth, animated sequence and the unintelligible blur exemplifies how the limits of vision could be tested and reaffirmed again and again.

The introduction of the zoetrope in 1834 signaled a fundamental change in the relationship between the spectator and apparatus. Lauded as a toy that amused both young and old, the zoetrope could accommodate a larger viewing party arranged around the spinning drum. The zoetrope's ability to enrapture a bigger audience meant that multiple people could simultaneously see and react to the same optical phenomenon at the same time, creating a shared spectatorial experience distinct from the phenakistoscope's individualized test of vision. Because of this arrangement, the zoetrope's users had varying levels of engagement. It invited fluid roles of operator and spectator, permitting the onlooker to look over the top of the drum (when the images would appear as a blur) or to look through the drum's slots (where the moving image would snap into focus). The range of interactions is nicely illustrated by an image of a large parlor-sized zoetrope at the center of a group of onlookers ranging from infants to adults (figure 3.2). The image's vantage point is level with the zoetrope's drum, so the viewer sees the semblance of an animated sequence represented through the slots.

Like representations of the phenakistoscope, which show busy social scenes, this image reveals a great deal about the zoetrope in action. The figures are clustered tightly around the toy on the table, positioned below a globed chandelier. Although the chandelier may have been gas lit, this scene of domestic harmony was likely to have been lit by kerosene or paraffin lamps, preferred methods of illumination because the soft, warm qualities of light they produced evoked the comfort of the domestic interior, as opposed to the perceived brightness and industrial connotations of gas lighting.[49] Studying the gazes of the people in the picture reveals that they are not all transfixed by the device but are largely watching one another. Notably, the only subjects in the picture watching the zoetrope are the children, who are positioned at eye level around the slotted drum. The adults tower over the zoetrope—a vantage point from which the images would appear only as a blur. Their faces are cast not toward the moving images but toward the children watching them, suggesting that their pleasure is derived less from the device's marvelous effects and more from observing the children's happy reaction to the toy. The infant in the picture interrupts this chain of observation and surveillance. Held above the zoetrope and apart from its mother's body, the young child's hands are outstretched—not toward the spinning optical toy—but toward the glass globes of the chandelier above. The baby's apparent disinterest in the zoetrope reaffirms the developmental logic of optical education. Much as Little Susy learns about her senses one by one, the baby in the image is not ready to process

Figure 3.2
Parties using the zoetrope. Top: Reproduced in Ruth Sunderlin Freeman and Larry Freeman, *Cavalcade of Toys* (Watkins Glen, NY: Century House, 1942), 245. Bottom: Caroline L. Smith, *Popular Pastimes for Field and Fireside; Or, Amusements for Young and Old* (Springfield, MA: Milton Bradley, 1867), 230. Courtesy of HathiTrust.

the rapid stimuli of the optical toy. Whereas the children in the picture appear delighted and enraptured by the zoetrope, the adults focus on watching the children watching. In this way, the demonstration of persistence of vision appears as both practice of generationally transmitted knowledge and a reflection of sentimental parental attitudes toward children that took shape over the nineteenth century.

Children were encouraged to actively participate in optical play not only as viewers but as exhibitors and performers as well. The 1867 rational recreation book *Popular Pastimes for Field and Fireside* describes a group of people gathered around the zoetrope with "one of the party keeping it in motion."[50] Like other images of optical toys in use, the accompanying engraving shows a group gathered in a handsomely furnished domestic interior (figure 3.2). A zoetrope sits on a large marble-topped table at the center of the room underneath a trio of globe lights with ten people gathered around. The people in the image regard the zoetrope with differing levels of focus. Children's heights are elevated: one young child is held in a man's arms, while the girl at the center of the image in the foreground stands on what is perhaps a footstool, her back to the reader as she watches the optical display. A man and woman at the right of the image converse with one another, the man gesturing casually to the zoetrope. Directly facing them, a young boy perched atop a chair points emphatically to the zoetrope, as though directing the couple's attention. The book imagines a child-directed exhibition, advertised by a homemade "high-flown handbill" with admission charged. The zoetrope's operation, it suggests, can be accompanied by oral commentary: "A bright boy or girl can add very much to the interest of the exhibition by witty descriptions."[51]

Traditions of such domestic optical shows also stoked fantasies of child-led exhibitions for paying audiences. In a serial titled "The Firm of Pixie and Prog," published in *Golden Hours Magazine* in the 1870s, two enterprising boys, Pixie and Prog, stage a magic lantern show for neighbors. The program, which included harmonica and drum music and lantern projections, culminated with a zoetrope display of pictures such as a tumbling man, figures playing leapfrog, and two strips found in Milton Bradley's first series. In one, titled Hash Machine, a mechanical arm perpetually feeds a man with a gaping mouth. Another—raining pitchforks—literalizes the idiom, depicting a man holding an umbrella taking long strides while literal pitchforks descend around him.[52] A decade after the zoetrope's introduction, the story framed the toy as the highlight of the exhibition, an attraction for which the audience's "enthusiasm knew no bounds."[53] Accounts of children staging such spectacles as entrepreneurial schemes linked optical play with economic gain and illustrate how optical play purported to transform children from inexperienced innocents to discerning spectators who had mastered and internalized the moving image.[54] When children played at staging shows for paying audiences, they displayed this perceptual mastery. Through the coordinated operation of the toys, musical accompaniment, and spoken commentary, they also controlled and interpreted visual phenomena for others. The quasi-public nature of such shows (real or imagined) points further to the pedagogical function of optical play as a kind of training for modern public life.

The praxinoscope, invented by Emile Reynaud in 1877, further changed the viewer's relationship to the moving image. Its notable change from the zoetrope is its use of mirrors to reflect the moving images instead of slots, making the animation smoother, brighter, and visible from more angles. The earlier thaumatrope, phenakistoscope, and zoetrope centrally invited viewers to consider the distinction between sensation and perception by allowing viewers to watch the spinning sequence the "wrong" way as blurred images. By contrast, Reynaud's praxinoscope with its mirrored prism in place of a slotted shutter "perfected" the moving image by presenting only a smooth, animated loop. A variation of the device, the praxinoscope theater developed in 1878, included a wooden mask decorated with a theatrical proscenium arch affixed to the front, which delineated a fixed perspective from which to view the animation and screened the rest of the spinning mechanism from view (figure 3.3). The praxinoscope could incorporate its own light source in the form of a candle with a lampshade, which evenly lit its smoothly moving images and made the device less dependent on ambient light. Such features improved the quality of the animated sequence and reduced the tendency to view the illusion in the "wrong" way.

In an 1882 book of popular science experiments and principles for young readers, Gaston Tissandier remarked on the way the praxinoscope theater masks its inner workings: "By this clever and entirely novel optical combination, the mechanism of the contrivance is entirely lost sight of, leaving only the effect produced by the animated figures, which fulfil their different movements on the little stage."[55] The toy's inner workings

Figure 3.3
Reynaud's praxinoscope theater (side view). Courtesy of the Bill Douglas Cinema Museum, University of Exeter.

were further obscured by its paper strips, which had black backgrounds instead of white, making the printed figures appear to move in virtual space. Although the praxinoscope theater simply placed the praxinoscope in a wooden box with a cutout stage to frame the moving image, the addition of the mask privileges a single vantage point from which to view the motion sequence and thematizes the viewer's position as that of a theatrical audience member. The surrounding box apparatus conceals the toy's internal mechanism, emphasizing the illusion as a spectacle of motion rather than demonstrating how the toy works. The separation between viewer and apparatus that the praxinoscope theater maintains is exemplary of what Gaudreault and Dulac characterize as a "viewer mode of attraction," as opposed to the player mode associated with earlier persistence-of-vision toys.[56] This is a significant departure from toys like the phenakistoscope or zoetrope that required more user accommodation to "work" effectively and, in so doing, prompted consideration of their underlying perceptual principles. The praxinoscope theater did not demand that its viewer interrogate the image it produced.

Erkki Huhtamo classifies toys like the phenakistoscope and the zoetrope within a broader tradition of non-screen-based "peep media" extending back to the fifteenth century. In homes, Huhtamo contends, devices like the eighteenth-century zograscope (a lens-based viewing device that emphasizes depth in a two-dimensional picture) "invited social interaction rather than visual seclusion and solitary introspection," a practice carried into the nineteenth century with toys like the phenakistoscope and zoetrope.[57] Whether accommodating a single viewer or a large group, these toys required not only visual but also embodied participation within a lively social atmosphere. Unlike later peep moving-image devices like the Kinetoscope (1894) and the hand-cranked Mutoscope (1897), whose hooded lenses produced "a space that would immediately identify itself as somehow separate from the world," persistence-of-vision toys did not always immerse their users.[58] Rather, their pleasures were tied to the permeability they offered as viewers dropped into and out of the spectacle at play. As pictures of these toys in use attest, users' attention was often divided—shifting among the toy's animated sequence, the group of friends and family gathered, and competing media forms, such as prints spread across the parlor table. The ability to tune out and return to the moving image again and again—instantaneously and on demand—habituated children to the experience of persistence of vision and cultivated a model of attention fit for an increasingly complex mediascape.

Whereas instructional texts established a hierarchy of sensory and cognitive processes through metaphors such as the servant, optical toys invited children to understand their eyes through experiential play. Whether envisioning the eyes as servants to the rational and moral center of the brain or experiencing the thrill of the moving image in the company of family and friends, children came to understand vision as embodied and subjective. Fundamentally social, home optical play functioned as a microcosm of the social world writ large. This play permitted children to test and refine their visual acuity in a controlled setting and to comment on and respond to optical displays around others. Persistence-of-vision toys enabled the exercise and display of discernment and scientific knowledge, preparing children to successfully navigate a world populated by those who might manipulate them through optical deception. Each toy's material attributes shaped audience participation in particular ways, encouraging audiences of varying sizes and inviting some to interact and others to watch. Furthermore, the extent to which each toy disclosed its inner workings varied, thereby affording play experiences that ranged from experimental and exploratory to those that were more centrally spectatorial than ludic.

These ways of seeing and understanding vision were thus connected to a broader sense of personal autonomy and empowerment—virtues key to the production of the middle-class subject. Although optical devices tricked the eye and reaffirmed an understanding of vision as flawed, they also encouraged viewers to revel in the momentary lapse of control to enjoy the optical illusions created. The condition of spectatorship thus depended on a conception of the eye as subject to deception—calculated in the increments between zoetrope and phenakistoscope slots. Yet there was a solidity to this deception in the scientific explanation underlying its production. Optical play rendered the observer complicit in new visual regimes, working vision into terms that were legible and could be interpreted as scientific data. In subjecting the gaze to such instruments, Sara Danius suggests, "the scientific articulations of the observer's physiology are made compatible with new arrangements of power that emerged in that period, in particular, the science of labor and the related rationalization of the human body."[59] This process of subjectification, however, also engendered a powerful sense of recognition and belonging that took shape at the perceptual level. As individual viewers experienced the moving image for themselves within the broader social context of home recreation, they engaged in shared opportunities for discerning spectatorship. Understood as instructional and entertaining toys for children, optical toys thus did not necessarily provoke anxiety. Rather, they were mechanisms through which new perceptual competencies and their accompanying social orientations were established. At the levels of form and content, these toys solidified a relationship between particular ways of seeing and a social imagination of individual autonomy, potential, and the possibility for economic growth.

Work, Play, and Bodies in Motion

The social contexts of optical play and the formal attributes of the devices themselves forged new media cultures in which children's spectatorship was understood as active and grounded in sensory-driven science education. Optical toys and the discourses that framed them reinforced white middle-class identity by cementing reliance on a rapidly institutionalizing scientific authority, characterized in part by increasing demarcation between branches of science—physiology, chemistry, physics, biology.[60] These emerging fields enabled the users of optical toys to cement the sensory basis of their individual subjectivity in scientific expertise. The scientific appeals of home optical play were especially enticing to members of the middle class whose senses of self were not anchored to longer generational legacies and for whom long-term economic stability was not an assurance. Yet the scientific proof undergirding these toys—like the toys and their animated sequences themselves—was tautological. Such devices, writes historian of science Iwan Morus, perform "the work needed to make us believe what we see in science."[61] They operate according to a circular logic, at once demonstrating and thereby verifying the phenomenon of persistence of vision.[62] In his *Outline of Psychology*, early experimental psychologist Edward B. Titchener suggests the zoetrope's self-affirming nature, writing, "In all these cases, vision is the test of vision; we know from the eye that the eye has deceived us."[63] In the same way, the toys' animated motifs reinforced the experiences of middle-class life. Drawing on familiar visual conventions, they depicted moving sequences of work and play, artisanal and industrial labor, all synchronized to the same pleasurable tempo.

What kinds of subjects did optical toys depict, and how did these animations help children understand themselves and their social positions? Images on optical media like phenakistoscope disks and zoetrope strips were produced in a variety of qualities. Some, like Ackermann's hand-colored phenakistoscope disks in the 1830s, are exquisitely rendered by known artists. Lithographed media from about the 1860s on—such as the disks accompanying a phenakistoscope produced by the French ladies' magazine *Journal des Demoiselles* as the "Pantinoscope" and Milton Bradley's zoetrope strips—included considerably less detail. In many ways, "bold [images] with blocks of colour and heavy outlines" were optimized for optical media, because, as Stephen Herbert points out, "fine detail would be lost due to the inevitable blurring of the viewed image." Herbert notes that many figures were thus produced with black faces, a design choice he attributes to both: "optical reasons" and "the usual purpose of exploiting racial stereotypes for amusement."[64] Here it is clear that nineteenth-century racial politics and visual conventions are inextricably linked, for the animated worlds that optical toys set into motion calibrated the eye to a reality organized and stratified by multiple markers of racial and economic difference.

Shapes and figures are commonly rendered in silhouette on optical media, which has the effect of both abstracting them and racializing them. The silhouette, Michelle Dacus Carr writes, is a "manirhetorical" medium, which "functions as a form of profiling, or meta-coding, in the racial narrative of the U.S."[65] Tracing the silhouette in the United States, Carr connects it with scientific racism as a visual strategy that "collapses visual, verbal and oral rhetorics into an ideal form for racial representation."[66] Silhouette figures in optical media appear rendered entirely in black, or sometimes in colored clothing, raising the question of whether the black ink denotes shade or skin tone. For instance, one disk accompanying the *Journal des Demoiselles*'s Pantinoscope advertised to young ladies in the 1860s features a dark horned figure disappearing into an oversized urn, the figure's design and repeated hiding action possibly reinforcing associations between blackness, devilishness, and mischief (figure 3.4). In another disk, a bell ringer's skin is rendered entirely in black but is set against the figure's red shirt, blue cap, and blue trousers, making the racial identity ambiguous. Still others used more stereotypically racialized visual conventions. Milton Bradley's Wood Sawyers zoetrope strip features a clothed man with dark skin whose silhouette exhibits stereotypical African American physiognomic features, such as oversized lips. Another, titled Chewing Gum, represents a grotesque large-headed figure with a gaping mouth and huge red lips that open and close.

Conversely, white subjects in optical media are easily identified by skin tone that conforms to the light "background" of the paper or cardboard strip or disk, effectively assuming whiteness as a neutral or normative position. Some have tan, peach, or pink coloring applied to their faces, producing a ruddy complexion. These visual conventions reflect formal considerations—such high-contrast imagery does show up with clarity in spinning optical toys—but they also link optical toys to racial themes and representational conventions across children's media. For instance, Heinrich Hoffmann's widely reproduced collection of cautionary tales, *Struwwelpeter* (translated as *Shock-Headed* or *Slovenly Peter*), includes "The Story of the Inky Boys," about a trio of white boys teasing a black man on a walk. As punishment, the boys are dipped in ink and become black themselves.

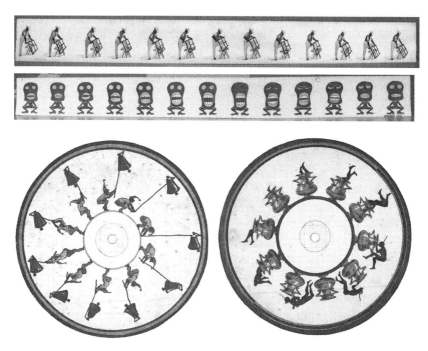

Figure 3.4
Top: Milton Bradley zoetrope strips, Wood Sawyers and Chewing Gum (1867). Bottom: Phenakistoscope disks from *Journal des Demoiselles* (1867). Top: Courtesy of the Strong National Museum of Play, Rochester, New York. Bottom: Collections of Museo Nazionale del Cinema–Turin.

In most retellings, the story undercuts its racial lesson, critiquing racially based ridicule yet also inflicting blackness as a punishment.[67] In the story's final image, four black figures walk in a line, the ink-dipped white boys rendered in crude silhouette, appearing less human in relation to the "black-a-moor," who is rendered in more detailed shading (figure 3.5). In the 1885 A. N. Myers publication of the story (and likely others), the image was rotated ninety degrees counterclockwise to fit on the page, producing a linear composition that recalls zoetropic arrangements.[68]

The racial hierarchy that the silhouette implies is consistent in optical media produced by several publishers (many of whom produced authorized or pirated copies of one another's work). These conventions suggest a broadly shared understanding of the kinds of bodies and subjects that should be represented with care. Following this logic, it is not surprising

Figure 3.5
Image accompanying "The Story of the Inky Boys." Heinrich Hoffmann, *The English Struwwelpeter, Or, Pretty Stories and Funny Pictures for Little Children*, 31st ed. (London: A. N. Myers & Co., 1885), 11.

Figure 3.6
Phenakistoscope disks with full-color and silhouetted figures. Collections of Museo Nazionale del Cinema–Turin.

that the figures of animals—when not the main subjects—were also reproduced in silhouette or simplified form. In one Ackermann disk, a corpulent man in fine attire and rendered in fine detail dines on a pig, while a dog depicted in vaguer blacks and browns lunges at the plate (figure 3.6). In another, a woman beats a man over the head with a stick, while a series of squirrels in silhouette run on a wheel in an inner ring of animation—perhaps an unexpected pairing, or a nod to a long-lost idiom. In one disk, a man on horseback pursues an ostrich with a spear. Both the man and the ostrich are drawn and colored in detail, while the horse is silhouetted. High-contrast black-and-white imagery is used in various ways to support the polar logics of racial and class superiority, abstracting and objectifying certain human forms and distinguishing people from animals, people from machines.

Artists and illustrators also commonly chose to represent tools and machinery in bold, silhouetted form. To similar effect, the gears, machinery and other prevalently reproduced objects that broadly gestured to industrialization simultaneously represented labor but also distanced it from the users, visually relegating it to a high-contrast backdrop. Recurring themes of industrial and artisanal production, of folk play and contemporary pastimes, shaped spectatorial identity by modeling lived experience as consisting within these two categories and synchronizing them to the same tempo. Images of work and play in motion represented the laboring body with the same precision and fluidity as the workings of machinery, advancing a logic of the factory worker as another cog in the larger industrial apparatus—an idea later elaborated on by figures such as Frederick Taylor and Frank and Lillian Gilbreth. Such depictions may have held special importance for children preparing not for lives of manual labor but administrative, clerical, and intellectual work, potentially including the oversight of the very industrial processes that optical toys referenced.

The phenakistoscope and zoetrope's content celebrated the advancements of industrialization, commonly reproducing images of machinery in motion. Media historian David Robinson has remarked on this "fascination with machinery," pointing specifically to an early set of disks made for the phenakistoscope by London publisher E. Wallis, which featured imagery such as a sawmill cutting a log in half. This series was "endlessly reprinted or pirated," and it is difficult to relegate the recurring motifs of gears, wheels, and mechanical parts to any single regional or national context.[69] Many disks designed for the phenakistoscope by artists such as Joseph Plateau and Simon von Stampfer, Thomas Talbot Bury, George Cruikshank, and others, are densely populated by gears propelled by people and animals or running autonomously, modeling relationships between men and machines and lauding the tireless efforts of industrial technologies (figure 3.7). Industrial iconography was especially well suited to the phenakistoscope, André Gaudreault and Nicolas Dulac assert, because of the toy's formal constraints—best geared toward subjects that can be represented within "a 'world' in which everything was governed by circularity and repetition, a world which annihilated any hint of temporal progression."[70] The cyclical rather than linear temporality of these animated sequences formally replicated the tireless logic of mass production, perhaps a means of imagining an ideal, indefatigable modern condition.[71] What is more, these toys' images produced a kind of mass aesthetic or "group performance"—a line of machines churning in time, a row of dancers pirouetting in sync—suggesting an industrial scale.[72]

This common imagery not only suggests the extent to which gears, levers and other mechanical contrivances had become familiar visual elements but also implies bodies and machines working in smooth, seamless harmony. Peter-Paul Bänziger and Mischa Suter contend that the body is a core site at which productivity has historically been understood: "It is only in the body—moving, deploying its energy, expending itself—that notions of productivity take concrete form.... As the linchpin of productivist assemblages of production [it] has remained remarkably stable despite all the promises of rationalization and automation."[73] Represented in optical

Figure 3.7
Phenakistoscope disks with mechanical motifs. Collections of Museo Nazionale del Cinema–Turin.

toys, fantasies of industrial technologies effortlessly performing their duties often extended to the representation of laboring bodies. In other cases, such as the sawmill, the body vanished entirely, leaving steam engines to churn, windmills to turn, and gears to spin autonomously, rendered in bold, black lines. The child's ability to observe and manipulate representations of machinery and laboring bodies in play may have held special significance as an opportunity to normalize and control those forms of work.

As the child spun the phenakistoscope or zoetrope, the worker or machine *did* appear to "tire" as the device slowed. However, by thematizing the worker's fatigue as simple inertia as the toy slowed down, these animated sequences minimized considerations of rest and replenishment, instead aligning the worker's toil with child's play, whereby the child needed only to give the toy another spin to set the whole scene in motion again. Tendencies to disregard, romanticize, or even erase the working body were prevalent in proindustrial treatises, such as Andrew Ure's *Philosophy of Manufactures* (1835), which, Joseph Bizup argues "avoids any reference to human labor," save for descriptions of child workers in the cotton industry (itself highly racialized), whose labors are characterized principally as sport and play.[74] Children's industrial labor was thereby characterized as play, justifying such work, while the white middle-class child's play was coded as their "work," thus naturalizing the set of relations that made optical play possible. Similar corporeal lessons on labor and class were reinforced in nineteenth-century movable toy books, such as those discussed in the following chapter. For instance, Lothar Meggendorfer's *Lustiges Automaten-Theater/Comic Actors* (ca. 1890) depicts a number of social types often organized by occupation in complex pull tab-activated scenes. Hannah Field argues that these mechanical features "encourage repeated pulling; child readers perform work with the book that matches the smaller repetitive movements—the drudgery—of the mechanical figures' tasks, even as they remain excluded from those tasks in real life."[75] Likewise, children engaged in optical play were more likely to encounter machines like those depicted by persistence-of-vision toys not in close bodily (and often dangerous) factory encounters as working children did, but as playful images, detached from the grim inequalities they perpetuated.

Boys playing in their parlors might aspire to one day manage such factory work. Accordingly, their labor would come to centrally involve vision and surveillance, making the exercise of viewing moving parts in an optical toy a particularly productive pastime. Optical media that featured mechanical motifs then furnished boys in particular an opportunity to observe and play with representations of machinery in action from within the context of their homes. The zoetrope's potential for more formal industrial education was realized by at least one writer for *Scientific American* in 1869, who noted "how valuable [the toy] would be to show the action of machinery, to illustrate mechanical movements. A machine or its parts might, by its use, be presented in actual, or rather apparent motion, showing not only the parts of the machine and their relations, but also their action."[76]

Iconography not only sustained a fantasy of modern industrial efficiency but also referenced modern and folk leisure activities. Jugglers, tumblers, and tightrope walkers frequently appear, as well as men riding velocipedes, couples dancing, musicians, and animal acts with bears, monkeys, and dogs. Whether depicting work or play, optical media synchronized organic and mechanical movements to the same inexhaustible rhythm. In animating human, machine, and animal figures in motion, they linked living and mechanical actions and obscured any notion of fatigue.[77] Just as the animated gears spin endlessly without friction (other than the phenakistoscope or zoetrope itself spinning), the dancing couple never tires, the juggler carries on, and the woman pumping water draws on an endless supply. From the rotation of a bicycle wheel and the fiddler's bow to the whir of windmill blades, the motion was confined to a sequence of ten or twelve discrete images. Phenakistoscope disks depicted both labor and leisure with the same tempo, regularity, and precision, all governed by the increments of the illustrations. Thematically, these animations celebrated rhythms of daily life structured between work and play. They also supported analogies between the worker's (or reveler's) body and the movements of machines, instilling the value of a tireless modernity by effortlessly depicting a potentially endless cycle of motion. Thematizing the worker's body in this way continued in early motion pictures, such as William K. L. Dickson's film *Blacksmith Scene* (1893), shot at Thomas Edison's Black Maria studio, the first film to be exhibited in the kinetoscope in 1893. At approximately a minute in length, *Blacksmith Scene* features a trio of smiths rhythmically hammering at an anvil. After a few cycles, they momentarily set down their hammers and each takes a swig of beer, then resume their synchronized work. In his analysis of the film, Charles Musser draws connections between the anachronistic blacksmith's shop and the work culture within Edison's own company.[78]

While optical media trained the eyes of the leisure classes, the toys' effects analogized the bodily training of manual workers whose volitional movements might be transformed into automatic behaviors. In his *Handbook of Psychology*, John Clark Murray likens the fusion of images in the thaumatrope and zoetrope to the fusion of a series of discrete bodily actions performed repeatedly until they blur into an indivisible unity. Murray claims that "it thus appears that actions, originally voluntary, may, by frequent repetition for a length of time, be removed from the sphere of human will into the sphere of those natural forces that form the human constitution."[79] He suggests that a physiological change is wrought during this automating process, arguing that through practice, the body can adapt to the rhythms to which it is subjected: "nerve-tissues ... become so pliable after repeated practice of the movements ... [actions] which at first are performed with deliberate and even painfully conscious efforts of volition, come to be carried on automatically after a while."[80] Optical toys had metaphorical utility for early experimental psychologists and were also widely taken up as standard laboratory apparatus. Hugo Münsterberg's catalog of equipment to accompany the Harvard laboratory's display at the 1893 World's Fair included a zoetrope, a kaleidoscope, and five hand stereoscopes with pictures, among other optical devices.[81] In a 1900 issue of the *American Journal of Psychology*, British psychologist E. B. Titchener recommended that newly formed laboratories include twelve Milton Bradley colored spinning tops, a "stroboscope, with 12 photographic strips ... [and] 6 double stroboscopic discs," and a set of cards with optical illusions on them.[82] In both theory and practice, optical toys thus helped in imagining how all visual and manual experience could be absorbed into an industrial logic. Early psychology practitioners reinforced the social and economic divisions that such a visual paradigm established.

Yet to view optical toys as exclusively cyclical, reinscribing the clean logic of industrial expansion, would neglect still other motifs that confronted the tidy loop of work and play with chaotic visual spectacles. In particular, many phenakistoscope disks feature animated sequences in which the figures depicted refuse to remain fixed in place, instead moving freely across the disk's surface. These animations are identified by their spiral-shaped appearance, such as one in Plateau's first set sold by Ackermann, which depicts a green-faced figure (figure 3.8). Spun in one direction, the grotesque figure appears to emanate from the center of the disk to the edge. Spun in reverse, the gaping-mouthed face appears to vanish into the center of the disk. These spirally arrayed images overtook the edge and cascaded over the sides, sometimes actually extending beyond the circular form, such as one disk featuring a scurrying rat disappearing over the side of the disk and one with a slithering snake disappearing over the side. In these examples, the edge of the disk itself is cut around the figure of the rat and the snake, giving the three-dimensional appearance of a metaleptic breach of a drawn figure entering into real life.[83] These animations express a delightful excess, suggesting the image's inability to be contained. Rather than gesturing to the repetitious logic of industrial production, this imagery is unbridled, explosive, anarchic rather than rational. These disks evoke the surpluses and excesses of children's play, suggesting potentials for both discipline and delight.[84]

This kind of imagery points to the room-for-play possible in home optical recreations. Although habitus "makes possible [only] the free production of all the thoughts, perceptions and actions inherent in the particular conditions of its production," optical play at home offered both the physical and psychic space to nuance and expand those conditions, interrogating the "antinomies" within which the middle-class subject was confined.[85] This formulation is descriptive of children's potential for agency in play but is an equally apt characterization of the broader cultural imagination of children's media culture writ large—a self-perpetuating set of binary possibilities for education or corruption that resists reinterpretation of nuanced middle accounts. Although optical toys were calculated to discipline the

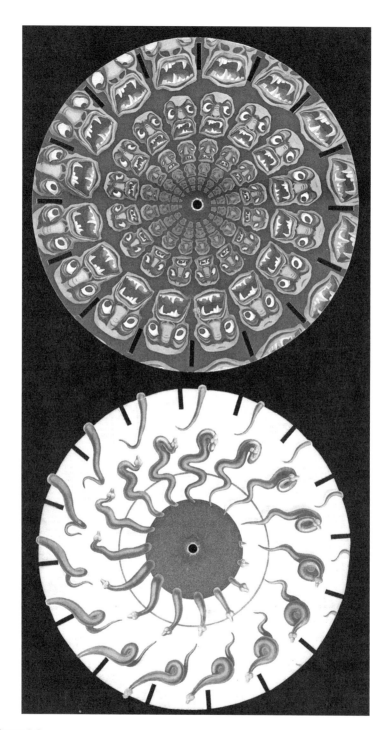

Figure 3.8
Fantascope (phenakistoscope) disks with green-faced figures and slithering snakes. Joseph Plateau and Rudolf Ackermann (London, 1833). Princeton University Library.

gaze and fix it within social and industrial hierarchies, their motifs and contexts of use offered many other possibilities. These toys helped socially locate children, to be sure, but within the complex and contradictory terrain of modern childhood, where they were subject to the competing imperatives of normative linear development, and free, undisciplined child's play.

Conclusion

Within film theory, the notion of persistence of vision has long been a factor in characterizing the kinds of interactions viewers have with screen-based moving-image media, positioning the cinematic spectator as an active agent or a passive subject. Optical toys, as the means through which persistence of vision was introduced to young people, would help establish how children understood themselves as media audiences and part of how they came to understand vision itself. Within the nineteenth-century home, toys like the phenakistoscope and zoetrope facilitated the exercise and display of optical discernment: a way of performing white, middle-class sensibilities. Related children's texts advanced hierarchies of the senses through social and moral allegories, such as the characterization of eyes as servants to the intellect. Such frameworks also helped yoke new modes of scientific authority to existing social values.

By presenting an illusion of motion, these toys highlighted the distinction between how a viewer perceives something and the actual object seen. They thus challenged the visual epistemology that had, until the nineteenth century, grounded the viewing subject. For children, however, the discourses of failure and deficiency were always already built into how they understood vision. Because vision was positioned as a learned developmental competency, scientific rhetoric that acknowledged its limits and its vulnerabilities did not necessarily produce anxiety, but instead formed the parameters within which subjectivity was constructed. The rational, disciplined subject could thus both delight in the moving image and maintain a sense of mastery by understanding how it worked. In this way, these toys recast vision not as an intuitive process, but as one that required conformity to a kind of training and refinement, which would be commensurate with a capitalist work ethic characterized by efficiency, focus, and intention.

Close examination of these toys' material attributes and iconography imagines the kinds of social configurations that likely coalesced around them. Picturing these play spaces in turn helps better characterize the interactions that children had with these optical toys, not as entirely immersed in optical spectacle, but capable of dropping into and out of the illusion at will. Much like the museum visitors introduced at the beginning of this chapter, nineteenth-century optical play involved considerable trial and error, where children could choose to look or to look away. Nevertheless, such play was an opportunity to experience and internalize persistence of vision, and these toys were deployed to train children's tastes and sensory habits. Optical play was an occasion for seeing and being seen—a pastime enjoyed during privileged leisure hours that enforced a distinct outlook on vision and social life overall. Persistence-of-vision toys paradoxically empowered viewers to understand the principles underlying their vision by playfully pointing out its limitations. These devices set into motion a visual regime that has continued into the contemporary children's mediascape. At stake in this investigation, then, is an opportunity to explore the genesis of a long preoccupation with how young people are socialized into particular cultures of spectatorship, participation, and interactivity. Optical toys were not just the ludic devices that produced the same effects seen later in the cinema, but structures through which nineteenth-century youth learned about their own visual faculties. They shaped the ways that children engaged with some of the earliest moving images and informed the way they saw the world around them.

4 Movable Toy Books and the Culture of Independent Play

There is a curious picture book in the collection of the Cotsen Children's Library at Princeton: *Dean's New Book of Parlor Magic: Or Tricks for the Drawing Room*.[1] Its title is misleading; it suggests rational recreation literature—text-heavy books several hundred pages long, such as those discussed in chapter 1, not a slim picture book with movable parts. Traditional books of parlor magic—a subcategory of rational recreation literature—invited readers to bring magic off the page through detailed descriptions of tricks and scientific experiments with spectacular effects. They transformed readers into magicians, exhibitors, and operators. The book in Princeton's collection features six movable scenes, which include exoticized figures like a Turk, a fortune-teller, and a Chinese juggler. Despite its title as a "book of parlor magic" featuring "tricks for the drawing room," the tricks in Dean and Son's 1862 text are performed by the figures in the hand-colored wood engravings, whose movements are controlled by tabs embedded in the pages. It thus scales down a range of performative traditions from fully embodied experiences to illustrated vignettes enacted by children's subtle manipulation of paper and pull tabs.

Several of the book's six scenes, such as the Chinese juggler and a tightrope dancer, replicate motifs seen in optical toys. Others were designed for the reader to perform "tricks" for a small audience of friends. In one, "Cups and Balls," a Turk performer holds two cups over two balls—one red, one black (figure 4.1). Pulling the tab vertically manipulates the figure's hands up and down to conceal or reveal the balls underneath. Pulling the tab from left to right shifts the middle layer of paper—where the balls are printed—so that they appear to change positions while covered by the cups. The scene is described as a miniature performance, with one child manipulating the

Figure 4.1
"Cups and Balls" from *Dean's New Book of Parlor Magic* (London: Dean and Son, 1862). Princeton University Library.

pull tab for others: "Great amusement is given by asking your friends to guess what coloured Balls are under the Cup." In another, "The Wonderful Bell and Magic Mirror," a grinning jester raises and lowers a large bell onto a platform, and the reader's manipulation of a concealed cardboard wheel with a lever changes the image underneath, surprising viewers when the bell is raised. Without a title that indicates the book's interactive features, a researcher encountering this catalog record would either require knowledge of Dean and Sons as a publisher of movable titles, or note the catalog heading "Toy and Movable Books—Specimens," itself a notoriously broad and unreliable indicator.[2] Otherwise, this title might easily be mistaken for rational recreation and passed over by researchers looking for movable toy books. Yet this book's explicit references to parlor entertainment and its condensation of bodily performances into a handheld format reveal how the movable toy book refashioned traditions of rational recreation as experiences that children could enjoy independently in the mid- and late nineteenth century.

Dean's New Book of Parlor Magic was published over thirty years after the introduction of optical toys like the thaumatrope, phenakistoscope, and zoetrope. By the 1850s, many children who had played with persistence-of-vision devices in their earliest days were now parents. Movable toy books appealed to adult buyers who may have found in them familiar echoes of the rich visual culture of their own childhoods adapted in novel ways, thanks to printing techniques like the chromolithograph and advances in paper engineering. Sold alongside moving-image technologies like optical toys, movable toy books offered an emerging category of playthings for younger children in particular. The toy book industry flourished in the latter half of the century, making a variety of intricately illustrated titles available for consumption by middle-class children. These books are characterized by their nontraditional shapes and sizes, their novel use of paper and cardboard to make turn-up flaps, levers, and pull tabs for moving parts, three-dimensional effects, and, from the 1870s, their colorful chromolithographed images. Movable books were thus distinct media that introduced new modes of visual and manual engagement to children.

This chapter considers how movable toy books supported children's independent play and contributed to a media culture characterized by rich educational opportunities, on the one hand, and concerns about children's leisure time, on the other. Movables were new media that responded to and shaped changing conceptions of the child as a container of potential futures: either realizing the social, moral, and economic aspirations projected onto them or succumbing to a sedentary lifestyle, bad taste, and failed possibilities. Publishers promised parents that books could occupy children for hours with rich textual, tactile, and visual features that broadly appeared to align with Locke's approach to teaching literacy through play.[3] Simultaneously, movables perpetually adapted and reinvented familiar content such as fairy tales and cautionary tales. As publishers produced multiple versions of the same title, movables helped acculturate young users to different forms of storytelling and introduced children to a range of distinct formats.

Some commentary within publishing, religious circles, and mothers' advice literature saw in these objects a swelling media culture that threatened children's well-being. As movables condensed embodied play experiences to visual and manual manipulation, they kept children safe at home, yet they also advanced a leisure culture characterized by reduced bodily investment. Toy books were frequently identified within the broader children's commercial market as promoting indoor play at the expense of outdoor recreation. Religious leaders and members of the literary press also argued that the vibrant colors of chromolithography inculcated garish tastes, unlike the chromatic harmony associated with middle-class respectability. These concerns built on the tropes of "impression" and "exposure," which had come to dominate discussions of children's vulnerable eyes. These conflicting attitudes reveal movables as objects where overlapping conceptions of the child as both a symbol of futurity and an innocent in need of protection converged. Movables thus represent a site at which the polarized terms by which children's practices of media spectatorship are still framed today, within the poles of educational potential and ruin.

From Parlor Play to the Page

Toy books of the latter half of the nineteenth century such as *Dean's New Book of Parlor Magic* bridged traditions of mixed-age home optical play and young children's unsupervised play. Unlike popular infants' "furniture for containment," such as the high chair, swing, and jumper, which functioned as "benign mechanism[s] of external control" as baby nurses fell out of vogue, toy books occupied young children's busy hands and minds.[4]

Jumpers, while commonly endorsed as safe by experts, were also regarded as dangerous. One satirical article from the *New York Times* noted the baby jumper's ability to quiet "the surly infant ... of obtrusive oratorical habits" so effectively that the baby might be forgotten and left to bounce for days until it is "so thoroughly shaken up that no care or anatomical skill could repack its internal organs in such a way as to induce them to work smoothly."[5] The author wryly concludes that the inventor of the jumper's "memory is still lovingly cherished by tired nurses and the manufacturers of infant coffins."[6] Faced with occupying infants and older children, who came flooding home from school and conscripted younger siblings into "noisy sport" and "boisterous play," mothers turned to toy books, which promised to entertain and even coordinate play among differently aged children.[7]

Because of their association with literacy and optical recreations, toy books may have been especially attractive alternatives to furniture that isolated and immobilized the child, offering enrichment and mental escape rather than physical containment. Beginning in the late 1870s, Philadelphia-based writer and editor Jessie E. Ringwalt, who had by then had at least seven children, authored a series of articles in *Godey's Lady's Book* in 1879 titled "Fun for the Fireside: A Help to Mothers."[8] The first column in the series, "Playing at Optics," stresses the importance of teaching children of all ages "the true delights of engrossing [independent] occupation." It describes the large mirrors in parlors and drawing rooms as catalysts that inspire infants and "small philosophers" alike to be curious about the direction of light, reflection, and "the reversal of the image [which] proves frequently to be a great mystery."[9] Whereas optical toys were frequently advertised as appealing to "young and old" and shown in social company, Ringwalt's article expressly describes play scenes in which "the children will be content and merry, and the mother relieved from much anxiety as well as labor."[10]

Extraordinarily, Ringwalt describes a child holding a toy book up to the glass to observe the image in reflection: children "may often be detected turning them-selves in the position of the figures in an engraving, in order to settle whether the pictured boy is using his right hand or his left one."[11] In this optical lesson, the child mirrors the position of the figures in a picture book, scaling up the illustrations, just as the illustrated figures in *Dean's New Book of Parlor Magic* scale down tricks that might otherwise be performed in the parlor. This reduction of scale enabled the child to enact magic tricks, juggling, and other feats with the subtle pull of paper tabs. Operating the movable scenes in *Dean's New Book of Parlor Magic* required children to move the lever up, down, and to the sides, sometimes at different intensities (gentle or firm) and in a specific sequence. The "Wonderful Bell and Magic Mirror" scene, for instance, required the child to hold down the right side of the page to keep the bell positioned over the blank space while simultaneously moving the lever to rotate the concealed wheel to produce the "surprise" effect when the bell was lifted.[12] Shifting from full-scale embodied optical play to visual and manual engagement with paper pages, movable toy books condensed displays of visual spectacle for children to perform independently.

The second article in Ringwalt's series, also focused on optics, details experiments with shadows, monocular perception, and the directionality of rays of light. In illustrating "the danger of relying entirely upon appearances," her treatment of optical recreations reinforces the conventional link between optical discernment and broader concerns surrounding authenticity, sincerity, and truth. Like "Little Susy" in Elizabeth Prentiss's story described in chapter 3, Ringwalt envisions optical education as a means of compensating for vision's trickiness: "a little child can be taught to correct the errors of vision, by a slight knowledge of the science of optics."[13] Yet the column's appearance in a lady's magazine alludes to its secondary purpose: the introduction of such recreations to free up mothers' time. Although Ringwalt describes games that commonly require groups, such as shadow buff (where a person parades behind a back-lit sheet and an audience guesses the person's identity based on his or her silhouette), she imagines young children under the loose supervision of extended family members: "When intended only to furnish fireside fun for the little ones, the perfection of the effects produced is of little consequence. The actors are satisfied by their own share of the frolic, and kind aunts and loving grandmamas are required to furnish boundless sympathy and little criticism."[14]

Ringwalt's series values optical play as much for keeping children busy as for imparting important optical lessons. She emphasizes that shadow plays do not require "the help of more experienced hands" to set up and highlights children's gratification rather than the quality of the optical effects produced.[15] She even adapts activities for only children, noting that the preparation of shadow figures is a "pleasing occupation," in itself, to say nothing of the resulting show.[16] Nearly half a century after persistence-of-vision toys were introduced, their broader optical lessons persisted, yet the expanding commercial media culture valued not only the pedagogical merits of home recreations but also their basic ability to fill children's leisure time. Colorful and interactive movable toy books contributed to these efforts. Some books, such as *Peeps into Fairyland* (ca. 1896) explicitly thematized "parents who are too busy or too tired to tell their children stories" and "the scene of [adults] reading aloud [to children recurred as] a nostalgic trope," particularly within toy books.[17] Such representations romanticized adults reading to children, even as novel book formats invited modes of engagement that did not require parental participation. The preciousness and scarcity of maternal time was also thematized in some movable books, such as one image in Lothar Meggendorfer's *Aus dem Leben* (*From Life*) (ca. 1890). The picture features a mother rocking the cradle of a baby who refuses to sleep, the book's mechanical parts simultaneously moving the cradle and "the pendulum of a clock on the wall." The accompanying poem, "An der Wiege" ("By the Cradle") confirms the mother's preoccupation with her own vanishing free time.[18] Toy books were seen as of great value to "any mother who has tried to keep a knot of little ones quiet and happy through the long hours of a Sunday indoors," and advertisements issued promises that toy books "will occupy the attention of Children for days."[19] One ad for Walter Crane's *New Toy Books* (George Routledge and Sons) suggested that adult buyers will "wish to be young again, that we might stare at them for hours in rapt delight."[20] These notions of childhood as a precious and protected period, coupled with insistence on the attention movables commanded, demonstrate how toy books reinforced a new ideal of children's leisure characterized by mediated absorption.

It is difficult to catalog the immense variety of toy book formats available to children by the end of the nineteenth century. Produced in unusual shapes and sizes, toy books stretched the definition of book as far as it could go, with attributes like flaps, turn-ups, and lever-activated movable parts that set sequences of events into motion. Some produced three-dimensional effects, had semitransparent pages, and revealed hidden pictures with Venetian blind or "volvelle" mechanisms.[21] One series from the 1890s, Dean and Son's *Cracker Toy-Books*, literally "crack[ed] like a pistol" when read—a feature that one writer in the *Spectator* complained "can hardly be reckoned as literature."[22] Dean's Cracker books, another writer quipped in the *Literary World*, "give at least a shillingsworth of agony to parents, and sixpenceworth of extreme felicity to the nerveless youngster."[23] The literal and figurative explosions of variety in the commercial market also paralleled the expansion of content beyond religious tales to familiar secular genres such as the alphabet book, fairy tale, and cautionary tales. These formal and thematic changes gave way to an increased conception of toy books as novelties, yet they retained an aura of quality by way of their relationship (however tangential) to older, more didactic texts for children.

The expansion of the children's toy book industry was facilitated by advancements in paper engineering and color printing processes. Techniques from relief printing and hand-stenciling to chromolithography enabled the production of colorful images on a previously unrealized scale and flooded the market with vibrant illustrations. German artists and publishers such as Lothar Meggendorfer and Ernest Nister are regarded as leaders in color printing and mechanical techniques alongside British publishers such as Raphael Tuck, and Dean and Sons, and the New York–based McLoughlin Brothers. McLoughlin Brothers took off when John McLoughlin Jr. and his brother Edmund took over following their father's death in the 1850s and became the dominant publisher of children's books in the United States by the end of the century. Around 1870, the firm completed a new factory in Williamsburg, Brooklyn, where they pioneered advancements in chromotypography (a method of using zinc plates to produce colored images without the special equipment needed for chromolithography), although by the 1890s, they had largely upgraded to chromolithography.[24] The children's media culture that nineteenth-century toy books advanced also transcended national and continental boundaries. The absence and lax enforcement of copyright law led to widespread piracy across the Atlantic. McLoughlin in particular was quick to rip off works by Walter Crane and entire series, such as Frederick Warne & Co.'s (London) Aunt Louisa books, selling them for considerably less than the originals.[25] The American Antiquarian Society's collections include books by other publishers with penciled-in annotations that reveal McLoughlin's editorial decisions, such as variations on the social and racial stereotypes represented in British books for American audiences.[26]

Nineteenth-century movables built on a centuries-old connection between children's literature and toys and play. John Locke endeavored to transform early letter recognition and spelling into games by pasting alphabet letters onto the sides of dice, so that children would become literate "without perceiving it to be any thing but a sport."[27] John Newbury's 1744 *A Pretty Little Pocket-Book* was sold with an accompanying ball (for boys) or pincushion (for girls), similarly promoting a "union of literature and material culture [that] has defined children's literature since" that time.[28] Hornbooks, briefly discussed in chapter 2, were made out of materials including metal, wood, and leather; had handles; and featured alphabets and prayers, covered by a thin layer of horn.[29] Given this rich history, Gillian Brown contended, toy books' "metamorphic and mechanical" elements demonstrate "that what we have come to think of as unbook-ish characteristics are fundamental to books [and reading]."[30] Links between text and materiality are crucial for interpreting movables because they highlight the multiple ways that these objects may have "worked" in children's minds and hands, including how their content might have been interpreted "against" the didactic grain.[31]

Early movable formats demonstrate this interplay between form and content as they alternately supported and challenged one another. Religious flap or "turn-up" books, which enjoyed popularity from the seventeenth to the nineteenth centuries, tell the story of Adam and Eve, introduce mythical creatures like the mermaid and the griffin, and chronicle a man's acquisition of worldly wealth and subsequent death. These books are commonly titled *The Beginning, Progress, and End of Man* or *Metamorphosis*, emphasizing the spiritual and material transformations they represented.[32] Their interactive features, as the preface to one 1836 edition explained, were meant "to amuse the young mind, and at the same time convey moral and religious instruction; to blend at once morality with amusement, and remove the gloom from the face of religious precept."[33] Like a poem prefacing an 1819 metamorphic adaptation of *The Pilgrim's Progress*, titled "A Prospect of Heaven Makes Death Easy," these books' playful formats were supposed to soften the realization of impending mortality.[34]

Religious turn-ups were constructed from a strip of paper, folded with a series of vignettes combining verse with a picture split in the middle by a horizontal cut, forming two flaps that opened up and down. The verses

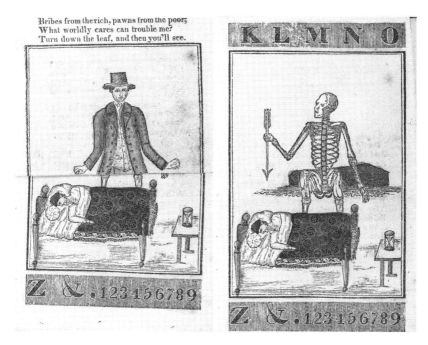

Figure 4.2
The man turns into a skeleton when the flap is lifted. Benjamin Sands, *Metamorphosis* (Cadiz, Ohio, 1835). Courtesy of the American Antiquarian Society.

initiated narrative progress by posing questions, then prompting readers to turn the flaps to advance to the answer—take, for example, Benjamin Sands's *Metamorphosis*, published in Cadiz, Ohio, and dating from the 1830s (figure 4.2) The image features a well-dressed wealthy man:

> Now I've got gold and silver store,
> Bribes from the rich, pawns from the poor'
> What worldly cares can trouble me?
> Turn down the leaf, and then you'll see.

Turning down the leaf reveals the same man, now on his deathbed. An hourglass on the bedside table signals death's approach. The larger image of the man from the waist up is still visible on the top leaf, looming over the bed. Turning the top leaf up replaces this figure with that of death, embodied by a skeleton, and a coffin in the background. Despite these books' didacticism, however, surprising scenes are produced along the way because turning each flap reveals only half of the next image. Eve is produced from

Adam's body; turning down the flap at her waist morphs her into a mermaid. A lion acquires a bird's head as one flap is lifted, transforming into a griffin before turning into an eagle.

Jacqueline Reid-Walsh argues that the surprising and unintended image combinations in religious flap books "afford ... play engagement both with and against the thrust of the religious narrative."[35] Despite their heavy religious messages, Reid-Walsh contends that they facilitated open-ended, perhaps even transgressive play. This would all change, she argues, with the considerably more elaborate movables of the mid- and late nineteenth century, which transformed the child's role "from agency to activity to spectatorship."[36] In more complex book formats, Reid-Walsh writes, "the ability of the child interactor to engage in numerous repeated actions is not the same as agency. The child interactor becomes a catalyst for the actions, but has no control over the power or direction of the motion, nor are the actions of his or her own choosing."[37]

The shift from agentic play to a passive form of spectatorship that Reid-Walsh charts resembles Gaudreault and Dulac's discussion of optical toys moving from a "player mode of attraction" to a "viewer mode of attraction."[38] The viewer mode, they explain, is characterized by an experience where the observer "fe[els] the presence of the apparatus a little less during the viewing." For instance, the user remains aware of the phenakistoscope's slotted disk, which stubbornly requires one "right" way of looking and emphasizes the toy as a device, not simply its content. By contrast, the later praxinoscope theater obscures the spinning mechanism behind a wooden mask or frame, and smoothly reflects and illuminates the content of the changeable paper strips in a mirror almost as a kind of stage or screen.[39] There are similarities between later optical toys, which privileged viewing over playing, and complex nineteenth-century movables, which Reid-Walsh argues permitted play but little control. Both design tendencies support engagement that requires less adult involvement. Like the "viewer"-oriented praxinoscope theater, which left comparatively little room for operator error and obscured its inner workings, the complex movables of the nineteenth century made colorful, interactive experiences accessible without adult assistance. Considered within the broader practices of rational recreation—themselves shifting—movable toy books played an important role in supporting children's unsupervised play.

Family Pastimes and Children's Playtime

Mothers and caregivers who sought to occupy children at home may have thus been attracted to movable toy books, which linked literacy, visual spectacle, and manual engagement without the need for adult oversight. Movable toy books exploded in popularity during the latter half of the nineteenth century alongside the growth of literature as entertainment. These concurrent developments are evidence of Karen Sánchez-Eppler's argument that the rise of fiction and "the concept of childhood … [as] associated with fantasy and fun … are not merely simultaneous—diverse escapist responses to the same social stresses—but are profoundly implicated in each other."[40] Toy books supported conceptions of white, middle-class childhood as a time of leisure, while their connections to expanded traditions of literacy education were perceived as informal supports to young children's learning. We know that children from across the social spectrum experienced public life in a range of ways, from attending the theater, the zoo, and other performances to riding new forms of transportation like the horse-drawn omnibus.[41] Middle-class childhood was distinguished by its association with domestic leisure in particular. This association was largely rhetorical—central to the characterization of the home as a moral center apart from the world—yet mothers' advice literature and the market for "furniture for containment" also reveal practical strategies to anchor and manage children at home. It is therefore unsurprising that movables commonly took public amusements as their subject matter, which reformulated (rather than replaced) a range of spectatorial practices for domestic enjoyment.

In both form and content, toy books adapted motifs associated with other visual media such as optical toys, the stereoscope, and the panorama. They gestured toward declining formats like the peep show, while promoting forms that were on the rise, such as the magic lantern.[42] Such design features and thematic tendencies made movables ideal media for filling children's leisure time by imaginatively whisking them off to distant places. Panoramic books, for instance, unfolded horizontally and offered a long sequence of views. "Panoramas," Hannah Field writes, "foreground the fact that pictures take time to parse, just as words do."[43]

Peep show books expanded in depth, imagining access to the Crystal Palace, Westminster Abbey, St. Paul's Cathedral, and the Thames Tunnel.[44] Other movables invited children to visit the circus and the zoo on demand.

These adapted formats did not replace middle-class children's public experiences, but as they reframed larger spectacles, movables reduced the risks associated with public life and provided children opportunities to practice diverse perceptual competencies in their everyday play. Moreover, as multiple versions of familiar genres and stories circulated, children encountered a range of formats and visual conventions, making such play itself a form of media education. Toy books, like optical amusements, offered new ways for children to negotiate the sometimes-conflicting imperatives to be both innocent and discerning subjects.

In the early 1880s, New York–based publisher McLoughlin Brothers produced a series of five Pantomime Toy Books of the stories *Aladdin*, *Cinderella*, *Sleeping Beauty*, *Blue Beard*, and *Puss in Boots*. Although no single toy book specimen exemplifies the diverse category of movables as a whole, several prominent features coalesce in the Pantomime Toy Books. Loosely inspired by the popular pantomime theatrical genre, these toy books were designed to resemble theaters, thereby remediating and adapting live performances for the home. They were also widely distributed by multiple publishers on both sides of the Atlantic. McLoughlin's series appears to be pirated or adapted from London's Dean and Son's identically named series from 1880, illustrated by Richard Andre (born William Roger Snow).[45] Dean and Son also apparently authorized a reproduction of the series by New York–based E. P. Dutton in 1880.[46] Transatlantic, issued by multiple publishers and based on broader public entertainment traditions, the Pantomime Toy Books exemplify the kinds of new formal elements, industrial strategies, and play practices that movables offered.

In these books, traditional pantomime characters such as Harlequin, Pantaloon, and Columbine often appear in a curtain call scene at the end, but the books otherwise retell each fairy tale in a straightforward manner—a distinction from live pantomime performances, which were often packed with intertextual references and socially relevant commentary. Each book has twenty-four pages of color illustrated plates in three sizes—small, medium, and large. The larger plates represented what the McLoughlin Brothers catalog called "five set scenes," while the smaller plates, which enacted smaller-scale transformations within those scenes, constituted "nine trick changes, making fourteen transformations in all."[47] The edge of the two outer leaves features a theatrical proscenium arch framed by box seats at the sides and musicians in an orchestra pit at the bottom, evoking a theatrical setting from the perspective of an audience member. The Pantomime Toy Books invited children to imagine theatergoing from the comfort of their own homes. Many titles had a version of the story printed in verse on the inside front cover and a prose version in the back. This design feature prevents words and pictures from being read simultaneously and assumes reader familiarity with the stories. The written stories come before and after the images and are sometimes even pasted to the inside covers, occupying the position of endpapers. In these books, text is at the periphery; the images are the showcase. This design leaves open considerable speculation about how young users experienced Pantomime Toy Books. While some movables supplied instructions to guide adult narrators, others were prefaced directly to children.[48] Given that the format separates looking and reading, it is possible that adults told the story, using the differently sized plates to manipulate narrative progression. Yet it is equally possible that children fulfilled publishers' promises that toy books could engross them for hours by narrating the tales themselves, taking delight in their ability to modulate the story's progression.

The books' differently sized plates divide narrative time and action into varying increments by associating different kinds of story events with different sized flaps, as one advertisement put it, "gradually developing the story to the end."[49] Turning the larger flaps commonly represents a change in setting and either concurrent or subsequent action. Smaller flaps mark shorter temporal scales, such as the introduction of a character within a scene. These varying spatial and temporal relationships contribute to the dramatic action by expanding or compressing time. In McLoughlin's Pantomime Toy Book version of *Sleeping Beauty*, for example, when the kingdom is put under a spell to sleep for one hundred years, five of the fourteen changes are devoted to showing members of the royal court as they slumber (figure 4.3) Turning the small- and medium-sized plates cuts to scenes of sleeping characters throughout the castle. The representation of one hundred years of story time in five illustrations compresses time (it takes fewer than one hundred years to turn the flaps). Yet within the book's economy, that a third of the pictures depict the characters asleep indicates a heightened interest in this part of the story.

This is a narrative episode dominated by enchantment, when an entire kingdom is under a spell. Emphasizing this interlude may have been a means of similarly enchanting young readers who, encountering this distinct book

Plate 1
Optical toy supplement to a December 1881 issue of *The Boy's Own Paper*. Courtesy of the Bill Douglas Cinema Museum, University of Exeter.

Plate 2
Image accompanying "The Story of the Inky Boys." Heinrich Hoffmann, *The English Struwwelpeter, Or, Pretty Stories and Funny Pictures for Little Children*, 31st ed. (London: A. N. Myers & Co., 1885), 11.

Plate 3
Phenakistoscope disks with full-color and silhouetted figures. Collections of Museo Nazionale del Cinema–Turin.

Plate 4
Phenakistoscope disks with mechanical motifs. Collections of Museo Nazionale del Cinema–Turin.

Plate 5

The kingdom asleep, two of five changes. *Sleeping Beauty*, Pantomime Toy Book Series (New York: McLoughlin Brothers, 1882). Courtesy of the American Antiquarian Society.

Plate 6
Autumn, Little Showman's Series (New York: McLoughlin Brothers, 1884). Courtesy of the American Antiquarian Society.

Plate 7
The Snake Charmer, Little Showman's Series (New York: McLoughlin Brothers, 1886). Courtesy of the American Antiquarian Society.

Plate 8

Before and after the cigar. *Naughty Girl's and Boy's Magic Transformations* (New York: McLoughlin Brothers, 1882). Courtesy of the American Antiquarian Society.

Figure 4.3
The kingdom asleep, two of five changes. *Sleeping Beauty*, Pantomime Toy Book series (New York: McLoughlin Brothers, 1882). Courtesy of the American Antiquarian Society.

format, experienced a familiar story in a new way. The flaps highlight the king and queen and their court—pages, lords and ladies, jester, butler, and maidens—in humorous sleeping positions, while the (optional) accompanying text describes the prince passing through gates and roving through corridors and staircases until he reaches the princess's bedchamber. The differently sized "trick changes" provided contemplative young readers occasion to meander through the quiet castle halls and spy the royal court and subjects in sleep, much as the prince does in the story. Impatient youngsters may have seen the colored plates as material obstacles to hasty narrative advancement, that demanded—if not contemplation—at least the manual investment of page turning to reach the next story event. Hasty progression is not rewarded; to skip over this sequence is to skip through a third of the story. The pleasure is derived by taking one's time. The book's structure also invites nonlinear exploration; in the archive, it is tempting to flip forward and backward between flaps to explore spatial continuities and disjunctures among the settings and figures. It is particularly appealing in moments when manually turning flaps simulates the characters' bodily movements, as when the young princess pricks her finger on the spindle. In this way, the book's formal elements uniquely control its narrative temporality, which in turn structured the lived temporality of children interacting with it.

The nineteenth-century theater, Marah Gubar argues, was a site "where sentimental notions of childhood innocence were enacted but also undermined, reflecting deep uncertainties in the culture as a whole about the nature of childhood."[50] When stage genres like pantomime and fairy-tale extravaganzas were adapted as movables, they similarly reflected a contested, even ambivalent attitude toward childhood innocence. Movables did so not only through their content, but in their function, as they provided parents who may not have known what to do with their children a way to engage youngsters during long leisure hours. By reproducing story events according to visual conventions closely associated with other children's picture books, McLoughlin's Pantomime Toy Books inevitably sanitized stage productions that were bawdy, raucous, rife with sexual themes, and often violent, which drew complaints by some worried about young audiences.[51] Keeping children occupied with "clean" versions of public amusements, movables thus helped to both constitute and sustain conceptions of innocent childhood as a time of both protection and education.

Figure 4.4
Autumn, Little Showman's series (New York: McLoughlin Brothers, 1884). Courtesy of the American Antiquarian Society.

Movables kept small hands busy and at the same time commonly exploited the passage of time as a narrative theme, linking children's spare time to seasons, years, and life stages. In this way, they effectively standardized time at different scales, from a quiet afternoon to the years of childhood and beyond.

Another McLoughlin series, the Little Showman's books, featured three-dimensional scenes that take their shape when the book is opened, recalling a peep show or the stereoscope's three-dimensional photographic image, popularized in the 1850s. Rather than facilitating gradual narrative progression, as the Pantomime Toy Books did, the Little Showman's books froze narrative advancement altogether and offered visual absorption in a single moment in time. The McLoughlin Brothers's first publication of these books was a compilation of pop-up pictures titled *The Mammoth Menagerie* from about 1882, which features a series of views of zoo animals in their enclosures. Each page displays a pop-up scene made of two free-standing paper panels, producing three planes of action. Some scenes have additional movable or protruding parts. Two years later, selected scenes from *The Mammoth Menagerie* were reissued as individual books. Each book includes a narrative written in verse, printed on the bottom inside of the cover when the book is opened. Readers could alternate between text and image, as the verse cues the reader's gaze to various parts of the picture. This arrangement would permit young children to enjoy the scenes without the text and older children to use the text as a prompt. By allowing children to manipulate them, movable books, such as these pop-up scenes, supported the same kind of experiential pedagogy that optical toys facilitated. Just as children likely regarded persistence-of-vision devices as intended or from alternate perspectives, "part of the fun of the three-dimensional movable is in looking at it from the top or the side, to see how the illusion of depth is created."[52] Such opportunities for scrutiny and investigation surely occupied children's time and attention.

In 1884, McLoughlin published a series of four Little Showman's books, each representing a different season (figure 4.4). The verse paired with an autumn apple-picking scene addresses the moody school-aged child preparing to return to school after an extended vacation:

> Though the days grow short and chilly,
> Every hour is full of joy;
> Being sad is being silly
> You should be a happy boy.

All the trees are gay and splendid,
With their leaves of gold and red;
Soon vacation will be ended,
But your school you must not dread.
For we all grow strong and ruddy
In the long vacation days;
But in school we learn to study
And improve in various ways.
So our time of play we'll treasure
And grow strong and well and bright,
Then go back to school with pleasure,
Where we'll learn to read and write.

This book captures the peculiar mixture of excitement and nerves children experience as they anticipate the beginning of the school year—a sentiment recorded in nineteenth-century diaries.[53] Like diary keeping as a means of accounting for time, the autumn scene prompts children to consider the signs of a new school year—changing weather and daylight—supporting a shift from an agriculturally oriented experience of the changing seasons to the institutionally imposed school calendar. The verse concludes by describing the baby in the scene, who eagerly looks on from a confined place behind a railing. Too young for formal instruction, the baby watches children on a seesaw—a movable element within the three-dimensional scene—with interest.[54] For the baby, this is an early experiential lesson in physics.[55]

By including text and image that work together or separately and characters of various ages, the autumn scene thematizes the passage of time while making the assumption of school attendance routine for both younger and older children. Structured around the changing seasons, this series of four Little Showman's titles endeavored to similarly structure the seasons of readers' growing-up years in the incremental hours of their leisure time. The combination of visually complex three-dimensional scenes, textual material, and movable parts like the seesaw offered entry points for engagement to children of different ages. If handled with care, these books could "grow up" alongside children, while the verses worked to socialize them as students and readers.

The Little Showman's books' marketing also positioned them as toy-like objects that coordinated children's cooperative play. One advertisement for the books, which appeared on the back of another McLoughlin Brothers title, imagined children discovering the books in a retail context: "If you visit a store where these books are spread out on the counters, and raise their covers, the likeness to a book will end in a charming surprise. Beautiful Tableaux will magically appear, Cages of Wild Animals will spring into being."[56] Noting the movables' resemblance to books, but emphasizing their toy-like attributes, the advertisement presumes a context where literacy is secondary to play. The ad goes on to suggest: "You will find yourself acting the part of a showman, and all the customers, particularly the little ones, flocking around to see the Show."[57] It is easy to picture the "Little Showman" figured in the series title as a school-aged child saddled with entertaining younger siblings. Perhaps they played collaboratively with little ones, animatedly reading the verse and directing their audience's gaze. Or perhaps they simply modeled the book's effects and then left younger children to their own devices. Like *Dean's New Book of Parlor Magic*, the "Little Showman" of the series title was meant to straddle roles as an independent reader and as a performer (perhaps for younger children). Although parents may certainly have experienced these playthings alongside their children, movables contained representations of performance and spectacle between their covers for children's independent consumption distinct from the multigenerational traditions of rational recreation.

As movables repackaged public entertainments for the home, they also made available additional opportunities for middle-class children to practice discerning spectatorship. Children had likely experienced the public amusements represented in movables—indeed, their familiarity with such public spectacles was probably key to the books' appeal. Yet visits to the theater and the zoo were not everyday occurrences. Toy book versions of these entertainments thus facilitated practices of spectatorial identity on a regular basis. In one Little Showman's scene, titled "The Snake Charmer," a mother and her children observe a theatrical performance by a man in traditional Zulu costume and a woman with a snake around her shoulders—whom the text identifies as his wife (figure 4.5). The optical journey that the accompanying text leads the viewer along follows a linear path through the image moving from back to front. The verse first directs the viewer's focal point from the back plane featuring the man, then to the woman in the middle, over whose shoulders a plump snake is draped. The woman's anglicized features may be reminiscent of another popular sideshow act,

Figure 4.5
The Snake Charmer, Little Showman's series (New York: McLoughlin Brothers, 1886). Courtesy of the American Antiquarian Society.

so-called Circassian Beauties, who performed as exotic exemplars of physical attractiveness.[58]

The third stanza directs the reader to the foreground, where the mother and her children watch. The verse draws attention to visual details like the man's "bright" costume and "gleam[ing] lance." Sonic cues evoking "native war song[s]" and hissing snakes recall the soundscapes of similar live performances, vividly described by one review in the *Spectator*: "The howls, yells, hoots and whoops, the shuffling, wheezing, bubbling, groveling and stamping ... form a concert to whose savagery we cannot attempt to do justice."[59] The scene was likely inspired by the rising popularity of Zulu stage acts such as the "Zulu Kaffirs" and "Farini's Friendly Zulus" beginning in the 1850s. Many performers advertised as Zulus were not actually from the South African ethnic group, and the "pseudo-Zulu" emerged as a kind of "stock comic character," much like a blackface minstrel. Some performances even included the revelation of a "Zulu" character's fraudulence.[60] Like spectators at a live attraction, then, the children looking at this toy book at home may have debated over the status of the man in the snake charmer scene as "authentic" or a "pseudo-Zulu," the scene furnishing a domestic adaptation of racialized discerning spectatorship.

In each of these titles, the viewer's mobile gaze through and across the planes of action is imagined to take time, analogous (if not equivalent) to the duration of a live performance. Theming toy books as public exhibitions, performances, and spectacles did not simply domesticate those experiences; they enforced an assumption that such practices of looking are durational in nature (whether the length of a trip to the zoo or the leisurely afternoon leafing through vibrantly colored pages). Other formats like the Pantomime Toy Books playfully reinterpreted a matinee or evening at the theater, effectively making a version of the Fairy Tale Pantomime available on demand. Much as movables domesticated forms of public spectacle as a means of filling children's leisure time, other consumer goods in the home worked to arrest children's vision and attention. For instance, Jessie Ringwalt's "Playing at Optics" column noted the engrossing qualities of the ubiquitous parlor mirror. Similarly, busily patterned nursery wallpapers of the nineteenth century, many of which featured imagery copied or adapted from children's books, reworked the images' associations with narrative, "oriented [instead] toward circuitousness and repetition."[61]

In their variety, intertextual, and intermedial appeals, movables also normalized a commercial children's culture saturated with new media formats. Densely printed ads on books' endpapers and back covers demonstrate how each title introduced consumers to a vast catalog—hundreds of books, including multiple versions of the same story. In one such advertisement, *Puss in Boots*, *Sleeping Beauty*, and *Cinderella* are all tales listed under the Pantomime Toy Books series and under Aunt Louisa's books.[62] Perhaps buyers debated among these versions, but such advertisements also promoted the purchase of multiple versions of the same story, where narrative events might be represented with slight variations. For instance, children familiar with the Aunt Louisa version of *Puss in Boots*, which was told in six pages of text accompanied by six colored illustrations, may still have been delighted by the Pantomime Toy version, which skillfully uses the small and medium flaps to emphasize the cat's deft tricks.[63] With a subtle turn of the flap, the cat smoothly catches rabbits in the bag and then presents them with a flourish to the king. The lion appears to magically transform into a mouse as the cat pounces. Conversely, while the Pantomime Toy version imaginatively represents key story events, early readers might have taken pride in the comparatively text-heavy Aunt Louisa version as they muddled through new words. As publishers stretched and reinterpreted content across diverse book formats, which themselves gestured to a wide range of entertainments, they advanced a nascent form of children's transmedia culture.[64]

As parents and publishers used toy books to keep children busy, the books' varied formats also acculturated children to engaging with new media and experiencing content in a range of ways. Movables provided middle-class children abundant opportunities to cultivate what might now be called media literacy and offered ways to both practice and play at the experience of public media spectatorship and consumption. However, as movables structured narrative time during children's leisure hours with colorful, interactive features, they also popularized play practices slightly at odds with traditional forms of rational recreation, which had involved fuller bodily investment, resourcefulness in gathering homemade materials, and a less commercial orientation toward play. For some, the pastimes and aesthetic sensibilities that movables encouraged contributed to a new media culture headed in the wrong direction.

Counternarratives and Cautionary Tales

Movable toy books offered distinct opportunities for even young children to play and read without adult oversight, and publishers bombarded consumers with thousands of choices.[65] Interactive book formats were suited to a range of genres, from fairy tales and alphabets to cautionary tales. Cautionary stories raise especially interesting questions of how movables' interactive features were imagined to instruct or discipline children. In their explicit aim to manage children's behavior, they also gesture toward a critique of movable book culture as a whole. Much like the bird-in-the-cage thaumatrope discussed in chapter 2, which allowed children to disregard admonishments about mistreating animals, movable cautionary tales visualized bad behavior to promote what Maria Tatar calls a "pedagogy of fear."[66] In so doing, they attempted to confine children's transgressive streaks to the affordances built into the page. Such books encouraged young readers to manually carry out misbehaving characters' punishments, to conscript children into the story's moral universe through corporeal engagement. Yet curiously, this same condensation of children's play from fully embodied movement to the focused manipulation of paper flaps itself came to be the subject of critique, presaging contemporary worries over children's sedentary behavior and attention problems. As the movable toy book industry addressed changing conceptions of children's innocence by occupying children in play loosely inspired by Locke's literary philosophy, a counterdiscourse of advice literature and literary and religious publications simultaneously saw toy books as threats to children's well-being.

McLoughlin Brothers seemed especially fond of cautionary stories. The company reproduced nearly two hundred books derivative of Heinrich Hoffmann's *Struwwelpeter* (Shock-Headed or Slovenly Peter), a work that has become emblematic of the genre in the nineteenth century.[67] The naughty children in Hoffmann's tales commonly meet with violent and even fatal ends: a girl burns to death while playing with matches; a thumb-sucking boy has his thumbs lopped off by a madman wielding giant scissors. "The Story of the Inky Boys" discussed in chapter 3 sees a trio of three boys fully dipped in a giant vat of black ink as punishment for ridiculing a black man. Movable versions of the stories illustrate the potential to both adhere to and subvert the story's lessons. In *Dean's Living Strewelpeter*, one story, "The Peculiar Fish," features a fisherman rescuing a boy, effected by a pull tab that manipulates the fisherman's upper body to draw a net from the water with a boy clinging to it.[68] Although the reader is meant to advance the tale by pulling the tab to rescue the boy, it is equally easy to push the tab back and plunge the boy under again—refusing to enact the story's narrative. Indeed, the tab's pushed-in position, which sees the boy submerged, is the book's reset position, necessary for it to fit back onto a shelf. Movables like this one contain the binary potentials of right and wrong, yet their formal features do not necessarily encourage children to adhere to the former.

McLoughlin's book *Naughty Girl's and Boy's Magic Transformations* (ca. 1882), illustrated by Justin Howard, uses flaps to heighten the behavioral lessons in its stories. The book contains several cautionary tales, four of them accompanied by richly colored plates attached to pages with flaps that fold open at the middle to reveal a new scene twice the size underneath. This way of representing key dramatic moments breaks actions into a before-and-after comparison perfect for cautionary tales. The top flaps depict the characters' misdeeds, and the scene underneath reveals the consequences. True to the title, several of the characters literally transform. An incessantly chattering girl named Polly is shown talking, and the scene below reveals her grotesquely transformed into a parrot. A girl who is always "scolding and fighting … biting and scratching" morphs into a cat. Distilling the narrative to two key moments, the Magic Transformation format focuses on the story's lesson: bad behavior and its results. The transformations are "magical" because the figures in both the top and bottom illustrations occupy the same position on the page, establishing a visual continuity that evokes a technique akin to a dissolve, made popular by the magic lantern.

Movables thus "gamified" cautionary tales. In fact, McLoughlin Brothers commonly used the same illustrations in both books and their toys and games, such as wooden picture blocks that "dissected" the image into cubes.[69] *Naughty Girl's and Boy's Magic Transformations* was also issued as a game with images cut into vertical pieces and mounted onto card for children to assemble or rearrange, thereby pointing to multiple narrative outcomes.[70] These tales were intended to confine bad behavior to the page and the imagination, sparing the child from fantastical punishments (as in animal transformation tales) or painful real-life consequences (as in Slovenly Peter). In another of the McLoughlin stories, "The First Segar," the top flaps depict a boy confidently raising a cigar to his mouth while his sister observes (figure 4.6). When the flaps are folded back, the boy is shown

Figure 4.6
Before and after the cigar. *Naughty Girl's and Boy's Magic Transformations* (New York: McLoughlin Brothers, 1882). Courtesy of the American Antiquarian Society.

choking and surrounded by plumes of smoke, his face swollen and contorted from crying. His sister looks on, laughing. The excessive smoke and the boy's anguished face, rendered in close-up, emphasizes his discomfort as a deterrent to readers. Yet such representations circulated alongside other products that stoked children's curiosities in other directions. Unitarian minister Charles Wendte, for instance, noted, "Your boy is delighted with the glimmer of his candy cigar, because he sees his father and elder brothers smoking. Soon, however, he is hiding in some obscure nook, and practicing with the real article in tobacco."[71] Importantly, many archival specimens of toy books bear "traces of children's reading—coloring-in, rips, tears, and other marks of damage," details commonly mobilized as evidence that children refused the behavioral lessons that books sought to impart (both in terms of their content and lessons in the proper treatment of books).[72] Yet "the [movable toy] book's disintegration" after rough handling did not necessarily prompt "the attendant disintegration of whatever it is that the book teaches to or expects of its child readers."[73] If an overarching aim of the movable toy book was to occupy children's home leisure time, then its purpose was often accomplished, whether the child read the book as intended or spent hours mutilating its pages. Toy books were objects of consumption and were likely consumed (and destroyed) by their users. In filling children's time, whether by sanctioned or transgressive ways, these books thus served a broader ideological function than what their content alone suggests.

Movable cautionary tales endeavored to represent bad behavior to prevent its surfacing in children's everyday lives beyond the page. Perhaps paradoxically, the play practices associated with toy books themselves came to be regarded as concerning behavior. Critiques were mounted on thematic grounds, with objections to secular or frivolous content, but they were also fascinatingly focused on form and function. Specifically, some people worried about the vibrancy of chromolithography and the sedentary play that movables encouraged. Even before the widespread adoption of chromolithography, commentators warned against the danger of excessive indoor play and overly vibrant color. A scathing piece on toy books printed in an 1830 issue of the *Episcopal Watchman* implores readers to consider the grave importance of "persons engaged in making compilations, or in producing new materials for perusal in the nursery, or in the construction of devices and ornaments calculated to draw the notice, and either to improve or injure the infant searcher after amusement and knowledge." Even in this early period, the author expresses his sorrow "that such immense quantities of trash should every day be placed within the ready grasp of our unsuspecting progeny."[74] Colored illustrations are central to the critique, characterized as "the most gaudy daubery imaginable, designed to catch the young eye, and to qualify the unformed taste, before it can discern the absurdity of a green sky, a yellow ocean, or a scarlet lawn."[75]

The role of "gaudy" colors in spoiling or inaccurately calibrating children's perceptual apparatus is a common refrain. An 1850 rational recreation text leans on common tropes of inscription and impression that are so inextricably tied to conceptions of children' exposure to improper content. It includes an image of two children bent intently over a book on a table:

> Here are James and Joseph looking at Picture Books. They got them perhaps from their Father. They look as if they were much interested in the contents of the books. They have laid aside their reading books to look at the beautiful prints contained in this one. Some of them are colored, and some are not. Of course the colored ones are longer looked at, and the ones the children are most impatient to see. For it is natural that the most gaudy things should strike the eye of a child first.[76]

Publishers like McLoughlin Brothers took this order of perceptual operations to heart, attempting to catch and focus children's gazes on colorful spreads. An 1893 McLoughlin edition of *Beauty and the Beast* is shaped like a theater, opening in the middle to revealing two half-length pages resembling a stage framed by a proscenium arch. Two sets of six colored pages unfold from the middle to reveal each subsequent scene. A blue velvet curtain frames the top of each page; the bottom features a wainscoting motif, where the text accompanying each scene appears. The colorful stage area, where *Beauty and the Beast*'s drama literally unfolds as the pages are turned, appears in stark contrast to the left and right margins framing the action, which are rendered in black and white and depict balconies brimming with spectators. These design decisions both assume and reinforce assumptions about what kind of imagery will "strike the eye of a child."

Movables prompted a second core complaint: that they discouraged children from spending enough time outside—a discourse that bears striking resemblance to twenty-first-century concerns about children's play.[77] One 1854 manual advised mothers "to throw away all false notions about gratifying your taste in having a slender, pale-faced, delicate boy at your side, dressed in silk velvet and linen cambric, who likes to sit in the parlor and work bookmarks in silk floss, or play checkers *very still* in the corner.... Throw such notions all aside, with the pictured alphabet and the pretty toy books." The manual ultimately argues that outdoor play is superior to "studying a pasteboard alphabet," an educational plaything emblematic of the deluge of similar products available to children.[78] Another manual acknowledged that "the busy mother is so delighted to see her child amuse himself quietly with his book, that she forgets he is losing what is a thousand times more important: exercise in the open air, and the habit of observation."[79] Accounts pitting active, embodied play against the comparatively sedentary visual and manual engagement required of toy books reverberate in the twenty-first century. In the 1860s, the movable scenes in *Dean's New Book of Parlor Magic* reduced bodily performances of parlor magic tricks to paper pull tabs. Over 150 years later, Scott D. Sampson describes a similar corporeal condensation in his 2015 book, *How to Raise a Wild Child*, lamenting children's video game cultures in which "bodily exercise is restricted largely to thumb gyrations."[80]

Movables' vibrant visual qualities also reflected generational tensions over a children's media culture that looked radically different from how it had appeared in the decades prior to the mid-nineteenth century. Although toy books replicated motifs also found in optical toys, adapted a range of familiar entertainments, and gestured toward traditions of rational recreations, chromolithography dramatically changed the appearance of industrially produced playthings. In 1873, the "Art for the Nursery" column in the London publication the *Athenaeum* reported: "We have before us a large batch of handsome and showy books for the delight of children: books such as, so far as colour and prices are concerned, were not within the reach of our fathers and grandfathers, or of ourselves in gone-by days. Our children are more fortunate in this respect."[81] Though the column anticipates the problems that color education would address in the 1890s, cautioning that "color, wrongly used results in chromatic atrocities," it maintains optimism of the growing field.[82] Twenty years later, in 1893, the same column offered a much sharper critique of several titles submitted for review by Dean and Sons: "*Dolly's Party*, which, apart from its chromatic atrocities, approaches imbecility, and is likely to foster bewilderment in the youthful mind; *The*

Venetian-Blind Movable Book, which, though gaudy, might be more stupid than it is, and is full of surprises."[83]

Worries over children's perceived declining outdoor play and exposure to gaudy colorful pictures represented an alternative narrative to that told by advice manuals and publishers who saw in movables quality literacy-adjacent content presented in engaging ways. Many of these concerns seemed grounded in an uneasiness in the relationship between children's tastes and the commercial media and toys available to them. In an 1884 article about Christmas gifts, the Unitarian minister Charles Wendte, who had held positions in churches across the United States, pined for his own childhood days, when children were satisfied with toys like blocks, tin soldiers, wooden dolls, and Noah's arks. These traditional toys, he sadly says, "would seem tame and poor to the present generation of children."[84] He takes special aim at toy books: "The sensational picture-book, with its gaudy illustrations, in which vulgar and hideous themes are grotesquely treated, imposes itself deeply on the infant imagination, and in after life the coarse tastes and cruel disposition of the man may be accounted for in no small part by this early perversion of the art instinct and moral feeling of the child."[85] Wendte's account reproduces the same kind of generational malaise and adult disconnect that historian Gary Cross would track in his discussion of children's toys and media produced a century later.[86]

Wendte's worries over "kids today" in the 1880s, with their insatiable appetites for novelty, reflect a tension at the heart of the concept of childhood innocence that gradually solidified in the late nineteenth century. Critics who warned that movables would spoil children's bodies and tastes grasped at an impossible, nostalgic past version of childhood—discord more commonly traced in later twentieth-century media. Yet it was the very conditions that made possible the figure of the child's leisure time at home that also appeared to justify the vast market of commercial goods designed to occupy that time. These conditions formed a complex causal loop whereby colorful diversions like movables both created and seemed to respond to children's perceived needs and tastes. Even as toy books imparted moral lessons and attempted to enforce good conduct, the new recreational and media cultures to which these books belonged were themselves subject to scrutiny. These books and the new leisure patterns they enforced coordinated the broader, sometimes contradictory, ideologies of the middle-class child at home.

Conclusion

Movables reshaped leisure culture in the second half of the nineteenth century, conveniently occupying young children in front of whom long years of leisure stretched ahead. Where Dean's 1862 *New Book of Parlor Magic* condensed rational recreation to the hand and eye, by the turn of the century, books would also remediate cinematic motion for the page. In 1898, London publisher Bliss, Sands and Co. published a colored version of *The Motograph Moving Picture Book*, a picture book with twenty-three wood-engraved scenes with lithographic color added and a special cover designed by Henri de Toulouse-Lautrec.[87] Each scene appears to come to life when a transparent overlay with a fine-lined pattern is placed over and moved across the image. The perception of motion is produced by the optical effect of a moiré pattern, which results at the points of intersection when one or more sets of lines (or dots) are superimposed. The subjects of many of the book's illustrations were seen across prints, lithographs, and cinema, such as the sensational scene of a burning house or the serpentine dancer, which, by the time of the book's 1898 publication, had been filmed by both Edison and the Lumière Brothers and had appeared in a variety of print publications such as *Frank Leslie's Popular Monthly*.[88]

Each image in the *Motograph Moving Picture Book* was accompanied by instructions about the proper placement and movement of the transparency. To get the full effect of the book's image of a mortar mill, for instance, the child was directed to "place the star on the Transparency over the star on the picture, tilt the Transparency very slightly up to the right and move very slowly up and down over the face of the picture."[89] Upon proper execution, advertisements noted, "Hours may be spent over [the book] with ever varying and surprising results," echoing the same time-filling promises common to publishers' appeals.[90] Children likely experimented with how the speed and directionality of the transparent overlay changed each scene's movement, actively creating and responding to moving images. Such experiences support Charles Musser's assertion that nineteenth-century observers were not "naïve, passive spectators awestruck by the lifelike moving image but active viewers making judgments and comparisons in relationship to other cultural works and their own everyday experiences."[91]

In their manipulation of narrative space and time, their direction of the user's gaze, and their adaptation of a range of other performance practices and media forms, movable toy books played an integral role in standardizing new conventions of visual and interactive storytelling. They supported a new visual culture characterized by a wide range of aesthetic and interactive conventions, and in so doing established and normalized new ways of looking that equipped children for a rapidly changing visual and technological landscape. Perry Nodelman argues that "in persuading us that they do represent the actual world in a simple and obvious fashion, picture books are particularly powerful deceivers … [they] are a significant means by which we integrate young children into the ideology of our culture."[92] Nodelman's choice of the word *deceivers* aptly gestures to the important role that images played in nineteenth-century children's culture, where many pedagogical practices of looking actively worked to unsettle any semblance of truth that visual perception assumed. The particular ideologies that movables worked to inculcate had as much to do with routinizing modes of mediated engagement and reinforcing assumptions surrounding children's leisure time as with the kinds of content represented.

The enormous variety of movable specimens also attests to how these books naturalized a new commercial culture itself, characterized by vibrant color, excess, and perpetual novelty. On the one hand, publishers' boasts that toy books' effects would occupy children for hours were likely regarded as testaments to these books' value. New commercial media like movables kept children indoors, quiet, and still, literally and figuratively fixing the child within middle-class domestic space. Yet others feared that the imaginative mobility that movables offered came at the expense of children's lived experiences. It would seem that publishers had created a market characterized by oversaturation of both book formats and the colors found in the images themselves, which later educators and manufacturers would work to tame and refine.

5   Color Education: From the Chaotic Kaleidoscope to the Orderly Spectrum

Milton Bradley's 1889–1890 Game and Toy Catalogue advertised a vibrant chromolithographed puzzle called the Smashed-Up Locomotive. Fully assembled, the puzzle depicts a steam engine on the tracks hitched up to a green tanker car, each part of the train meticulously labeled. The puzzle was sold in a "polished wooden box" affixed with "an elegant [picture] label on the cover." Unlike contemporary boxed puzzles, which customarily reproduce the puzzle's assembled scene on their packaging, the image on Milton Bradley's Smashed-Up Locomotive box differs dramatically from the image on the puzzle itself. Variations of this puzzle were likely available at least beginning in the 1870s, and the box was issued in at least two versions. On one, two figures stand at the bottom left of a landscape. They are half turned toward rocky ground and a field and horizon beyond. They are surveying a scene that is difficult to make out at first. However, close inspection reveals that the two are gazing at the spectacular disaster of a crashed train in the distance: train cars appear disengaged from their tidy line and the iconic locomotive cattle catcher is tipped sideways, sketched in simple black lines. The other version of the puzzle's packaging displays this violence with more clarity. A bold title rendered in bright orange letters, "The Smashed-Up Locomotive," dominates the foreground. Behind the letters is a scene of vehicular carnage. The locomotive cab pitches forward at an alarming angle. The cattle-catcher grill is mashed into the track. The windows are broken and the smokestack splintered in a ring of jagged remnants. Behind the locomotive, the green tanker car has fallen on its side; the wheels point skyward at an unnatural angle (figure 5.1).

The puzzle celebrates the mechanical marvel of the locomotive—a technology that underwent perpetual improvement and elaboration in the

Figure 5.1
Versions of Milton Bradley's Smashed-Up Locomotive puzzle, ca. 1890. Top: Box top with crashed train. Courtesy of Joe Seymour. Bottom: Finished puzzle. Courtesy of the Strong National Museum of Play, Rochester, New York.

nineteenth century—by visually reproducing it through another relatively new technology: the chromolithograph.[1] For nineteenth-century children, the puzzle's vibrant colors may have served as analogues to the train's motion, evoking speed and dynamism. The radical disjuncture between the complete, operational train in the finished puzzle and its smashed-up form—depicted on the box cover and evoked in the heap of unassembled puzzle pieces—brings to mind the promises of the locomotive's velocity and the danger of its motion run out of control. Versions of this puzzle exist in the collections of several institutions, including the Strong National Museum of Play and the New York Historical Society. It is striking in person because instead of a jigsaw puzzle's familiar rounded interlocking pieces, the "dissected" picture of a train is fragmented in only flat-edged pieces. Many pieces are shaped like rectangles, trapezoids, and square-like forms with missing corners. Over a dozen of the pieces are identically shaped and sized hexagons, making them materially interchangeable. Players thus cannot rely on finding the right fit based on shape, an affordance of the familiar jigsaw. Instead, the puzzle's successful completion is largely dependent on matching line and color, further emphasizing the chromolithograph's significance.

Bradley's Smashed-Up Locomotive was part of an industrially produced material world for middle-class children that by late century had become increasingly colorful. Alongside vibrant products made by Milton Bradley, Dean and Son, and McLoughlin Brothers, for example, a vast network of experimental psychologists, members of the medical community, and educators gathered interest in children's vision generally and color perception specifically. This range of practitioners shared concerns about how children saw, what they saw, and how color sense might be trained and refined to various ends. These critical activities both contributed and responded to a proliferation of colorful consumer goods available to children. By the century's close, color literacy was regarded as an essential skill—central to vocational training and linked to the refinement of children's aesthetic and spiritual sensibilities. Accordingly, several comprehensive systems of color education were developed to awaken children's senses and stress the importance of chromatic order and harmony. Color education purported to teach children how to see in an increasingly fast-paced and color-saturated world. The systemization and instruction of color prepared children for the workforce and cultivated their preferences in alignment with the aesthetics of the mass-produced goods available to them.

Educators and educational suppliers associated color literacy with the promise of a bright future, color ignorance with profound peril. Proponents of color education such as Milton Bradley, Louis Prang, and Albert Munsell all asserted its importance through a discourse characterized by risk and opportunity. On one hand, nineteenth-century life promised new and dynamic visual experiences—a visual paradigm that came to be embodied by the kaleidoscope, introduced in the early nineteenth century. Its visual allures notwithstanding, this beautiful, ever-changing and vibrant new world was also perceived as chaotic and distracting. By the end of the nineteenth century, color education—which stressed a common language and theory of color, as well as principles of color harmony—was framed as key to developing children's aesthetic, spiritual, and vocational sensibilities. Schoolchildren in the late nineteenth century used materials such as mechanical rotators, spinning tops, and colored disks to break down and reconstruct colors from their component parts. Such apparatuses functioned much like parlor play with earlier optical toys like the thaumatrope and zoetrope, which cemented new conceptions of visual literacy and reinforced practices of optical discernment.

This chapter explores the competing discourses associated with children's color perception over the course of the nineteenth century. Although the kaleidoscope's inventor, David Brewster, imagined its chief application in the design arts, the toy largely became known for producing unpredictable, ungovernable optical effects that users found pleasurable and absorbing. The device's association with unbridled chromatic experience was mirrored by its own intellectual property history, as Brewster's original idea was immediately swept into the market beyond his economic and scientific control. Despite the kaleidoscope's theoretical appeal to progressive educators, its association with distraction and fragmented focus may have discouraged pedagogues from incorporating it into formal instruction. Instead, the kaleidoscope sustained dual possibilities for conjuring vibrant images and supporting a model of distraction connected to growing concerns surrounding children's color blindness and color ignorance, which helped form the conditions for systems of color education to flourish. At the same time that colorful consumer products saturated the children's market, physicians, psychologists, and educators worried that undetected color blindness (as a congenital disorder) and color ignorance (as a result of poor education) represented grave threats to children's development, vocational choices, and even public safety.

Systems of color education, such as those developed by Louis Prang and Milton Bradley, responded to these fears. Proponents of color education sought to standardize and quantify the chromatic spectrum—aligning art, science, sensation, and perception. They took a progressive pedagogical approach, leading with student observations and interests, perhaps best exemplified by Bradley's spinning tops and color mixing wheels. Combining the visual perception of color and motion, spinning tops and mixing wheels fitted with disks of various color combinations could be spun to demonstrate how colors combine from component parts. These devices relied on persistence of vision—the same perceptual phenomenon that animated earlier optical toys—and allowed pupils to test and verify hypotheses about these properties of color. Color wheels and tops represent another site at which optical experimentation and play were central in childhood education. In contrast to the kaleidoscope and the model of attention with which it was associated, the persistence-of-vision devices used in color instruction purported to control and systematize the chromatic experience.

Kaleidoscopic Playscapes

Over half a century before Milton Bradley's colorful, explosive locomotive found its way into children's hands, Scottish scientist David Brewster (1781–1868) invented the kaleidoscope, a device that would become emblematic of Victorian visuality writ large. The best-known optical toy to engage with color, its countless textual invocations are what media archaeologist Erkki Huhtamo refers to as "discursive kaleidoscopes," key ways of understanding the device's meanings in nineteenth-century contexts.[2] Its "discursive manifestations," Huhtamo contends, "can be read as symptoms of a creeping transition into the cultural condition we call 'media culture.'"[3] The kaleidoscope invited users to see the world in new ways. After Brewster invented the kaleidoscope around 1815, it was patented, then manufactured by London optical instrument maker Philip Carpenter beginning in 1817. However, the device was exhibited in London before manufacturing under Brewster's supervision was underway, and soon London and Paris were flooded with hundreds of thousands of knock-off kaleidoscopes, for which Brewster received no compensation.

Brewster lamented that this sudden proliferation exposed innumerable people to the device's dazzling effects without an accompanying explanation of its underlying principles or practical applications.[4] The toy's runaway success would parallel the model of attention with which it came to be associated—dynamic, perpetually shifting, and ungoverned. The attraction of the device as a toy dominated its reception over Brewster's other hope that it might be applied "as a mechanical means for the reformation of art according to an industrial paradigm."[5] Instead of an integral instrument in the areas of decorative arts and designs, capable of continuously and automatically conjuring colorful images that might be made into industrial products, the sensational toy came to function powerfully as a colorful diversion and a linguistic trope to characterize the multifaceted quality of modern urban experience. Helen Groth, for example, has charted the kaleidoscope's literary power across the works of authors such as Percy Bysshe Shelley (who coined the term *Kalleidoscopism*), Lord Byron, Samuel Taylor Coleridge, and the Scottish poet Anna Jane Vardill.[6] Groth writes, "The kaleidoscopic metaphor captures a sense of celebratory 'multiplicity,'"[7] calling to mind a liberating, freeing experience and introducing the observer to a dynamic array of visual delights.

Given the device's association with multiplicity, it is little surprise that the word *kaleidoscope* itself came to be used to describe miscellany or omnibuses.[8] The diversity of the objects reflected in the kaleidoscope's cell, ranging from bits of colored glass and wire to beads and lace, mirrored the exhaustive assortment of contents in rational recreation texts popular throughout the nineteenth century. Like rational recreation literature, which widely sampled games, pastimes, science, and magic, the kaleidoscope offered a seemingly inexhaustible parade of aesthetic experiences. Just as recreational literature meant to entice children with its wide-ranging coverage, the kaleidoscope served as a metaphor for progressive sensory-based pedagogy that aimed to interest viewers. In her 1886 teachers' manual, Massachusetts-based educator Louisa Hopkins recommended that if primary schoolteachers responsible for large, diverse classrooms "present things to the child as in a kaleidoscope; he will give his absorbed attention to this presentation of interesting phases in a prepared, but unannounced sequence, which will reveal more to him in a few minutes than an hour's task-work."[9] With her kaleidoscopic approach, Hopkins assumed children's natural "restlessness," and accordingly, she advised teachers to structure their classes with "a frequent change of theme, the senses leading, the mind following, growing and strengthening and rejoicing in acquiring knowledge concerning all which his senses or his imagination seize upon."[10]

Even as the kaleidoscope served as a metaphor for a multifaceted, interest-driven approach to sustain pupils' attention, the kaleidoscope itself was less likely to be found in the nineteenth-century schoolroom. Instead, the toy that had been so prominent in public would eventually move into the home. One reason that the device was adopted more widely in homes than in schools is that although it opened up new configurations of visual experience with dazzling images, it was also implicated in cultural discourses of attention and distraction. Like many other Victorian optical toys outfitted with peep holes and lenses, the kaleidoscope mandated a spectator immersed in the reflected image. So-called Kaleidoscomaniacs, argues Erkki Huhtamo, disappeared into the colorful images that the instrument produced, often at the expense of their immediate physical surroundings. Huhtamo offers insightful analysis of a nineteenth-century engraving, *La Kaleidoscopmanie ou les Amateurs de bijoux Anglais*, which depicts observers riveted by the kaleidoscope, oblivious to their loved ones being seduced behind their backs.[11] Jason Farman recalls similar early nineteenth-century accounts of engrossed kaleidoscope users, arguing that the toy "represented the fleeting attention of a population who were easily bored, fascinated by illusions, and distracted from social interactions in the public sphere."[12]

It is easy to recognize contemporary analogues of such mania in the ubiquitous figure of the mobile device user so absorbed by the screen that they fall or collide; Huhtamo links this historical topos to contemporary examples such as a woman in Reading, Pennsylvania, whose fall into a mall water fountain in 2011 while on her phone was captured by security footage and subsequently viewed by millions online.[13] Contemporary discourse combines similar concerns about speed and distraction. Analyses of heightened pedestrian risks are coupled with changes such as local regulations outlawing looking at cell phones while crossing the street and the modification of public infrastructures like dedicated cell phone pathways for mall patrons.[14] Two hundred years before, people peering into the kaleidoscope inspired similar concerns, the device in people's hands symptomatic of a modernity that could be both vivid and beautiful but also jumbled and cacophonous. In this way, the kaleidoscope cast the visual terrain as potential spectacle and potential peril.

Children were particularly vulnerable to the kinds of distraction that the kaleidoscope offered. Educator Louisa Hopkins's proposal to address children's "restlessness" in schools by presenting content in a kaleidoscopic manner implied that students had short, disorganized attention spans—a view in keeping with other expert discourses. The child's developing sensory apparatus was perceived as a priority by early experimental psychologists, for instance, who characterized children's attention as unruly and in need of direction. In his 1892 textbook, *Psychology*, William James articulates the attributes of children's vision:

> Childhood is characterized by great active energy, and has few organized interests by which to meet new impressions and decide whether they are worthy of notice or not, and the consequence is that extreme mobility of the attention with which we are all familiar in children, and which makes of their first lessons such chaotic affairs. Any strong sensation whatever produces accommodation of the organs which perceive it, and absolute oblivion, for the time being, of the task in hand. This reflex and passive character of the attention … makes the child seem to belong less to himself than to every object which happens to catch his notice.[15]

Critically, James's account frames the mastery of perceptual skills in terms of agency, yoking the child's autonomous attention to a gaze that is active rather than "passive." In this formulation, the ability to see and act from a purposeful position were key elements in the formation of sentient subjectivity. In a similar vein, educators sought to organize and direct children's interests, to train the senses and adopt habits that would lead to good patterns of reasoning and judgment.

Educators and experimental psychologists encountered challenges when faced with real children as students and subjects whose behavior did not always conform to expectations. In 1894, educator and psychologist George W. A. Luckey conducted an experiment on peripheral color vision at Stanford University. Luckey used a device called a perimeter: a darkened, semicircular rod affixed to a wall, which formed a kind of panorama around the subject at eye level. Colored beads were pushed from the periphery toward the center of the rod until the subject, with one eye covered, was able to correctly identify their color.[16] Conversely, subjects were asked to identify the point at which color information left their field of vision, tested by starting the beads at the center and moving them toward the periphery. The procedure required children to keep their eyes fixed straight ahead as the bead approached or receded from their field of vision. Luckey's young subjects evidently had great difficulty maintaining this focus, and many results had to be discarded when children's eyes darted around. Working with children's undisciplined eyes, Luckey complained, "at times became very annoying."[17]

While concerns over attention and distraction so central to the kaleidoscope featured prominently in education and psychology, the kaleidoscope itself did not disappear, even as its novelty declined. By the 1820s, the kaleidoscope was no longer a popular public sight, but it would eventually be taken up as a parlor amusement in the last quarter of the nineteenth century.[18] In the United States, Charles G. Bush was the most prominent manufacturer of parlor kaleidoscopes, which are distinguished from handheld models by their slightly wider tubes and their attachment to tabletop stands. Bush patented several improvements on the device's design in the 1870s, including the addition of liquid-filled glass ampules in the object chamber and an opening at the side of the object chamber to easily allow users to change the household items they placed in the device.[19] The ability for children to independently use the device was a key factor in the parlor kaleidoscope's design. In his 1874 patent for a folding kaleidoscope stand, Bush specified that the toy's setup should be easy enough "that a child can separate the parts of the stand or reunite them in a moment."[20] The kaleidoscope's domestication has been interpreted as a retreat from public life that isolated and distracted users.[21] Yet its role as a children's device opens up other readings, particularly around its function to invite new forms of playful visual mobility. The parlor kaleidoscope's contents simulated the busy, dynamic public world, inviting children to adopt a "kaleidoscopic" gaze as a domestic rehearsal.

When the kaleidoscope was brought into the parlor, it did not leave the world behind, but brought the world with it, within its tube. The range of materials commonly placed in the kaleidoscope's object cell became a kind of microcosm. Brewster's writing on the subject recommended putting objects such as twisted brass and iron wires, lace, beads, live insects, and salt crystals into the device's transparent cell.[22] The *Magazine of Science and School of Arts* suggested using semitransparent or shiny material such as bits of copper wire and colored foil, as well as "opaque objects, such as a seal, a watch-chain, the second's hand of a watch, coins, pictures, gems, shells, flowers, leaves and petals of plants."[23] This advice to experiment with both natural and manufactured objects transformed the kaleidoscope's cell into a user-authored cabinet of curiosities that could be set into motion and observed. Bits of metal, glass, lace, string, nails, buttons, and other "trinkets" represented the stuff of everyday life to which children had access and that the kaleidoscope could present in new ways.

In some instances, the incorporation of the kaleidoscope in the parlor seemed to inspire a shift in the conception of domestic spaces themselves in more optical terms. One curious account published in *American Agriculturist* around the same time that Bush popularized the parlor kaleidoscope encouraged readers to make a "piano kaleidoscope" with the polished gloss of a hinged piano cover as two reflective surfaces. Readers were instructed to prop up the hinged piece of the cover with books at the appropriate angle, then to cover it with a shawl to make an oversized kaleidoscope tube in which larger household goods such as statuary and candlesticks could be exhibited.[24] Unlike the parlor kaleidoscope, fashioned from wood and displayed on a handsome stand, the article describes a playful scene with children (or adults) manipulating furniture, moving books, and rearranging silver and brass objects that might otherwise ornament the mantel, transforming the room into an apparatus for kaleidoscopic looking. Still other kaleidoscopes had removable object boxes that could be replaced with multifaceted lenses—what we might call bug-eye lenses today—so that when users looked through the tube, their domestic environment appeared in multiple, tiny scenes.[25] Such activities refashioned household interiors according to a kaleidoscopic logic, providing opportunities for domestic experimentation that introduced the colorful dynamism of the public world to children in measured, controllable ways.

The kaleidoscope thus did not retreat from the natural and manufactured world, but brought it into new focus for young users. Within the parlor, children could navigate and explore this world at will—a possibility made central in the design of Bush's parlor kaleidoscope. Bush's 1874 patent for improved illumination and a changeable contrasting-color background for the kaleidoscope also outlines a "revolving object box," which turns at the end of the tube to move the colored objects inside.[26] Among the parlor kaleidoscope's most distinctive characteristics is its six protruding metal spokes around the circumference of the object box, which resemble the handles on a ship's wheel (figure 5.2). Attached to its tabletop stand, the parlor kaleidoscope was operated differently from the traditional model. Rather than rotating the entire tube to set the objects in motion, users of the parlor kaleidoscope instead grasped the spokes protruding from the object box much like a miniature ship's wheel and "steered" it around to see the colorful combinations form and change. In 1876, Nantucket-based Robert F. Macy iterated on the ship's wheel mechanism, with the addition of a "rotary agitator … in order to agitate and turn over the objects in the

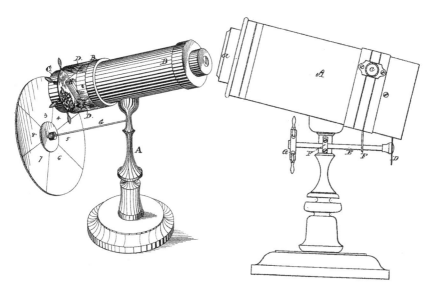

Figure 5.2
Patent figures showing ship's wheel-like components. Left: Charles G. Bush, US Patent 151,005 "Improvement in Kaleidoscopes," May 19, 1874. Right: Robert F. Macy, US Patent 174,690 "Improvement in Kaleidoscopes," March 14, 1876.

box."[27] Macy's patent quite literally shows a small steering wheel under the main tube, which, by means of a gear mechanism, would rotate the object cell. Although its placement on a tabletop stand in the parlor immobilized the kaleidoscope itself, these new design features materially and thematically invited young users to maneuver through complex visual experiences, evoking a sense of visual/virtual movement.

If parlor kaleidoscopes enabled children to imagine navigating through colorful environments, then they also acknowledged that such visual voyages unfolded over time—that they had both duration and velocity. These valences of kaleidoscopic looking, associated with speed and temporal progression, run alongside the toy's association with multiplicity and distraction. A block of text widely adapted and reproduced in juvenile recreational literature reinforces this relation between the device's valences of speed and multiplicity:

> The following curious calculation has been made of the number of changes this instrument will admit. Supposing the instrument to contain twenty small pieces of glass, &c. and that you make ten changes in each minute, it will take the inconvenient space of 462,880,899,575 years, and 360 days to go through the immense

variety of changes it is capable of producing. Or, if you can take only twelve small pieces and make ten changes in each minute, it will then require 33,264 days, or 91 years and 40 days, to exhaust its variations.[28]

Pointing to the practically countless combinations formed by twenty small beads, the passage speaks not only to the kaleidoscopic image's variability; it also attributes duration to that image by noting the hypothetical rate of "ten changes each minute." The kaleidoscope's evocation of colorful multiplicity and temporal progression made it an ideal metaphor for considering the tremendous industrial and technological changes shaping everyday experience, as well as for reflecting on those changes over the course of one's life.

In his 1884 Thanksgiving sermon delivered at the Brooklyn Tabernacle, the Rev. D. Thomas De Witt Talmage drew parallels between the kaleidoscope's splendors and the speed and abundance wrought by industrialization. Talmage painted a picture of a rapidly industrializing nation, remarking on projects such as the completion of the Northern Pacific and Southern Pacific Railroads. He preached, "The canals are blocked with freight pressing down to the markets. The cars rumble all through the darkness and whistle up the flagment in the dead of night to let the Western harvests come down and feed the mouths of the great cities." Shifting from the scale of industrial networks in motion, he wrote that in the wake of such dynamism, "the memory becomes a kaleidoscope," likening the movements of modern life to the device's colorful image.[29]

Talmage's sermon used the kaleidoscope as a rhetorical mechanism to invite the congregation to recall past life scenes: summers, winters, hardship, abundance. He introduced each remembered vignette as a "turn" of the device, an oratory strategy linking the kaleidoscope's central metaphorical connotations of multiplicity and temporality. The poet Martin Farquhar Tupper similarly linked the kaleidoscope's shifting scenes with temporal progression. His poem titled "Life" begins with a child peering through the device and passes through scenes of optimistic blue, "sobered gray," "Religion's purple light," and the "[sickly] … yellow lust of gold." He notes the device's perfection as a metaphor: "So, ever changing day by day, every man's life is but a kaleidoscope."[30] Whereas the parlor kaleidoscope, with its ship's wheel, implied a user-guided experience through a dazzling, colorful environment, Talmage and Tupper's metaphorical evocations envisioned the toy as a kind of time-traveling device, the contents settling after each turn to recall struggles, successes, the changing fortunes experienced over the course of a lifetime. As material artifact and metaphor, the kaleidoscope thus projected back while also propelling its user into a fast-paced and vibrant future.

Upon its introduction, the kaleidoscope was a runaway hit that could not be contained by the parameters of patent law, instead proliferating wildly. It was not put to use primarily (as Brewster had originally aimed) as a tool for the design arts (although such possibilities added to its advertised merits), but instead for the fleeting visual delights it offered. Accompanying its more widely recognized metaphor of multiplicity was the device's capacity to evoke motion, duration, and speed. The device put objects into motion for users' enjoyment, the unpredictable movement of the objects in the cell like the dynamism of the industrializing world, in which complex processes and enormous objects were similarly set into motion.[31] That the kaleidoscope did not find wide application in schools reflects its unbridled visual paradigm, associated with spectacle and distraction. Instead, it was brought into homes, where its motion was rationalized, the user's course guided and controlled as though steering a vessel. As one book of rational recreations put it, the toy's production of such beautiful images was "no romance, but a mere dry and simple mathematical truth."[32] The kaleidoscope brought the colorful experiences of the public world into the home, where children could test and explore their visual limits within a safe context. As it combined color and speed, the kaleidoscope represented both the promise and peril of modern life, much like Milton Bradley's Smashed-Up Locomotive puzzle, which lauded the steam engine while centralizing the specter of catastrophe. These possibilities associated with color literacy, as well as the dangers connected with color ignorance (and the condition of color blindness), would form the framework to support later color education efforts.

Chromatic Possibilities and Perils

The kaleidoscope would endure as a popular amusement that dazzled the visual senses and was "to the Eye what Music is to the Ear," but it was by no means the only plaything that brought color into children's everyday experiences.[33] As early as the late eighteenth century, Maria Edgeworth remarked on the short-term attraction of colorful commercial goods for children, warning that "the glaring colors, or the gilding of toys, may catch the eye, and please for a few minutes, but unless some use can be made of them, they will, and ought, to be soon discarded."[34] As explored in the previous chapter, a robust trade of movable toy books across the Atlantic brought brightly colored illustrations into children's homes and hands beginning in the mid-nineteenth century. Chromolithographed images extended beyond the page onto other products, including metal toys imported from Nuremberg, the world's epicenter of toy manufacturing at that time.

Synthetic dyes "enabled ... manufacturers to reproduce virtually any color, creating possibilities for great visual variety and for even greater visual chaos."[35] Milton Bradley complained that as new fashions and products swept the market each season, manufacturers fabricated not only the goods themselves but also the evocative but imprecise color names to describe them. Colors like "zulu," "woodbine-berry," "calves' liver," "mummy brown," and "dragons' blood red" were alluring for marketing, but would prove difficult to classify and replicate.[36] Children's playscapes were thus flooded with color. This vibrant world caught children's attention, stimulated their interests, and invited them into a culture of consumption of colorful goods.[37] Yet the proliferation of ever more colorful consumer products also ushered in new concerns that linked color to speed, overstimulation, and a prevailing sense of disorientation. These attitudes helped form the conditions possible for the development of systems of color education, even as producers of color education materials commonly also produced the commercial wares that exemplified the very chromatic disorder they purported to combat and tame.

The color instruction curricula that gained traction in the 1890s responded not only to the desire to elevate children's tastes and refine consumer habits but also to new dangers that the increasing saturation and speed of everyday life posed. Color blindness was regarded as a vocational hazard in industries such as railroads, where color recognition was central to signaling systems. By midcentury, Wolfgang Schivelbusch argues, railroad travel had been so widely adopted that the imminent threat of accident had receded from regular public discourse—absorbed, accepted, and rationalized as a part of contemporary life. Yet just under the surface, the gripping fear of the accident remained, to be "reawakened" by any disruption or alteration of the train's ordinary operation.[38] The growing awareness of color blindness represented just such a condition to reinvigorate uncertainty around high-speed railroad travel.

The fear of train collisions led to widespread color-blindness testing of railroad officials, such as the evaluation of over one thousand French railroad workers in the early 1870s.[39] Following a crash in Lagerlunda, Sweden, in November 1875 that killed nine people, ophthalmologist Frithiof Holmgren hypothesized that one or more of the crew members on the northbound train had been color-blind and had thus failed to detect the red, green, and white lamplights thrown by signalers along the route. This belief led Holmgren to devise a required test for color blindness and to the publication of an 1877 monograph, *Color-Blindness and Its Relation to Accidents by Rail and Sea*. The accident received global attention, both because of the class status of the passengers involved and because of the spectacular wreckage it produced, which was captured in a Swedish newspaper illustration by Carl Larsson and reproduced in woodcut around the world.[40] The accident helped cement a perceived correlation between visual defects and forms of vehicular catastrophe uniquely tied to modern transportation technology. The train crash thus became a genre of spectacle reproduced in many forms, including children's playthings. One 1886 holiday toy review described an exploding mechanical train. During play, "the smoke stack and roof of the engineers [sic] cab are blown off and the locomotive is entirely wrecked."[41] Such a toy might be the same kind of "catastrophe coach" to which Walter Benjamin refers in his review of Karl Gröber's 1928 history of toys: *Kinderspielzeug aus alter Zeit*. Benjamin describes grotesque faces smiling unsettlingly "on the lids of the parlor games and the faces of the character dolls" and children's giggles in response to "the ingenious 'catastrophe coach' that fell to pieces, as expected, when the train crashed."[42] Milton Bradley's colorful Smashed-Up Locomotive puzzle encouraged children to assemble and "smash up" the train repeatedly, modeling the same macabre play pattern that highlighted the steam engine's marvelous capabilities, as well as its high-stakes risks.

Inspired by Holmgren's method of color-blindness testing, Boston physician Benjamin Joy Jeffries oversaw the testing of 27,927 Boston secondary school students in the years following the crash at Lagerlunda, publishing his findings in an 1880 report.[43] Jeffries's preoccupation with visual defects in education (concerning both students and teachers in training) had been ongoing since at least the 1860s. In addition to testing on color blindness, he charted a range of threats to vision, such as nearsightedness. For Jeffries, good eyesight was a foundational element of a functioning economy, a concern linking "a bookkeeper who has to write and compute in some large concern six or eight hours a day" and "the mechanic in certain departments of shoe manufacturing." Vision testing and eye health were critical for both the educated classes and manual laborers "who are the muscle and sinew of our State."[44] In his color-blindness testing, Jeffries highlighted the urgent stakes of early color-blindness detection in boys' occupational training, particularly in instances where boys might otherwise apprentice in their fathers' trades:

> I found color-blind children of railroad engineers in our Boston schools whose one idea was to follow their father's employment. In a Savannah school I found two brothers color-blind whose father was a Savannah pilot. Fortunately, the present United States laws would prevent these boys taking up their father's profession. But only where there is *danger* from color-blindness should warning be given as to the child's future. In all employments where a recognition of color is important the color blind are debarred, as experience amply proves. It is cruel to let them unconsciously take up occupations in which their defect will surely cause them to fail, sooner or later.[45]

Jeffries's discussion of career paths disrupted traditional expectations that boys would (and even could) follow in their fathers' professional footsteps. Color-blindness testing emphasized children's specific limitations and capabilities, assuming individuals reliant on their own skills (rather than on multigenerational legacies)—whose mixture of natural abilities, hard work, and luck formed the conditions of possibility for their economic fortune. Although the percentage of color-blindness among boys that Jeffries detected was relatively low (4.2 percent of 14,469 boys), the scale of the testing suggested color blindness as a risk looming over all of childhood. This was so not only for those seeking occupations in which the condition posed a danger but also to those who would waste their precious youth training for careers in which they would not succeed. Testing for the condition should occur early, Milton Bradley appealed in his manual *Color in the School-Room*, lest the child's "lifework … turn out a failure, owing to the wrong choice of an occupation through ignorance of the existence of color blindness."[46] Much like Elizabeth Prentiss's character "Little Susy" discussed in chapter 3 had to protect her eyes from both exposure to unsavory sights and excessive wear, the discourses surrounding color education saw in color deficiencies both grave threats and practical risks that young people's energy would be wasted pursuing work for which they were unsuitable.

Dr. Jeffries's work with schoolchildren focused principally on the detection of color blindness as a special occupational danger, yet he also came to regard color ignorance as a significant impairment—particularly among boys, who are both disproportionately prone to the condition and whose education had not significantly concentrated on color sense. Even in their early teens, Jeffries observed, the boys he examined in Boston and Baltimore often did not know color names and struggled to accurately attribute colors to objects. He wrote, "It seems almost impossible that a bright boy of fourteen, not color-blind, should not know the word *green*, or be able to apply it."[47] Color sense had traditionally been the domain of girls and women, responsible for maintaining chromatic harmony at home and in fashion. Chair of physics at Columbia University and color theorist Ogden Rood surmised that such expectations "seem to have brought [women's] sense of colour to a higher degree of perfection than is the case with men, who ordinarily neglect cultivation in this direction."[48] Jeffries's testing helped advance the argument for color education in public schools and also revealed the impact of such data collection practices in individual students' lives. In a climate of little regulation and confidentiality, Jeffries maintained a list of the individual boys found to be color-blind, which he offered to make available to interested employers, a decision he justified by citing public interest.[49]

In his testing of both "mixed race" and "purely American" children, Jeffries did not find that "color-blindness is more frequent as we descend the social scale," though only 102 of his nearly 15,000 male subjects and 94 of his female subjects were African American. In the mid-1880s, Washington, DC–based ophthalmologist Swan M. Burnett did conduct Holmgren-based color-blindness testing on 1,359 African American boys and 1,691 African American girls—considerably smaller samples.[50] Burnett, who was married to children's author Frances Hodgson Burnett, "established the first eye and ear clinic in Washington, DC, and treated all who came there, including indigent and African American patients.[51] Thus, although some testing of racial minorities was being undertaken, the differences in these practitioners' samples nevertheless reflect the racial motivations determining which children were prioritized as the most urgent recipients of color education and the cultural and economic potentials it held.

It was both from within and in response to this flurry of commercial, psychological, and medical considerations of children's experiences of color that several systems of color education were advanced near the turn of the twentieth century. Color instruction systems, such as three methods developed by Massachusetts-based men—Albert Munsell (1858–1918), Louis Prang (1824–1909), and Milton Bradley (1836–1911)—sought to train children to make sense of their colorful environments and endeavored to supply the commercial goods necessary for such training. Munsell was influenced by Ogden Rood's *Modern Chromatics with Applications to Art and Industry* (1879), which he encountered while a student at the Massachusetts Normal Art School. Notably, he was inspired to use a spinning globe as an apparatus to mix colors. Munsell would go into the production of art supplies, including crayons, based on his theory. He formed the Munsell Color Company a year before his death in 1918, which would ultimately be acquired during the 1920s by makers of Crayola crayons Binney and Smith.

Lithographer Louis Prang entered the trade in the 1850s and later studied lithography in Germany, regarded as a center of cutting-edge lithography technique. He successfully produced and sold art prints and maps during the Civil War, and greeting cards, for which he was widely known. He published his educational manual, *Color Instruction*, in 1893. After having established a successful business with his board games like The Checkered Game of Life (1860) and other amusements like the zoetrope (1867), Massachusetts lithographer Milton Bradley grew interested in the philosophies of the burgeoning kindergarten movement in America. Bradley began publishing and manufacturing educational materials, such as a series of kindergarten learning materials known as "gifts" and "occupations," including materials such as small sets of wooden solids cut into different units, shapes for parquetry, straight and curved lines for pattern making, and materials for paper weaving. Bradley would publish four books on color education within a ten-year period: *Color in the School Room* (1890), *Color in the Kindergarten* (1893), *Elementary Color* (1895), and *Water Colors in the School Room* (1900).

Before committing their resources to the systematic instruction of color, Prang and Bradley had splashed color across the surfaces of an array of consumer products without considerable concern about its systematic deployment or interpretation. Yet as the number and range of colorful consumer products increased, so too did the desire to standardize and systematize color from within both specialist and popular communities. Having a strong eye for color was a highly valued artistic skill set, and proponents of color education such as Munsell believed these skills were not innate but "teachable."[52] Bradley, Prang, and Munsell all manufactured a range of materials for use in color education, including wooden beads, paper tablets, dyed fibers, watercolors, crayons, and colored paper mixing disks. The cylindrical colored beads in Dr. Luckey's peripheral color vision experiment, for example, were known as Hailmann beads: spherical, cylindrical, and cubed wooden beads manufactured by Milton Bradley that could be sorted according to shape or color and strung on strings to form patterns. Yet the materials in isolation were of little use without training and instruction on how to implement them in the classroom. In 1894, Providence, Rhode Island–based education writer Edith Goodyear (1867–1952) complained about the "array of material[s]" available for color education, which included "colored blocks, colored beads, colored sticks, pegs, and lentils; colored tablets, colored slats, colored mats crayons and papers."[53] Yet, she lamented, students' classroom work with these materials was "executed in precisely the same defiance of the laws of color harmony which characterizes the primitive handiwork of the most untutored savages! And this is the nineteenth century!"[54] Goodyear's sentiments about color in the classroom may have found continued traction after her marriage to Vermont public school superintendent John Lincoln Alger, who went on to head the Rhode Island Normal School.[55] In a series of articles for the *Journal of Education*, Milton Bradley similarly noted the "chaotic state" of color education in America as the twentieth century approached.[56]

By the early twentieth century, school building design and decor were also prominent safety and hygiene concerns. Educational publications targeting both urban and rural readerships noted the importance of schoolroom aesthetics in ensuring harmony and coordination among spatial and material elements of the classroom. Physicians agree, wrote Jennie Paine in the *School Board Journal*, "that colors have considerable influence on the mental and physical condition of children and many cases of severe nervous headache and nervous irritation have been traced to poorly colored school room walls."[57] One Vermont superintendent cautioned teachers against both extremes of "faded" decorations and "gaudy advertisements, and loud colored chromos," advocating a balanced classroom: "cheery, quiet, and restful in its colors, decorations, and atmosphere."[58] A bulletin issued by the Prang Educational Company discouraged the use of "colors from the red end of the spectrum," in schoolroom design, which "are injurious to the eye" if stared at for a prolonged time.[59] Recommendations stressed notions of balance and harmony—for example, painting dark rooms in warm colors and overly bright rooms in cool colors—and periodicals noted that the educational value of classroom decor, principally pictures and statuary, could be reduced if not properly coordinated with wall, ceiling, and floor colors.[60] Color produced dangerous threats and exciting opportunities for nineteenth-century children. Accordingly, educators, medical and psychological professionals, and commercial interests increasingly regarded the color of classroom environments and learning materials with special urgency. Color education advocates would endeavor to develop the best methods of instruction that reflected assumptions about children's learning. The legacy of persistence-of-vision and optical toys played a key role in this process.

The Rise of Color Education

Prang, Munsell, and Bradley's systems of color instruction shared the aim of developing a common system that would facilitate communication about colors, "bringing the color knowledge of artists and scientists together."[61] Color systems sought to standardize the physiological and psychological dimensions of color—the sensation of light acting on the retina and the mental perception of that stimulus—thereby bridging external and internal phenomena. Like Bradley's, Munsell's system was a "compromise between physicists and psychologists" offering an "agnostic" position that straddled physiological and psychological conceptions of color.[62] In his 1890 *Color in the School Room*, Bradley advocated for both a universal standard of reference, so that everyone could agree exactly *what* color was being looked at, as well as a nomenclature to identify each color, so that everyone would agree on how to name or describe the color seen.[63] "We cannot have measurements without standards," wrote Bradley in the preface to his 1895 book, *Elementary Color*. Likening the systematic treatment of color to measuring spatial distance, he continued: "By the foot or the metre we measure lines and by the divided circle we measure angles."[64] The drive to classify color in this way aligned with broader interests in standardization, including the nineteenth-century obsession with what Jimena Canales calls "microtime," measured in tenths of a second. These small, temporal increments came to govern transportation and communication technologies like the train and telegraph, as well as internal processes—the time between a stimulus and a response.[65]

The color-mixing apparatuses that color educators developed would come to be "standard device(s) in every psychology laboratory," where they were used in the measurement of the "psychological experience of color and the relationship of the physical laws of color mixture to the anatomy and physiology of the eye."[66] Psychologist Herbert Nichols described experiments in color perception at the laboratory at Harvard where subjects were exposed to different color combinations to determine the most harmonious pairings. Such findings, Nichols explained in an article in *McClure's Magazine*, might offer explanations for maxims such as "when things look gay, time seems short," noting that "psychology seeks the laws of such happenings."[67] He also described tests "studying the effects of colors on judgments of time." Experiments measuring these variables, Nichols explained, could answer questions such as, "Do the colors of a rival's bonnet really grow more glaring the harder they are looked at? To explain this is to touch on a social as well as an esthetic problem."[68] E. W. Scripture, who trained under G. Stanley Hall and went on to found the experimental psychology laboratory at Yale, described similar studies concerning the psychological principles of optical illusions in women's dress. In his textbook *Thinking, Feeling, Doing*, he suggests that women's dresses are often adorned with bows and ornaments because adding such visual cues segments their bodily space, thus making them look taller.[69] Accounts like these are fascinating glimpses into the psychological and social issues that color science purported to address. They reveal a deep-seated belief in the ability to objectify and quantify the chromatic experience.

This same drive to rationalize color carried over into educational practice. Through analogies, Bradley rationalized color within the terms of scientific objectivity: "As in language so in color, there are certain scientific facts which must be learned, just as the rules of language are learned."[70] Despite rhetorical strategies used to apply the rule-based qualities of language to color, color instruction manuals discouraged teachers from introducing colors through their names, instead favoring emotion-driven and experiential encounters. Bradley and Prang cautioned that colors should first be experienced and recognized as sensations rather than simply memorized. Words lacked scientific precision and could thus lead to inaccuracy or confusion. To begin with a color's name—identifying an object as green, for example—did not take into account what, precisely, an individual saw, thus risking the establishment of a sense of color literacy founded on misperception. This was precisely the problem that Dr. Jeffries had observed in his color-blindness testing.

Color educators also imagined young learners in much the same way that early experimental psychologists characterized children—subjects whose attention must be captured and directed on a corrective course. Edith Goodyear's 1894 article in *Primary Education* stressed that color instruction involved children both "unlearning and forgetting" prior experiences with unharmonious color combinations in everyday life and that young pupils had to be reached before their senses had been "blunted."[71] The connected beliefs in children's impressionability and fickle attention spans were at the heart of color education. Nineteenth-century educators drew inspiration from earlier child-focused philosophies like those of the Edgeworths and developed commercial products that purported to facilitate such education. For example, Bradley elaborated on and materially reinforced his interpretation of Fröbel's kindergarten approach through the production and sale of gifts and occupations. Similarly, the classroom object lesson, a method that gained traction in the United States in the 1860s, valorized hands-on learning and investigation of material things to develop students' patterns of reasoning. Like advocates of the whole-word method of literacy instruction described in chapter 2, proponents of the object lesson implored educators to "present to children things before words, ideas before names. Train them to observe, to do, and to tell."[72] Color curricula also emphasized the importance of experiencing colors as sensations or holistic ideas first, then breaking them down to be studied in component parts. Examining colors as elements of a broader system or spectrum would help students generate knowledge that could be reproduced and applied in everyday life.

Prang's 1893 manual insistently reminded educators to use a child-centered approach, asserting that pupils should learn about colors *"under conditions of free self-activity."*[73] It encouraged teachers to initially let children have unrestricted access to boxes of colored paper tablets for free play and to record children's activities, noting which colors children preferred and whether children grouped colors harmoniously or by contrast. Subsequent color matching tasks were followed by activities like one in which students were supposed to pretend that colors were a family and arrange them according to which members appeared most closely related.[74] Still other materials were meant to "enthuse ... the children with a feeling of color which can be developed in no other way."[75] Prisms hung in classroom windows and sunlight refracted in soap bubbles could facilitate discussions about the solar spectrum and rainbows, to be paired with a range of readings in teachers' manuals. Prang's guide, for example, traced the meaning of rainbows in Greek and Norse myths and offered related Bible passages and short poems by Tennyson and Coleridge.[76] Prang assumed students whose interests could easily be extinguished and cautioned instructors from being "prescriptive" or "imposing," warning that "this work must not be made mechanical, and must not be in any way forced."[77] His method began with color recognition, moved to more complex qualities such as tint and shade, and incorporated conversations about color and ornamentation in historical cultures, such as color combination and harmony. Less strictly sequential, Bradley's *Elementary Color* included theoretical issues in color, definitions, and examples of experiments to be carried out with color mixers and spinning tops.

Optical Play in the Classroom

The use of spinning tops in color education exemplifies instructors' appeals to student interests and attention, linking earlier persistence-of-vision toys like the zoetrope to formal education near the end of the nineteenth century. While materials like colored papers found frequent classroom application, color educators sought a method to mix colors that treated color as a property of light rather than relying on the mixture of pigments. To accomplish this, they turned to the apparatus and methods pioneered at midcentury by Scottish physicist and mathematician James Clerk Maxwell (1831–1879). Maxwell arranged colored paper disks on a simple, flat-headed spinning top. Disks had "a small hole in the centre to admit the spindle of the top, and were slit along a radius from the circumference to the central hole. By this means," Maxwell's 1882 biography explains, "two or more discs could be placed together, and by turning one relatively to the others, more or less of any particular disc could be made visible from above."[78] While working on a fellowship at Trinity College, Cambridge, Maxwell arranged these colored disks in different combinations on a spinning top divided into one hundred equal parts, which allowed him to observe different color combinations and to record the precise proportions of the component colors making up the mixture—for example, three-quarters red, one-quarter orange.

This method led to Maxwell's first color-related publication—a paper titled "Experiments on Colour," which he presented at the Royal Society of Edinburgh in March 1855. Color mixing with paper disks on a spinning top enabled a greater degree of precision because by such means, any color combination could be identified as the top spun, and then broken down and analyzed into its component parts, with the proportion of each contributing color clearly measurable. Such standards would thus be timeless, universal, and communicable, just as later proponents of color education had hoped.[79] A few years later, in 1859, British surgeon John Gorham also published a paper using a color top to explore principles of color contrast and harmony. Despite their interests in different aspects of color, "both Gorham and Maxwell … agreed on the key benefit of colour tops, namely, that they enabled a quantitative approach to colour phenomena."[80] This tradition of experimentation with color tops demonstrated both the potential utility of toys within scientific inquiry as well as the legitimacy of toys within later educational settings.[81]

It is unsurprising that James Clerk Maxwell found inspiration for his laboratory practice in a simple spinning top. Maxwell had been fascinated by optical toys since childhood. His older cousin, the painter Jemima Wedderburn Blackburn (1823–1909), was a frequent visitor to his home at Glenair, and together they took particular delight in the zoetrope and phenakistosope. Maxwell's 1882 biography chronicles some of their original designs for these optical toys—an uncommon account of children making and playing with such media. James and Jemima designed and constructed many phenakistoscope disks. Their homemade designs followed familiar motifs for the time, such as a galloping horse and circus performer leaping through hoops, a cow jumping over the moon, a dog chasing a rat, a tadpole metamorphosing into a frog, mechanical and clockwork arrangements, and, perhaps foreshadowing his interest in color, "intricate coloured patterns of which the hues shift and open and close as in a kaleidoscope."[82] Maxwell's fascination with optical toys would be ongoing; in the 1860s, he fabricated an improvement on the zoetrope that replaced the narrow slots with wider concave lenses. This modification enhanced the viewer's field of vision and corrected for the small degree of distortion produced

Color Education

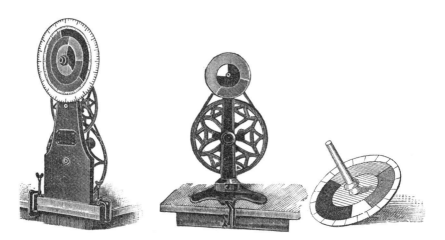

Figure 5.3
Bradley's color wheels and top. Milton Bradley, *Elementary Color* (Springfield, MA: Milton Bradley, 1895), 31–32.

by the conventional zoetrope's operation.[83] The development of Maxwell's professional pursuits from his childhood toys, play, and experimentation represented the ideal educational trajectory set forth in works of rational recreation literature for juvenile readers, such as Paris's *Philosophy in Sport*.[84] Building on this tradition, color instruction, with its progressive approach and use of materials like spinning tops, promised to combat the dangers of color ignorance through means that purported to appeal to children's playful inclinations.

Milton Bradley sold Maxwell disks along with two main apparatuses for mixing them. Crank-operated color mixing wheels (which showcased large, vertically mounted color disks) allowed teachers to demonstrate the principles of mixing to the whole class. These rotators were available in two varieties (figure 5.3). The premium version, a "high school" model (available with a set of disks for ten dollars) featured a large base that needed to be clamped to the edge of a table. The primary school version (available for two dollars), was free standing, as well as smaller and lighter. Teachers were instructed to use color wheels to model the process of combining and adjusting color ratios, forming hypotheses, and testing the results. In keeping with preoccupations around color, vision, and velocity that pervaded nineteenth-century thought, *Color in the School-Room* specifies a speed at which teachers should operate their color wheels. The text recommended a minimum of fifty revolutions per minute—spinning the rotator too slowly would produce "a dazzling effect," which is "unpleasant."[85] Bradley promised that color mixers could capture student interest, so "there need be no fear of want of attention on the part of any pupil."[86] These demonstrations were opportunities for participatory engagement led by student observations and hypotheses. The twenty-fifth anniversary edition of kindergarten proponent Edward Wiebé's *The Paradise of Childhood* recalls an example from a kindergarten classroom in which the teacher approached a group of pupils admiring their classmate Bessie's new dress. When the teacher asked the students to identify the color of the dress, she received a range of responses. The teacher invited Bessie to stand at the head of the class next to the color wheel, while she spun the disk and adjusted ratios of blues and greens as directed by student input until a match was found.[87]

In the classroom, teacher demonstrations of color mixing with the large wheel would be followed by individual student experimentation with Bradley's spinning color tops, which permitted "the children to attempt to repeat the wheel experiments … and thus produce [the results] for themselves."[88] Bradley's top, available for six cents each or fifty cents per dozen, consisted of a cardboard base affixed to a wooden spindle with a nut to hold the colored disks in place. Promotional materials described the top in children's hands both at school and in the home, implying the practical application of color instruction, and the top as a device that extended formal lessons into children's everyday lives.[89] Correct operation of the top itself was considered a skill; Bradley noted that "there will be in every school some children who are exceedingly awkward in the manipulation of the top, until the happy day arrives when all school children are graduates of kindergartens."[90]

In praise of the top, experimental psychologist E. W. Scripture remarked that with the toy, "every experiment and demonstration with colors can be made by the child himself directly on the desk." He added that "the intense interest of the children in adjusting the disks and spinning the top renders the instruction efficient to a degree unattainable before," rationalizing the method's appeal to students within a logic of productivity.[91] One can imagine students watching with anticipation as the teacher demonstrated the color wheel, anxiously awaiting their turn to play with the spinning tops themselves. Perhaps tops and disks were distributed prior to the demonstration and students were instructed to leave them at their seats. Perhaps the toys and disks were stored in a drawer or cupboard to be distributed when the time was right. While E. W. Scripture described a classroom scenario in which students remained at their desks to play with their toys, it is easy to picture tops spinning from desks onto floors as students accidentally or purposefully lost control. More permissive instructors may have even, on occasion, invited students to seek other surfaces—the seats of chairs, the floor—transforming the classroom into swirling groups of color. Such classroom experimentation gave students hands-on opportunities to learn about color mixing through trial and error, a pedagogical approach that institutionalized the same sentiments toward sensory-driven productive play that had characterized rational recreation in the home for decades. Both at home and school, optical toys and spinning tops linked ongoing scientific investigations of movement, velocity, and vision in the popular imagination. In fact, as Joshua Yumibe explains, it was "the physiological study of color afterimages [that] led to the theorization of persistence of vision … [which] in turn grounded the cinema apparatus historically."[92]

Unlike earlier moving-image toys that used slots as shutter mechanisms to bring spinning pictures into sharp relief as animated sequences, color spinning tops combined colors from their component parts in a blur so that children could construct and deconstruct precise shades. In classroom exercises, the student began with an object whose color they wished to match, for example, Bessie's new dress or a commercial product advertised in the color ecru. They then selected disks thought to represent the colors that made up the object's color and tested the combination by spinning the top adjusting the ratios of the component colors until they matched. Ecru, for example, was an orangish yellow made up of 12 parts orange, 15 parts yellow, 17 parts white, and 56 parts black. Neptune, a greenish blue, was made up of 13.5 parts green, 2.5 parts blue, 11 parts white, and 73 parts black.[93] The interplay between the color top at rest and its composite color produced in motion resembled the practices of looking that were common in home optical play, as when children alternately peeked through the zoetrope's slots to watch the animated sequence and watched from overhead as the images blurred together. Color mixing experiments required the top to be stopped and started repeatedly to test and adjust color ratios until a match was found. These tops thus shared with optical toys both a reliance on persistence of vision and a playful experimental and experiential method by which children mastered visual knowledge that would have everyday applications.

These applications extended beyond the top's ability to identify the colors of consumer products and would also come to include the top's adoption within anthropological research in the early twentieth century. Researchers found in the top "the most effective way of measuring blackness as opposed to any other color."[94] Charles Davenport, who began his teaching career in the Zoology Department at Harvard in the 1890s and went on to author *Heredity of Skin Color in Negro-White Crosses* (1913), appreciated the top's portability for fieldwork and the purportedly "neutral" means of measuring colors through the systematic adjustment of disks and the "unbiased" spin of the device. Ultimately, the top's scientific qualities were lacking, as Michael Keevak argues: "The color top demonstrated nothing less than that the names 'Yellow Race' and 'Red Indians' were both 'expected' and 'deserved'" according to the racial logic of Bradley's colored paper and the devices for spinning it.[95] Like earlier color-blindness testing, such experimental practices presumed white children as the observers and beneficiaries of the top's chromatic pedagogy, advancing the assumption of whiteness as a normative racial identity and other colors as differentiated from that white base.

Color tops and mixing wheels thus represent another way that persistence of vision was instrumental in children's visual education in the late nineteenth century, expanding the visual paradigm that earlier optical toys set into motion. In *Color in the School-Room*, Bradley mentions persistence of vision in conjunction with the zoetrope (which he had also sold since 1867), and in his later *Elementary Color*, he references the "fiery circle"—that widely reproduced domestic experiment explored in chapter 2: "It is a fact well known to every boy that if he rapidly whirls a lighted stick the fire at the end produces the effect of a circle of light, which phenomenon is explained by a quality of the eye called retention of vision, by which the impression made by the point of the light remains on the retina of the eye during an entire rotation."[96] Such pedagogical and ludic devices were not merely playful, Yumibe contends, but "worked to shape the viewer's subjective perception to an orderly system that rationalized space, time, and color in ways that would bridge one person's individual experience to another's."[97] Via color education, Bradley codified the importance of persistence of vision, its significance extending from a key part of the performance of optical discernment in the parlor to a formal academic practice.

Conclusion

During the nineteenth century, children were introduced to an ever-expanding range of colorful products, which helped to shape public discourse about children's experiences of color around two poles. On one end of the spectrum, the kaleidoscope's dynamic, surprising images promised perpetual novelty and absorption. On the other end, experiments like George Luckey's aimed to define and delineate the child's field of vision in regimented ways, even as such experimenters struggled with their subjects' tendencies toward distraction. The child as a consumer, media spectator, and modern subject was situated among these positions. Systems of color education near the end of the century mitigated between these two extremes. They acknowledged both the urgent importance of a standardized color sense and the necessity of tapping into color's allure for successful pedagogy. Cultivating children's understanding of color primed them as modern subjects in a variety of capacities—as consumers, employees, and stewards of the white middle-class home. Ruling out color blindness and distinguishing it from color ignorance represented a further means of feeling in control in the wake of accelerating modern experiences that increased the stakes, enabling mobility and communication but also risking bodily injury or catastrophe on a larger scale. As color cascaded across material goods and before the child's eyes, it helped chart out their potential futures slung between progress and peril as the new century approached.

Seen within the context of broader practices of rational recreation and informal education, color instruction and the commercial apparatus necessary for its implementation made significant contributions to the establishment of a visual paradigm characterized in part by the exercise of color literacy. The analogies that color educators advanced between color instruction and other academic areas such as language, music, and geography framed color as a link that would unify students' knowledge across a range of subjects. Prang's materials emphasized color training's practical and spiritual import, capable of unlocking "all other primary work—language, number, and place ... in ways that will most surely attract the child and awaken his interest."[98] Such rhetoric supported color literacy as an urgent priority and helped carve space for the topic within school curricula. Practitioners in industry, education, psychology, and medicine agreed on the importance of color literacy for children of many backgrounds. Whether they would grow to be locomotive engineers, industrial designers, or wives furnishing homes, color would be central to their personal, professional, and community-based experiences.

Both Bradley and Prang's systems were built on the premise that color training might help refine pupils' senses, advancing a rule-based system of color so that "taste" could be standardized, rather than a lofty, floating term.[99] Color needed to "be embodied in a system of rules," explained Bradley's *Color in the School Room*, because "otherwise it will never be understood by people whose intellectual capacity is not above average."[100] Exemplified by classroom exercises like the kindergarten class matching a pupil's dress to a precise shade on the mixing wheel, color instruction endeavored to synchronize students' understanding of color with the aesthetics of mass-produced commercial goods.

Color sense was thus similar to forms of visual knowledge promoted by rational recreation and informal science literature—other cultural discourses that linked perception to particular social positions and values. Like optical toys created illusionistic displays around which children could practice optical discernment, knowledge of color theory, such as color names, complements, harmonies, and contrasts, demonstrated socially acceptable standards of visual recognition and beauty. Together, these skills represented the "right" way to see aligned with commercial and scientific developments of the nineteenth century. Efforts to tame color—from the unpredictable jumble of the kaleidoscope to the orderliness of the chromatic spectrum—paralleled many other cultural shifts brought on by the subject's changing experience of space and time through new communication, transportation, and entertainment technologies. In the wake of such technological flux, the move to standardize color represented one way that educators imagined controlling children's visual experiences. Color instruction thus assuaged anxieties not only about the threat of catastrophes like train crashes but also the stability of the individual development of the middle-class subject, who learned to see the world in new ways.

6 Democracy and Discipline: Object Lessons and the Stereoscope in American Education, 1870–1920

The image of a woman standing at the edge of a cliff at Glacier Point in California's Yosemite Valley stands out in the New York Public Library's digitized collection of stereoscopic views (figure 6.1). Published around 1902 by the stereoscopic firm Underwood & Underwood, the card is a pair of albumen prints mounted side-by-side, each of the same scene. The images were captured from a few inches apart to simulate the slightly distinct perspectives of the left and right eyes. Like most digitized optical media, this surrogate image provides a valuable reference, but the contemporary observer misses the experience of seeing the image through the historical apparatus for which it was designed.[1] When viewed through a stereoscope, the mind unites the two images to produce an illusion of depth. To the viewer peering through the device, the woman and the ledge on which she stands pop out as a single flat plane, set apart from Yosemite Falls and the Sierra Nevadas in the distance. The expanse of the Yosemite Valley is evoked in the perceptual space that appears between the two planes. The effect of depth that the stereoscope produces differs from how the same scene is perceived in person. "In the stereoscopic image," writes Jonathan Crary, "there is a derangement of the conventional ordering of optical cues." The device consolidates and flattens each discrete plane, so that the resulting image "has no unifying logic or order."[2]

Although this image's location is clear, the photographer and subject are not specified. Similar stereo views of small groups of men and women seated casually along the ledge at Glacier Point were published by the firm Strohmeyer & Wyman around 1894, four years after Yosemite became America's first national park. In one, a man stands facing the camera, his hands on his hip; a second man is casually lying on his side, leaning on his

Figure 6.1
"Nearly a mile straight down, and only a step, from Glacier Point (N.W.), Yosemite, Cal." Miriam and Ira D. Wallach Division of Art, Prints and Photographs, Photography Collection, New York Public Library Digital Collections, New York Public Library.

elbow, his face propped in his hand. The New York Public Library has six copies of images of this same woman at the edge of the rock, distinguished from one another by the subtle changes in her skirt as the wind blew. These images all feature the same caption, "Nearly a mile straight down and only a step," hinting at both the figure's precarious position and the scale of the rock features and valley below. Stereo photographer Henry A. Strohmeyer's image library was taken over by the New York–based firm Underwood & Underwood around 1901, so this image is likely republished from that archive. By the early twentieth century, the stereoscope's popularity as a parlor amusement had waned, but firms like Underwood & Underwood and the Meadville, Pennsylvania–based Keystone View thrived, largely by employing college students to sell boxed sets of stereo views door-to-door and by selling these sets with accompanying materials to schools.

In the late nineteenth and early twentieth centuries, tens of thousands of schoolchildren had access to this image in their classrooms. Underwood published a manual, *The World Visualized for the Classroom*, that aided teachers from elementary to high school in incorporating the stereoscope and its images into lessons. The manual was written by Frank McMurry (1862–1936), an educator from Indiana who later studied at Halle in Germany and would go on to teach education at the University of Illinois and, later, at Columbia. McMurry's book refers to this image, Underwood number 290, three times. It is referenced in a twenty-two-image sequence of California sights (as one of five representing the Yosemite Valley), as one of five illustrations to accompany a reading of John Muir's 1912 work, "The Yosemite," and, less logically, as an illustration to go along with a line from Longfellow's 1855 epic poem, *The Song of Hiawatha*: "From his footprints flowed a river."[3] As this image was appropriated for educational use, its meaning changed. Notably, the woman at the center of the image is not mentioned in McMurry's manual. As students gazed into the stereoscope in the context of lessons on California's natural beauty, were they meant to see beyond the woman at the edge of the cliff? How did the stereoscope—as a medium designed to furnish vivid and direct sensory impressions—work to make this woman disappear?

Raising these questions unearths a link between the stereoscope's afterlife as an educational medium and the popularity of object-based pedagogy from the 1860s to the early twentieth century. Contrasted with earlier pedagogical models that foregrounded written literacy and memorization, the object lesson mandated learning through the senses, offering pupils exposure to and experience with real things in nature. The visual and tactile attributes of optical devices like the stereoscope echoed the logic of the object lesson. The stereoscope's use of photography and its striking effect of depth lent the medium a valence of authenticity and truth. In schools, the stereoscope thus not only manifested a phenomenon of binocular vision but also functioned as a medium through which other subjects might be taught. As a consequence of the stereoscope's use in classrooms, students were trained in a systematic method of processing visual information that transformed the act of looking into an exercise in efficient scanning and discrimination. Stereo views and the teaching materials that accompanied them naturalized the way of looking that the stereoscope demands. As teachers adopted the device for classroom use, its visual paradigm and the perspective it enforced came to substitute the stereoscope's mediated virtual image for lived experience.

The stereoscope was transformed into a pedagogical medium in the United States beginning around the 1870s through the 1920s as an extension of object teaching. During this period, the stereoscope experienced a resurgence of popularity largely due to firms like Underwood & Underwood and Keystone View Company, which targeted institutional markets like churches and schools with their packaged stereo views. The device found new application in American schools in part because the three-dimensional image it produced appeared to align with the tenets of the object lesson. Like the object lesson, the stereoscope's proponents claimed, the device offered sensory experiences that invited close observation, activated reasoning, and prompted educated responses. Because of its ability to illustrate distant sights, the stereoscope held the democratic potential to introduce new experiences to diverse student populations regardless of location or economic status. However, by arguing that the stereoscope offered a new kind of mental reality, the rhetoric surrounding the device's educational application conflated a highly mediated experience with in-person physical encounters. While providing students virtual mobility, the stereoscope and the conditions under which it was used also worked to discipline and standardize students' practices of looking. It was thus a behavioral tool as much as a technology for sensory enrichment. Examining promotional and pedagogical materials alongside teachers' firsthand accounts suggests that the new mobility the stereoscope offered was inseparably linked to strategies of classroom management, the regulation of student behavior, and the cultivation of students' fields of vision in structured ways.

Extending the established argument that stereoscopy enabled a new kind of virtual travel, this chapter considers the ideological ramifications of standardizing these new experiences for schoolchildren. Locating the stereoscope within the educational discourses that propelled it into the classroom reveals the connections that its use bore to the methods and objectives of object teaching. While deployed with the purpose of providing students with direct sensory impressions, the stereoscope simultaneously functioned as a disciplinary agent. Although it offered young users exposure to the world, the guidelines governing its use regulated the nature of students' sensory experiences, thereby codifying a kind of visual literacy and outlining a set of acceptable practices for how children should perform the act of looking. The stereoscope's promoters took advantage of the rapidly institutionalizing field of experimental psychology, which promised educators empirically grounded advice on how best to teach children. Psychologists' beliefs that educators could cultivate or eliminate particular personality traits and habits "just as a trainer shows the athlete how best to apply his powers and the surgeon cuts out a hindering tumor" authenticated a range of new pedagogical technologies and approaches, including the stereoscope.[4] Psychological research on visual and mental experiences shored up confidence in the stereoscope as an educational medium, and as educators put faith in the stereoscope's virtual view, they emphasized the mind over the body.[5] Engaging the visual and mental faculties, the stereoscope also physically molded students to conform to the standard of the ideal student. Through such corporeal lessons, Mona Gleason writes, "industrial workers and loyal citizens were cultivated, and hierarchies informed by race, class, gender, and ablebodiedness were maintained."[6]

A brief historical overview of the object lesson demonstrates how the stereoscope's visual and tactile qualities aligned with the observational skills and methods of sensory learning central to object teaching. Along with the object lesson, the new field of experimental psychology was institutionalized by the end of the century; both developments helped to popularize and authenticate a connection between physical sensations and mental processes that were critical to adopting the stereoscope. An analysis of recommended classroom activities and representations of children at work with the device point to the stereoscope's paradoxical function to both visualize the world while masking the pupil's immediate surroundings from view. The implementation of the stereoscope in schools was a continuation of nineteenth-century pedagogical practice that reflected the tensions and challenges that public schoolteachers faced. The device's dual functions as both an instrument for imagining social and cultural mobility and as a tool for disciplining students also exemplifies a progressive educational effort meant to maintain rather than transform the complex social world of the diverse turn-of-the-century classroom. By perpetuating a new kind of looking, the stereoscope opened new worlds and visual experiences to which students might not otherwise have access. However, it also helped to define the terms by which those worldviews were seen.

Object Teaching and the Stereoscope

The stereoscope found new application as an educational apparatus when its functions as scientific instrument and later popularity as a parlor amusement converged in the late nineteenth-century schoolroom. A laboratory model of the device, designed by Charles Wheatstone in 1838, was made to demonstrate the unstable, subjective nature of vision (figure 6.2).

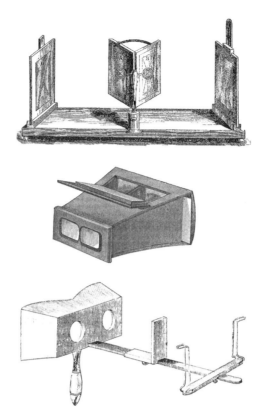

Figure 6.2
Top to bottom: Wheatstone mirror stereoscope, Brewster stereoscope, Holmes stereoscope.

Wheatstone's reflecting stereoscope was larger than later handheld models; it sat atop a table or stand and used two mirrors to direct images into each eye. David Brewster's boxlike model, introduced in 1849 as a consumer product, enclosed prismatic lenses in a handsome housing (usually wooden), obscuring its inner workings to enforce a user-friendly model of stable, reliable perception.[7] Brewster's lenticular stereoscope surged in popularity following its display at the Great Exhibition in the Crystal Palace in 1851. There, it attracted the attention of throngs of visitors, including Queen Victoria.[8] The stereoscope soon became a global sensation, manufactured by multiple opticians. By the 1856 publication of his book *The Stereoscope: Its History Theory, and Construction*, Brewster reported that around half a million units had been sold, with photographers dispersed globally to produce content.⁹

Classrooms were generally equipped with a third iteration of the device, the so-called Holmes model, which, in most forms, featured a viewing hood trained at the image situated on an adjustable rack. First introduced by Oliver Wendell Holmes Sr. in 1861, this version of the stereoscope saw myriad variations, partially because Holmes did not patent his design. Holmes's initial model had a hood, but the rack that held the stereograph in place was not adjustable. The same year, Joseph L. Bates developed a hoodless model with a sliding cardholder, which he did not patent. In 1862, a foldable model with an attached magnifying viewer was made, and the following year, a Holmes viewer mounted on a tabletop pedestal was issued. Stereoscope hoods were made in a variety of materials, including cardboard, wood, leather, and metal, and were thus available at a range of prices.¹⁰ Marketed under several names by numerous companies, the Holmes format combined the adjustable qualities of Wheatstone's experimental apparatus with the ready-made ease and portability of Brewster's version, making it an optimal classroom technology that could be in heavy use by multiple students.

These design changes paved the way for the stereoscope's adoption in classrooms. In January 1920, the first issue of the journal *Visual Education* remarked on the stereoscope's transformation in form and function, saying the device "has now been moved from the marble-topped parlor table to a trunk in the dusty attic, while thousands of new ones are finding daily use in American schools."¹¹ Pioneered by educators such as Anna Verona Dorris, who authored *Visual Instruction in the Public Schools*, the newly institutionalized visual instruction movement in the 1920s emphasized technologies as instructional aids, exploring the utility of devices like the stereoscope, magic lantern, and motion picture. Bolstered by publications such as *Educational Screen* and national organizations, the visual instruction movement gained significant popularity between 1918 and 1928.¹² However, the sensory pedagogy at the heart of visual instruction has longer roots in the history of the object lesson—a teaching approach introduced in the early twentieth century that found widespread success in the United States beginning in the 1860s. The method and philosophy of the object lesson furnish crucial context for understanding the stereoscope's adoption in schools.

In large part, the stereoscope's popularity as an instructional aid in the late nineteenth and early twentieth centuries rested on the same philosophical tenets of the object lesson. Supporters of the object lesson were inspired by Locke and the Swiss educator Johann Pestalozzi (1746–1827), both of whom integrated material objects into instruction. Today, the term *object lesson* evokes a vague notion of learning with objects or the use of objects as examples or metaphors.[13] During the nineteenth century, however, the educators who developed object teaching imagined objects at the center of a systematic, multistep process. Object lessons used concrete things (for example, a rock, a shell, a piece of cloth, or a sheaf of wheat) as the starting point to develop observational and reasoning skills. These sensory observations then served as the basis for drawing conclusions, connecting concepts, and communicating ideas to others.[14] Charles Mayo, who had studied with Pestalozzi, and his sister Elizabeth's books *Lessons on Objects* (1830) and *Lessons on Shells* (1832), outlined a sequential pedagogy that began with a student's careful sensory observations of an object (a piece of glass, a block of type, for instance). This examination was followed by an analysis of the object's abstract qualities, drawing conclusions, and classifying and connecting objects across categories. Finally, students learned to communicate their findings in written or verbal form.[15] Key to the process was not necessarily the acquisition of knowledge about the specific object, but honing the observational, intellectual, and communicative skills that could be applied to any object.

Pestalozzi's philosophy was popular in US teacher training beginning around the 1830s, and the object lesson became popular across the United States.[16] In the late 1850s, Edward Austin Sheldon (1823–1897), the superintendent of the Oswego Board of Education in upstate New York, was introduced to object pedagogy, including commercial products to support it. Preassembled specimen boxes like cabinets of curiosities were commercially available and could be used in classrooms alongside teacher-assembled collections. Sheldon was joined by like-minded educators such as Norman Calkins (1822–1895), who became the superintendent of New York City's schools in 1862, taught at the Normal College at the City University of New York through the 1870s, and played a prominent role in the National Education Association. Educators like Sheldon and Calkins would transform Pestalozzi's original notions of object-based pedagogy into highly structured teaching methods "ordered around particular objects and pictures."[17]

One manual published from the 1860s through the 1890s aimed at teachers of five- to ten-year-olds, called for a "systematic culture" for the senses to be taught in schools,[18] much like color instruction sought to name and order the chromatic spectrum. As a method, the object lesson "summarizes an entire constellation of attitudes about the value of scientific learning, rational inquiry, and individual autonomy."[19] Indeed, by furnishing "a language and a mode of looking that shaped larger cultural patterns and concerns," the object lesson cultivated structures of thought that aligned with, rather than challenged, the prevailing social order.[20]

At first look, the object lesson may appear to contemporary sensibilities as an approach designed to foster what today would be considered critical thinking skills. Object teaching was promoted in contrast to rote memorization as a more stimulating, open-ended approach. During an 1872 roundtable discussion, one Ohio educator argued that rather than "cramming" knowledge into students' minds, the object lesson should not simply impart specific content but should "teach the child to see, then to think, then to express the result of the seeing and the thinking."[21] William N. Hailmann, an early proponent of kindergartens in America, remarked that "object-teaching is founded on the fact that the knowledge of the most trifling empirical fact, as well as of the greatest abstract truth, can reach our mind only through the senses, either directly or indirectly, with the assistance of memory and imagination, on the fact that *we learn by observation.*"[22] These sentiments recall other forms of inquiry-driven pedagogy that took hold in the nineteenth century in the broader expansion of secular public education. However, the habits of mind that teachers sought to naturalize through object teaching were calculated to stabilize rather than transform a social world arranged by raced, gendered, and class-based hierarchies.[23] When the object lesson extended to the stereoscope, the spectrum of sensory habits was reduced to the visual, and educators came to emphasize virtual over physical experiences. In this way, the stereoscope's broader legacy was the maintenance of established social hierarchies through the training of children's gazes calibrated to the instrument's simulation of reality.

Unlike the earlier persistence-of-vision toys, which informally cultivated practices of optical discernment in the home, object lessons formalized children's sensory training in schools. While not centrally concerned with visual deception, object teaching nevertheless responded, at least indirectly, to the lurking specters of dishonesty and inauthenticity by providing skills to aid in the evaluation of sensory evidence and potentially unsavory interests.[24] A critical approach to connecting disparate objects in fluid networks based on use, region, history, material, or industrial process "gave children and adults a way to make sense of the diverse things at the center of late-nineteenth-century capitalism." By the end of the nineteenth century, Sarah Anne Carter writes, object lessons also likely worked "to allay fears about the control of an increasingly abstract and distant market."[25] Focusing on objects was one way to fix shifting, speculative values in immediate, tangible things. Brewster himself suggested the stereoscope's key role in object-based pedagogy for the masses. Without the basic skills of reading, writing, and arithmetic, he explained, "the humblest of our race is unfit for any place in the social scale." Yet he also argued about the profound importance of learning about the world more generally, through connections among things. An advocate of secular education, Brewster argued that religious lessons alone left the pupil "utterly ignorant of everything above him, around him, and within him,—ignorant, too, of the form, the magnitude, and the motions of his terrestrial home,—ignorant of the gigantic structures which constitute the material universe,—ignorant of the fabrics which industry prepares for his use, and of the luxuries which commerce brings from the ends of the earth and places at his door."[26]

The object lesson helped children link things to one another, but through its emphases on sensory observation, mental contemplation, and written or oral reports, it also clarified the relationship between the individual mind and the external world. Its pedagogical flow from observation, to analysis, to written or visual response tracks a continuous line from external phenomena to internal impressions, back to communication to others.[27] These were the same kinds of physiological and mental pathways that philosophers of mind and later experimental psychologists endeavored to understand, often using instruments thought to record the speed and intensity of mental phenomena.[28] Practitioners of so-called brass instrument psychology relied on apparatuses constructed to measure and produce time and to capture subjects' responses.[29] In his *Principles of Psychology*, in print from the 1850s into the twentieth century, Herbert Spencer explains, "That which distinguishes Psychology from the sciences on which it rests, is, that each of its propositions takes account both of the connected internal phenomena and of the connected external phenomena to which they refer."[30] As the object lesson connected direct sensory impressions with intellectual responses, it thus modeled the links between the senses and the mind that early psychologists would explore. This shared pedagogical and empirical commitment helped certify the stereoscope's visual effects as a suitable substitute for physical encounters.

Though the stereoscope's heyday as an instructional medium would come in the twentieth century following Underwood and Keystone's marketing efforts, the object lesson's institutionalization was pivotal to the optical device's success. Instructional aids such as specimen collections and Oliver and Boyd's object-teaching cards with small samples mounted on card with accompanying text were joined by chromolithographed pictures such as those produced in collaboration between Norman Calkins and lithographer Louis Prang. Pictures were regarded as adequate substitutes if physical objects could not be found, even if they restricted analysis to the visual.[31] If pictures were acceptable proxies, the stereograph's simulated tangibility heightened the picture's appeal. As one ad explained, "Pictures present but two dimensions. The Stereoscope supplies the missing link."[32] Early materials like Hart and Anderson's *The World in the Stereoscope* (1872) specifically framed the stereoscope as an aid to object lessons, emphasizing depth as an added quality: "Object-teaching in its different forms is a feature of instruction in the best schools. When the objects themselves cannot be presented, pictures of them are frequently used.... But the photograph is superior to any other picture, and the stereoscope adds wonderfully to the value of the photograph."[33]

Set against this broader educational backdrop, the stereoscope was reborn as a medium for object teaching. In the 1880s, two Kansas brothers, Bert and Elmer Underwood, founded Underwood & Underwood. The company gained prominence through a campaign of door-to-door sales and the publication of maps and guidebooks to accompany packaged sets of stereo views. Underwood marketed the stereoscope and its images as a comprehensive "travel system," in which stereographs were organized by place or subject and sold in groups. Expert endorsements from educators and psychologists lent authority to both the images and the mental and physiological processes involved in stereoscopic looking. The company's copyrighted map systems further authenticated the product, linking individual stereo views to specific geographical points. Underwood boasted a full travel library of world sites that were organized for specific markets, such as school groups, grades, and age ranges, making them easy to buy and easy to teach.[34]

Underwood publications such as Albert E. Osborne's *The Stereograph and the Stereoscope: With Special Maps and Books forming a Travel System*, and Frank M. McMurry's *The World Visualized for the Classroom*, joined Hart and Anderson's earlier *The World in the Stereoscope*, which all supported educators in incorporating the stereoscope into their classes. Underwood's major competitor was Keystone View Company, founded in the 1890s. Keystone also produced interpretive materials to accompany their stereographs, opening a dedicated Educational Department in 1898.[35] Like Underwood, Keystone marketed stereographs in sets, cross-referencing views so that a single stereograph would find relevance in a variety of subjects. Keystone's first teachers' guide was published in 1907, to accompany its hallmark set of six hundred stereographs. In 1920, the company produced a pared-down version of two hundred images for primary grades, and four years later, an extended educational set of one thousand views was produced.[36] Keystone acquired Underwood's image library in the 1920s, and the company continued to market to schools well into the twentieth century.

In his extensively researched survey of the history of the stereoscope and stereograph, William Darrah points out that "it is difficult for us to evaluate the influence or effectiveness of these visual aids. Millions of children were taught by them. In 1922 Keystone boasted that every American city with a population of 50,000 or more had adopted the 'Keystone System' for its public schools."[37] Teachers' correspondence, educational journals, and instructional manuals and materials demonstrate the experiences students were meant to have with the stereoscope. Expert endorsements from educators and psychologists praised the stereoscope as an instructional aid on the grounds that it furnished the same kind of immediate sensory engagement that the object lesson encouraged. *The World Visualized for the Classroom* contains a statement signed by fifteen psychologists asserting that a stereoscope user's experience "is such that he would get if he were carried unconsciously to the place in question and permitted to look at it. In other words, while this state of consciousness lasts, it can be truly said that the *person is in the place seen*."[38] Such affirmations of the stereoscope's abilities solidified the device's status as an educational medium and attested to the realism or objectivity of its three-dimensional image.[39] Psychologists' certification that the stereoscope produced the "actual" experience of travel contradicts the decades-old practices of optical discernment that persistence-of-vision toys sought to instill. Rather than foregrounding the disjuncture between experience and perception, the stereoscope industry and its supporters endeavored to sell the mediated gaze as the "real" thing.

Submitting to this paradigm of mediated vision created many opportunities for students. Psychologists, educators, and particularly its distributors saw the stereoscope as fulfilling the promises of democracy by extending diverse experiences to a broad population of students. Underwood salesmen were trained to emphasize to potential customers that, with the stereoscope, one no longer needed to be rich to travel.[40] Albert Osborne noted that with geography lessons through the stereoscope, "the range of experience of the average child can be incalculably increased."[41] At a moment when direct sensory encounters were of paramount importance in education, the stereoscope's ability to facilitate travel experiences across a wide socioeconomic spectrum and in far-flung local and regional schools was a great asset.

Repackaging the Stereoscope for Schools

The stereoscope industry could capitalize on the broader popularity of object teaching—itself one mechanism that progressive educators employed to fulfill the promise of the reforms Horace Mann had initiated in the 1830s. By the last three decades of the nineteenth century, school systems that had been organized piecemeal at state and municipal levels began to resemble the beginnings of a national system.[42] Public schools were often crowded and culturally and linguistically diverse, and the pedagogical focus on images and objects may have also been perceived as a more universal starting point for students and teachers with dramatically different levels of preparation. "By 1909," as Underwood and Keystone developed their travel systems, the US Immigration Commission conducted a survey that found "57.8 per cent of the children in the schools of thirty-seven of the nation's largest cities were of foreign-born parentage."[43] Instructors' manuals do not often comment directly on these challenges, which are more likely to surface in educational journals. Yet materials for teachers provide a fascinating window onto the stereoscope's ideal intended uses, with special attention on the visual and mental experiences it conjured for students.

Educators used stereographs to teach a range of subjects; manuals accompanying boxed stereo views boasted detailed tables of contents and indexes that covered topics such as agriculture, architecture, biography, botany, child life, cities and city life, civic betterment, English composition, geology, manual training, mythology, physical geography, products and industries, human races, and transportation.[44] Much like a stone in an object lesson could function as a catalyst for thinking about geology, historical tools, or contemporary mining, stereo views were curated by subject specialists and educators hired by Underwood and Keystone, then strung together in different narrative and thematic sequences. Topics varied widely, including industrial or agricultural processes, architectural tours, and geographical travel through cities, countries, and regions. Selected scenes were grouped to illustrate prose, poetry, and essays. Each stereograph acquired a distinct meaning when placed in a given narrative chain and paradoxically functioned as both a detailed, precise example and an interchangeable component in a potentially infinite series of views. This organizational method ensured that packaged views had maximum versatility.

A single stereo view, for example, Underwood's number 42, captioned "Street peddlers' carts on Elizabeth Street—looking north from Hester Street, NY," is referenced multiple times in Frank McMurry's *The World Visualized for the Classroom* (figure 6.3), It is found in a fifty-one-view sequence illustrating the mid-Atlantic states, preceded by a view of "palatial homes and hotels of Upper Fifth Avenue" and followed by a view of the steel frame of a skyscraper in progress.[45] In a subsection of the "Civic Betterment" category, the scene exemplifies an "unattractive" tenement, while in the "Home Economics" section, it is included alongside images of markets in Venezuela, Brussels, Cairo, Algiers, Jaffa, Jerusalem, and Shanghai to support the assertion that "women have done valuable work" to improve sanitary conditions.[46] It is listed as "a good residential section of N.Y. City in the Revolutionary days" in a sequence of war-related sites; as a scene to accompany Amelia E. Barr's book, *The Belle of Bowling Green*; a scene to accompany Paul Leicester Ford's *The Honorable Peter Stirling, and What People Thought of Him*; and a scene to accompany Jacob Riis's autobiography, *The Making of an American*.[47] Within these narrative groupings, this single scene served as a regional placeholder and a historical marker of the American Revolution. It was meant to spur nostalgia for the days of New York's rising merchant class (in the case of Barr's novel) and to stoke sympathies related to urban reform, in the case of Riis's life story. Evoking sentiments of nationhood, squalor, progress, and nostalgia, the image functioned as both a concrete example and a flexible subject invested with a range of meanings.

Democracy and Discipline 195

Figure 6.3
"Street peddlers' cart on Elizabeth Street—looking north from Hester Street, New York City." Miriam and Ira D. Wallach Division of Art, Prints and Photographs: Photography Collection, New York Public Library Digital Collections, New York Public Library."

Extensively cross-referenced stereo views made the stereoscope applicable across a range of topics, yet these endlessly recombinatory narratives threatened to decontextualize images otherwise invested with realism and specificity. Interpretive captions grouping views together often emphasized different aspects of the image, and some commentary proved contradictory. For example, Keystone view number 292 depicts a domestic scene of a woman pressing a corn tortilla on a stone while one girl looks on and another shapes a tortilla by hand. The image is visually bisected by a handmade broom propped diagonally in the background. A basket of corn and the stone tools for pressing the meal are visible in the foreground (figure 6.4). The view is listed multiple times throughout the *Guide to the Keystone "600 Set."* In the "Production and Manufacturing" section, it is described as depicting a "primitive way of preparing corn for the table," while in a section devoted to precious stones and quarrying, the pupils' attention is drawn to the view's example of "primitive pottery in other countries."[48] Several additional textual references refer to the instruments or methods depicted as "crude" or "primitive."[49]

The human subjects in the tortilla-making scene are also objectified in the service of lessons about race and culture. Under "Racial Geography," a

Figure 6.4
"Tortilla Making, Salvador." Keystone view number 292. Elihu Burritt Library, Central Connecticut State University.

caption informs readers that "these are especially good types of the Indians prevalent through Central and South America," directing attention to the people rather than the tortillas.[50] The view is also one of five stereographs depicting Central America in the "Political Geography" section accompanied by the comment, "The common people of the Central American states are so ignorant that the governments (republic in form) are very unstable. Revolutions are very common and very destructive. The common people have little share in the government."[51] The scene is juxtaposed with an image of a goat being milked in a Norwegian fjord under the "Community Civics" section, noting, "Life and health were almost wholly dependent upon the efforts and the arrangement of the family itself."[52] A section on "preparing and serving food" notes the scene's cleanliness: "Cooking though primitive may be clean, as you can see. Here again the woman begins her work with the corn on the cob. Compare this kitchen with your own and tell where you think the better results can be obtained." Conversely, a section labeled "Health Habits—Cleanliness" in the "Hygiene" section accompanies the same view with a caption reading, "Uncleanliness in preparing food is the cause of numberless disorders."[53]

Like object lessons, which used physical specimens for pupils to draw connections among people, places, and things, each narrative thread with which Keystone's number 292 is associated highlights different elements of the image: stone, corn, woman, children, dirt. In classroom exercises, the context and larger goal of the lesson would dictate the conclusions students drew from this image. Yet the image's interpretation as illustrating artisanal processes, to signify political unrest and familial self-reliance, and particularly to make contradictory inferences about the setting's sanitation, render it unstable. Most problematic, the intended interpretive pathways drawn through the image reduce its ethnographic subjects to objects. In most of the manual's references, the woman and children making tortillas in Keystone's view number 292 are marked as racially and culturally "other," although in one instance, the view is characterized as a "family scene," gesturing to a connection between the viewer and the people in the image.[54] Within nineteenth-century classrooms, "the bodies of African American and Native American graduates [often] provided material evidence" of the civilizing effects of school, commonly through techniques such as before-and-after photographs.[55] People became object lessons, their instrumentality in demonstrating some higher truth often in tension with their individual humanity, much like Underwood's view of Glacier Point disavows the woman at the edge of the rock who arguably occupies the image's focal point.

These contrasting functions, as concrete images attributed with realism and as interchangeable pieces in thematic sequences with predetermined goals, foreground the stereo view's role in the classroom not only as an optical instrument that offered new views of the world but as a tool to enforce entirely new ways of seeing. The decontextualized, seemingly careless worldview that these lessons appear to advance is at least partially understood within the broader pedagogical context of the object lesson.[56] In object teaching, the physical specimens themselves were less important than the habits of observation and reasoning they were employed to cultivate. Similarly, Underwood and Keystone operated on the assumption that images do not hold singular meanings but are sensory pieces, which, if thoughtfully assembled by a careful observer, help make the world knowable. Of course, the worldview projected by the stereoscope industry was one in which empire and industry reigned. These attitudes were asserted not only through the stereoscope's content but through its very form.

As a medium that makes unique demands of the user's visual and mental faculties, the stereoscope's lessons had as much to do with teaching *how* to look as they did with *what* children saw through the lenses. Jonathan

Crary echoes this point, suggesting that "the content of the images is far less important than the inexhaustible routine of moving from one card to the next and producing the same effect, repeatedly, mechanically. And each time, the mass-produced and monotonous cards are transubstantiated into a compulsory and seductive vision of the 'real.'"[57] The classroom activities and discourses that supported the stereoscope in schools reveal a striking contrast between the new worlds introduced through the device and the visual discipline it instilled.

Mind over Matter

To focus on the seductive flow of the stereoscope's inexhaustible stream of images underscores that sensory training was the real goal of such object lessons. Whereas lessons using physical specimens encouraged students to hone their skills through a combination of sensory registers (one could touch feathers and minerals, taste and smell spices), lessons through the stereoscope demanded physical accommodation of the child's eyes to the apparatus. Even as they certified the stereo view as a "real" or even superior experience, many educators and psychologists acknowledged that stereoscopic looking was itself a learned skill that required practice and expectation setting. Herbert Spencer noted that the two images of a stereograph do not come together without "persevering contemplation," and even then, "there are some eyes which to the last fail in combining them; and to which they continuously appear conflicting and confused."[58]

Similar to persistence-of-vision toys such as the phenakistoscope and zoetrope, the stereoscope relied on a perceptual trick. However, its association with photography already lent it a different kind of truth value.[59] Moreover, unlike home optical play, object lessons through the stereoscope were emptied of their ludic potentials in order to authenticate the device as an educational medium. "Using stereographs is not play; it is work," began *The World Visualized for the Classroom*. The book cautions teachers against using the stereoscope as a student reward or incentive, a trap that educators might easily fall into considering the device's "wonderfully attractive" nature.[60] The college-aged sales agents that Underwood employed were advised to remind customers that "the tours are designed not to amuse or to entertain, primarily, but to instruct, to educate, to do the work, and give the satisfaction largely of travel itself."[61] To insist that the device required "work" and was not simply fun hinted at the physical and mental concessions students had to make in order to conform to the stereoscope's design.

In his 1911 manual for teachers, Hugo Münsterberg noted that observers scan the stereoscopic image differently from the way they would the same scene in reality. These "unnatural eye movements," Münsterberg warned, "produce a continual disappointment" if students are not adequately trained.[62] The difficulty, Münsterberg explained, was that although the stereoscopic image's "artificial plasticity suggests the attitude of reality," its representation of depth is simulated. Other three-dimensional media, such as the pop-up books discussed in chapter 4, combined pictorial representations of depth with actual depth as the paper planes unfolded in real space.[63] This physical quality, Hannah Field contends, ultimately reaffirmed visual epistemology for children, as "touch can confirm what the eye sees, even as an illusion is mounted."[64] By contrast, the stereoscopic image demanded that viewers accept its three-dimensionality in the absence of tactile confirmation. The stereoscope's 3D image falls short of expectations, according to Münsterberg, because although it evokes what the corresponding view might look like in person, the eyes' distinct physical movements across the stereo view image betray its artificiality. Through the stereoscope, the eye sees but does not *feel* the image. This distinction was rationalized by the stereoscope industry through the assertion of a hierarchy of physical and mental experiences, the latter of which was lauded as superior.[65] Through this reasoning, the stereoscope's mediated view was certified as a sufficient substitute for the "real" thing. This is not to say that students naively mistook the stereoscopic image for reality, but as they were repeatedly reminded of the virtual view's "realism," a strong pressure was exerted to buy into the stereoscope's visual paradigm. The child's expectations thus had to be reconciled with the experience of stereoscopic viewing.

Münsterberg explained that "every educational step demands the subtlest adjustment to the perceptive conditions, which are steadily changed by the inner growth and training."[66] The instrument's ability to offer new visual experiences required the child's senses to be reoriented to its features. In one activity, all students were asked to study a stereograph as closely as possible with their unaided eyes, followed by a period during which a few stereoscopes circulated through the room to allow for in-depth examination. Students were then asked to share what they had seen.[67] Perhaps the exercise was a way to manage crowded classrooms equipped with too few stereoscopes, or perhaps it was a thoughtful pedagogical choice. Regardless of the motivation, the exercise recalled the less structured perceptual practices of home optical play, where children alternated between looking at the zoetrope or phenakistoscope the "right" way and the "wrong" way to see the difference. The stereoscope formalized what had been a fluid interplay between sensation and perception in home contexts, requiring the child's concerted effort in order for the stereoscope to "work" as intended at school.

Students practicing these skills learned how to look within the thematic context of the accompanying interpretive materials, for instance, in the opening example of Underwood's view 290 of Yosemite's Glacier Point. The granite rock formation may stir an evocative connection to Longfellow's *Song of Hiawatha* (though a geographically inaccurate one, as Longfellow's poem is set near Lake Superior). The scene logically pairs with John Muir's environmental writing about the Yosemite Valley. Yet within the context of stereoscopic lessons, the way Underwood suggested this image be used in the classroom played a trick on students: it made the woman at the end of the rock seem to disappear. Like the woman's body, which vanished from consideration in the stereo view's accompanying materials, students gazing through the stereoscope experienced a peculiar distancing from their bodies.

In the stereoscopic gaze, the observer forfeits a degree of bodily autonomy in exchange for mental mobility. How else could impoverished children in densely packed urban schoolrooms or sparsely furnished, poorly heated rural schoolhouses visit India, China, or the Grand Canyon? Characterizations of the stereoscope's lenses as windows to the world beyond[68] emphasized a virtual travel experience during which it felt "easy and natural for one to lose all consciousness of immediate bodily surroundings and to gain *real experience of seeing*, of being *present in* the places themselves."[69] A Keystone promotional image depicting a boy gazing into a stereoscope evokes the visual world accessible through the device. A photograph of a dense cityscape is cut into a triangular shape and collaged in at the end of the stereoscope, suggesting the boy's mental projection—a world widening beyond the stereoscope's lenses (figure 6.5). This rich world could be accessed by the mind through the eyes. The boy's straight posture alludes to the stereoscope's ability to discipline the rest of his body in the process, implying a correlation between the pupil's orderly body and the reverent

FIG. 46. Using a stereoscope

When the stereograph is seen through this binocular instrument an impression of depth, or third dimension, is received

Figure 6.5
Visualization of stereoscopic looking, Keystone View Company. Reproduced in Anna Verona Dorris, *Visual Instruction in the Public Schools* (New York: Ginn, 1928), 136.

gaze into the device. Just as movable toy books furnished a way to engage the imagination through visual and manual means alongside "furniture for containment," the stereoscope cultivated habits of attention alongside transformations in the nineteenth-century classrooms organized around students seated at desks.[70]

Stereoscopic looking bypassed the tactile stimulation experienced during physical travel, captivating and even temporarily immobilizing its user. The stereoscopic impression was so vivid, some promotional material suggested, that salesmen were reminded that potential customers might require a tap on the shoulder while testing the device in order to bring them back to the present place and time.[71] This corporeal reorientation became so pervasive that it even surfaced in discussions of in-person sightseeing. One author in 1899, for example, proposed that students model the physical attributes of the stereoscope with their bodies, recommending "the use of the hollow of the hand as an impromptu stereoscope," encouraging students to play at "stereoscopic" looking with their unaided eyes.[72] Unlike Spencer and

Münsterberg, who stressed the mediated qualities of stereoscopic vision, Underwood's manual for traveling sales agents boasted that the device offered an experience "such as a tourist would get by a bodily trip," asserting its capacity to replicate (rather than simulate) physical travel. While such a sentiment implies that the body follows the mind in such experiences, the manual continues in a contradictory vein, expressing the stereoscope's capacity for the "liberation of our minds from the limitations of our bodies."[73] The stereoscope thus afforded pupils new experiences, but it did so by reinforcing a new way of seeing that substituted lived experience with mediated vision, thereby obscuring the distinctions between these two modes of perception. It was no coincidence, however, that this "liberation" of the mind was also a convenient strategy for controlling students' bodies.

The mental mobility that the stereoscope encouraged could ultimately be learned and internalized as an instinctive way to interpret the world. Educators' responses to the stereoscope reveal a second goal of such instructional methods: classroom management. As promotional materials claimed the device's ability to replicate (not simulate) physical travel, this same certification of virtual travel also resulted in classrooms characterized by quiet, stereographic viewing. In one sense, the stereoscope responded to the "problem" of children's attention conceived more generally. Children's scattered attention and inability to focus for sustained periods of time were at once considered natural characteristics of their development but also characteristics that required intervention.[74] In a chapter on object lessons for kindergarten teachers, Mary Tyler Mann and Elizabeth Peabody, the latter of whom founded the first English-speaking kindergarten in America, explain: "A child is not able to direct its own attention; it needs the help of the adult in the unfolding of the mind, no less than in the care of the body."[75] As George Luckey's experiment on children's peripheral color vision discussed in the previous chapter attests, children's restless, noncompliant bodies were fundamentally misaligned with the attributes of the ideal psychological subject (even as many psychological studies endeavored to understand children's distinct perspectives). These are the same behavioral characteristics that would be valued in students. As a lens-based technology that literally trains its user's eyes to precise elements of a three-dimensional image, the stereoscope was ideally suited to the task of focusing pupils' attention. The hooded design of the Holmes-style stereoscope, which physically shut out immediate stimuli, transformed the child's unfocused look into a controlled, orderly gaze, uniquely enforcing these directives about children's attention and perceptual habits.

Instructional materials outlining exercises with the stereoscope echo this emphasis on disciplined looking. The Keystone manual, for example, suggests activities ranging from individual viewing at reference tables during independent study time to highly structured exercises that specified the sequence and amount of time that each student had to view a stereograph. A recitation study involved a series of stereoscopes, each loaded with a separate view to be rapidly passed down rows of classroom seats while one student orally delivered facts about places viewed. Designed to optimize efficiency, the exercise enabled every student in a class of approximately forty to view the series of images in a matter of minutes.[76] The Underwood manual similarly outlines activities that involved regimented transfer of stereoscopes between students at the sound of an auditory cue given by the teacher, and manuals included charts of seating layouts to demonstrate efficient schemes for distributing and passing stereoscopes in the classroom (figure 6.6).[77] Some feature seating charts for up to forty-eight students. These charts appear like football plays, marked with complicated legends and arrows indicating the stereographs' movement and directionality among student groups.[78] Timed classroom exercises in which children viewed and passed stereoscopes to one another following a grid-like system controlled how long and in what order children viewed stereographs.

The orderliness of the stereoscope's use, suggested one high school teacher, allowed children to focus more closely on the subjects depicted than physical travel allowed. Because of its ability to "enchain the attention," the teacher argued, "it may not be too sanguine to believe that a child may be made thus to know more of the real life of foreign or of distant lands than is often known by the hasty or careless traveler who visits them."[79] Such a statement inverts the object lesson's foundational rationale, asserting not only the stereoscopic view's superiority but also the visual and bodily attention of the media spectator over the in-person visitor. This logic, which justified rigid classroom exercises, likely appealed to late nineteenth-century public school teachers faced with large, diverse classes. Historian of education Lawrence Cremin paints a picture of the urban school in the 1870s and 1880s: "Problems of skyrocketing enrollments were compounded by a host of other issues. In school buildings badly lighted, poorly heated,

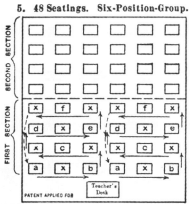 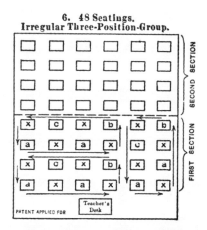

Figure 6.6
Seating charts explaining how to pass the stereoscope. *Philip Emerson and William Charles Moore, Geography through the Stereoscope: Student's Stereoscopic Field Guide* (New York: Underwood & Underwood, 1907), xiv.

frequently unsanitary, and bursting at the seams, young immigrants from a dozen different countries swelled the tide of newly arriving farm children. Superintendents spoke hopefully of reducing class size to sixty per teacher, but the hope was most often a pious one." He goes on to explain that it was "little wonder that rote efficiency reigned supreme."[80]

Anticipating rowdy and distracted pupils, Philip Emerson, an administrator and geography teacher who coauthored Underwood's *Geography through the Stereoscope* (1907), also argued that exercises with the stereoscope were preferable to field trips, which required teachers to expend the majority of their energy on disciplinary matters. He explained that the device "shuts away all the other impressions save the guiding direction of the teacher's voice, makes the conditions ideal for orderly, effective attention to the work in hand."[81] Emerson's tidy solution to classroom discipline seems borne out in images of schoolchildren attentively using the device in classrooms and libraries, implying the stereoscope's success in enforcing these behavioral expectations. Of course, instructors' writing and photographs indicate only intended disciplinary results, leaving open the question of students' own experiences and responses to the stereoscopic image.[82] However, teachers' commentary and the imagery that justified and sold the stereoscope in schools nevertheless attests to the central role that the stereoscope—an optical technology—played in the production of an ideal student.

Although a value placed on direct sensory encounters initially fostered the stereoscope's educational adoption, the classroom environment that instructors hoped to achieve paradoxically consolidated a broad bundle of potential sensations into a focused visual stream. Emerson quite transparently shared his hopes that the stereoscope would make his classrooms easier to control. Other commentators critiqued the stereoscope as an easy solution for unprepared and disengaged teachers, much like criticisms of movies in the classroom in the twentieth century. One short piece in *Illinois Teacher* complained: "There are many stereoscopes among us, and some might be had for our schools, doubtless; but of what avail will they be, unless behind them there is a live teacher? From some experience in school work, we are convinced that there is need of more mental activity among teachers, directed toward their daily work in the school-room. We speak advisedly when we say that too large a proportion of our teachers feel but little, if any, interest in their calling."[83] Packaged curricula and stereographs reduced the workload of "the nation's ill-equipped, poorly trained teachers" and endeavored to standardize the educational experience, including the sensory habits of the stereoscope itself.[84] Sarah Anne Carter points to similar shortcomings in the implementation of object lessons. Many educators evidently found the incorporation of actual objects in classrooms challenging and ended up reverting back to traditional memorization exercises.[85] Historical photographs reveal object lesson cards hung on walls as decorations rather than in students' hands. Such evidence raises questions about teachers' willingness or ability to execute lessons as intended.[86]

Conclusion

Before the visual instruction movement flourished in the 1920s, the stereoscope picked up on the call to sensory pedagogy that the object lesson had ushered into vogue. Charged by its associations as scientific instrument and parlor entertainment, the stereoscope was rescued from the attic thanks to its alignment with object-based pedagogy. In so doing, it institutionalized a new way of seeing and enforced a new standard of student decorum. The device's classroom application was designed to be efficient and productive, with activities designating the correct way to use the device and view the stereoscopic subject. While providing innumerable new opportunities for children to learn about the world, the stereoscope simultaneously restricted their scope of vision, rendering their bodies static while their minds were engaged. In seeking to fulfill the democratic ideals of providing a range of students access to the world, the stereoscope thus enforced a visual regime designed to discipline the student and standardize the visual learning experience. Stereoscopic travel systems controlled what children saw, and educators monitored the conditions under which they were seen. In broadening the potential number of visual subjects to which the pupil had access, the stereoscope also framed the boundaries and angles of possibility from which they learned about the world. Rather than being seen as a mediated encounter with the physical world, stereoscopic viewing was set apart as a superior object lesson capable of distilling its subjects into efficient, organized sequences of images. Such organization, in turn, focused and corralled students, guiding their observational and interpretive responses.

In reformulating what it meant to travel the world, the stereoscope fit into a constellation of other media technologies that changed relationships to space and time. Comparisons with the telephone, for example, helped position the stereoscope—already over half a century old—as a contemporary device for virtual travel, an instrument that "annihilates distance."[87] Alongside turn-of-the-century inventions such as the telephone or the electric light, which were met with both optimism and ambivalence, the stereoscope's resurgence as an educational medium required alignment with the cultural and commercial ideologies of late nineteenth- and early twentieth-century America.[88] The longer popularity of object-based pedagogy, alongside the newly institutionalized field of experimental psychology, together helped refashion the optical instrument for the classroom. To see the stereoscope as an object "connected to the world outside"[89] prefigured a kind of network mentality, inviting students to make connections among people, places, and things without even leaving their seats.

Fashioning a disciplined pupil who had free access to virtually endless sights and scenes, the stereoscope could control what children encountered in the world, and how they encountered it. In contrast to salacious stereoscopic views found in exhibition settings like penny arcades, educational stereographs, by virtue of both their contexts and use, not only aimed to produce ideal pupils but also extended the protectionist mantle of childhood to public schoolchildren from a variety of backgrounds.[90] The stereoscope industry's insistence on the advantages of the virtual view and its employment of experts to vet this view as better than a "real" trip also strongly contrasted with the decades-old practice of optical discernment that persistence-of-vision toys sustained. The stereoscope's visual epistemology required a concession—a willingness to accept the device's distinct arrangement of optical cues as a version of the real. Moreover, for underprepared instructors, the instrument was a boon.

The mental mobility stressed in conjunction with the stereoscope's adoption has analogues in contemporary education, where neuroscientific research forms a considerable body of literature from which educational theory draws. There are thus broader stakes in investigating historical classroom media technologies like the stereoscope.[91] They lie in thinking about the recurring challenges or perceived problems that educational media seek to address, the regimes of knowledge produced through the implementation of new technologies, and in the identification of all of the stakeholders in the transaction. Today, multimillion-dollar contracts are struck between technology giants like Google and school districts across the country.[92] The "Googlification of the classroom," Natasha Singer wrote in the *New York Times* in 2017, reflects pedagogical goals analogous to those in the nineteenth century, "driv[ing] a philosophical change in public education—prioritizing training children in skills like teamwork and problem-solving while de-emphasizing the teaching of traditional academic knowledge, like math formulas."[93] As of 2017, "more than half the nation's primary- and secondary-school students—more than 30 million children—use[d] Google education apps like Gmail and Docs."[94] Just as the stereoscope produced quiet, focused pupils, the technologies like the Apple iPad transfix and command students' attention in the classroom. One third-grade Virginia teacher whose class adopted iPads lamented rather than celebrated this new disciplinary regime. In terms strikingly similar to discourses surrounding the stereoscope, she admits that "tablets are portals to a million possibilities," yet argues that a little noise in the classroom and chatter among the students is integral to their learning and growth, more important than what is gained through the iPad's use.[95]

There are distinctive historical continuities here, but as this teacher's concern with her too-quiet classroom shows, the various ways that technologies and their "effects" are interpreted change. Just as students were trained to look through or beyond the woman perched at the edge of Glacier Point to instead consider the grandeur of her surroundings, the stereoscope enforced a form of bodily knowledge that valued the visual and mental experience over a primarily physical one. Conversely, today in the wake of mounting concerns over children's decreased outside play and increased screen time, the quiet and isolated experience of stereoscopic viewing would not necessarily be received as a best practice. Efforts to remobilize the stationary student can be seen in a range of products, from flexible, modular seating options to elastic "bouncy bands" affixed to chair legs to allow students to fidget in place. This marketplace is unsurprisingly supported by a range of expert literature that endeavors to reconnect the brain to the body.[96] Optical toys continue to circulate in markets filled with such new technologies and products. The conclusion of this book outlines how these toys have found new relevance in the contemporary home, gallery, and public spaces and explores the twenty-first century ideas about childhood that they help to construct and sustain.

7   Conclusion: Oversized Optics in the Digital Age

In 2014, the maker of science, technology, engineering, and math (STEM) toys GoldieBlox released GoldieBlox and the Movie Machine, a construction set with an accompanying storybook (figure 7.1) The book chronicles the efforts of Goldie and her friends to save their local film festival (cancelled due to a broken projector). To solve the problem, Goldie proposes they build a giant zoetrope to exhibit short films. Using step-by-step instructions, the book guides girls through the process of building their own zoetrope alongside Goldie and her friends. The kit comes with several preprinted and blank picture strips for girls to make their own animations and advertises a companion mobile app for additional experiments in stop-motion techniques. The cultural and economic conditions motivating GoldieBlox's production of a zoetrope kit in the twenty-first century share many features with those supporting the toy's initial sale in the nineteenth. Whereas optical toys originally responded to concerns about children's home recreation and cultivated the visual subjectivity of an expanding middle class, the GoldieBlox kit reflects anxieties associated with the decline of the middle class. The GoldieBlox movie machine, and many other zoetrope kits like it, frames optical play as STEM play, a pastime perceived today to be key to economic growth and opportunity.[1] The zoetrope's long life and its contemporary instantiation as a STEM toy demonstrate the enduring connection that optical toys have to the visual and cultural constructions of childhood. Such toys are not obsolete technologies displaced by newer media but are alive and well in today's playscape.

The GoldieBlox zoetrope joins a host of other contemporary optical kits in the STEM toy market, a defined industrial category that exploded in the first decades of the twenty-first century.[2] The continued manufacture and

Figure 7.1
GoldieBlox and the Movie Machine, 2014.

sale of optical toys as scientific playthings attests to their ongoing role as responses to preoccupations surrounding children's educational play in times of economic uncertainty. In the *New Yorker*, GoldieBlox founder and CEO Debra Sterling explains the generational shifts in the economic landscape that motivated the company's formation: "'When I grew up,' Sterling says, 'the jobs that your parents wanted you to be was [sic] a doctor or a lawyer.' ... 'But now I think an engineer or a scientist or someone in technology is becoming a coveted job.'"[3] Today, contemporary optical toys are not centrally framed as devices for the practice of discerning spectatorship. Nevertheless, their sensory pedagogy reflects familiar prevailing anxieties surrounding children's learning, attention, and the cultivation of critical observational skills that can be widely applied.

Conclusion

Retail shelves and online marketplaces of STEM and STEAM (the A standing for art) toys recall nineteenth-century interpretations of the Edgeworths' "rational toy shop—" the toy cupboard where zoetropes and kaleidoscopes would be found alongside hoops, sticks, kites, and other playthings that could be put to productive ends.[4] Mountain View, California–based KiwiCo. is a purveyor of subscription-based STEAM kits for children and youth. Browsing KiwiCo.'s offerings—broken down into six product lines of kits for users ages birth to over sixteen—is much like perusing the table of contents from a nineteenth-century rational recreation text. Do-it-yourself kits with activities and apparatuses for experiments in chemistry, astronomy, physics, design, and more promise to make kids' domestic environments into laboratories of learning after school and on weekends. KiwiCo.'s inventory is peppered with optical toys and kits for visual experimentation. The company has sold sets to make kaleidoscopes, thaumatropes, and zoetropes, as well as spinning tops, a color experimentation kit, a Wheatstone-style stereo viewer, and a "kinegram" machine, which animates pictures using what is known as the "barrier-grid" or "picket fence" technique—producing the same moiré effect that *The Motograph Moving Picture Book* used in 1898. Framed in the language of critical media literacy, KiwiCo. endeavors to "help ... kids think big and act like creators and producers instead of just consumers."[5] This valorization of "maker" culture is a departure from nineteenth-century sentiments that more explicitly celebrated (tasteful) consumption. Yet, like KiwiCo.'s nineteenth-century counterparts, optical toys today continue to aid in the construction of young subjects whose senses and habits of mind are perceived as requiring alignment with future social and professional aims.

Meant for home use and sold through a subscription model, KiwiCo.'s products respond to parental dissatisfaction "with traditional curricula that don't offer their children the kind of content and pedagogy that will best prepare them for a career of innovation and problem-solving."[6] A 2018 report produced by the Toy Association, the trade organization, explains that the STEM/STEAM movement "grew out of two intertwined needs—a workplace that demands STEM skills and an educational system that can pipeline people into those positions." The movement has thus influenced changes in American national policy, education, and the toy industry.[7] Capitalizing on at least a latent critique of public education, the STEM/

STEAM toy industry actively contributes to a broader neoliberal educational agenda by suggesting the individual child/student as the locus of potential and the family as the core unit responsible for that growth.[8] Such toys belong to a much larger legacy of what Rebecca Onion calls "the science extracurriculum"—a set of products and practices (indeed, a whole mind-set) that values stimulating "a child's joy in science, as practiced independently in leisure hours."[9] The "maker" movement represents one contemporary instantiation of such informal popular science pedagogy, resulting in organized Maker Faires and publications like *Make* magazine, which Josef Nguyen argues "indexes broader interests in making, crafting, and other forms of hands-on material engagements that proponents frame as both necessary for the future and a form of resistance to contemporary modes of labor, production, and consumption."[10]

Unsurprisingly, until fairly recently, the beneficiary of such extracurricular exploits has long been figured as middle class, and often white and male. Like the related nineteenth-century tradition of rational recreation, these supplementary opportunities have aided in the construction of a productive and rational adult subject: "Children's scientific entertainments often cost money, and the children who were entertained by these sometimes-expensive toys and books were embodying a rational style of leisure, one that channeled their impulses toward novelty-seeking in favorable intellectual directions."[11] Today, as they are coordinated across nonprofit, state-sponsored, and commercial sectors, STEAM initiatives speak "to the desire to prepare our children for the workplace by educating and providing the skills they need to succeed; thereby helping our nation and its citizens to globally compete and prosper."[12] Thus positioned within the nested narratives of citizenship and individual economic growth, optical toys today embody a drive to mold children into productive social subjects, much as they did in the nineteenth century.

The terms by which this subject position is constructed and understood reflect a distinct set of social and economic pressures within twenty-first-century American and, to an extent, European culture. These toys' marketing iconography and packaging envision an inclusive world of aspiring STEAM professionals, featuring boys and girls of multiple racial and ethnic backgrounds eagerly clustered around kits. GoldieBlox joins several other companies that make STEM/STEAM toys aimed at girls, including Roominate and Nancy B's Science Club. A girls' line produced by science toy company 4M, STEAM Powered Girls, sells a zoetrope labeled as an "optical mood lamp," complete with "lovely patterns," suggesting a kind of "pinkification" of the zoetrope that in fact naturalizes it as a "boys' toy." The racial and gender diversity imagined in such imagery notwithstanding, these toys further retrench the assumed socioeconomic status of those engaged in optical play. Positioned, as they were in the nineteenth century, as supplemental to formal education, these toys function similarly to other fee-based extracurricular activities like musical or sports lessons and reflect a middle-class domestic habitus characterized by parental guidance and productive play.[13]

Of course, the promises of STEAM toymakers to transform kids into "makers," not just "consumers," falsely assumes these two positions are separable. The growth of this industry to begin with was largely perpetuated by a reconsolidation of the economic landscape that resulted in lost opportunities in the middle and working classes. Peter Tremin begins his recent book with a visual metaphor, noting that "growing income inequality is threatening the American middle class, and the middle class is vanishing before our eyes."[14] If optical toys once proliferated to meet the presumed needs of a growing middle class (and, in their deployment, helped actively constitute that identity position), then their enduring popularity reveals a continued belief in their capacity to visualize and materialize the promise of middle-class mobility. As staples of the nineteenth-century child's toy box, optical devices made routine a distinct discerning and optimistic outlook that anchored a particular figure of the child. As contemporary STEAM toys, these same devices sustain a similar aspirational child figure—a project focused less exclusively on their visual paradigm and more on their ability to coordinate multisensory engagement with the critical thinking skills considered necessary for twenty-first-century life.

The zoetrope's ability to survive as an educational staple has required an interpretive shift to highlight its tactile rather than visual elements. For instance, German toymaker Haba produced an optics kit that includes several solid beech building blocks, belts, gears, wheels, and paper media (disks and strips) that can be built into a variety of optical machines, including color mixers and zoetropes.[15] The kit is part of the company's Discovering Technics line, which includes several expansion sets. Although the ability to showcase optical phenomena such as persistence of vision adds to the toy's appeal, its design indicates its broader appeal as a modular construction set. Bright orange pieces allow children to connect the naturally finished wooden blocks in multiple configurations; these flexible components and contrasting colors emphasize building and experimentation as core intended play patterns. In contrast to nineteenth-century paper and cardboard zoetrope templates, this set focuses on open-ended building as much as it does on optical experimentation.

Similarly, instead of centering on the optical principles underlying the zoetrope's operation, the GoldieBlox kit focuses on problem-solving and teamwork skills. In the first three (of eight) steps outlined in the kit's storybook, the reader follows along as Goldie constructs a series of seemingly unrelated objects: a spatula, her friend's skateboard wheel, another friend's drum.[16] Goldie's real skills come into play when she creatively reappropriates and synthesizes these disparate things to construct a belt-driven zoetrope, thereby saving the town's film festival. Enlisting the support of her friends, Goldie builds a large-scale zoetrope to exhibit one-second movies, gesturing toward the contemporary association between the nineteenth-century device and animated .gif files.[17] Today, optical toys are valued less for their engagement of visual properties (which, in isolation, risk association with "passive" screen cultures) and more for their requisite manual engagement—their capacities for hands-on tinkering and experimentation. Moreover, the larger-than-life and hands-on iteration of the zoetrope that Goldie and her friends build recalls the uptick in recent zoetrope-inspired art installations and advertising campaigns, connecting twenty-first-century optical play to new possibilities in the creative industries.

Scaled-Up Optical Toys in Art and Culture

The tactile ethos of optical toys within contemporary children's STEAM culture carries over to a spate of recent zoetrope-inspired artistic practices and advertising stunts. In museums and galleries, in public parks and plazas, and in digital form, gigantic zoetropic creations continue to amaze and delight multiple publics. Fine artists such as Gregory Barsamian, Peter Charon, and Mat Collishaw produce large-scale kinetic sculptures that use physical objects sculpted or 3D-printed in specific attitudes of motion like the drawn images along a zoetrope strip. These individual objects are mounted on enormous motorized racks and platters capable of spinning at high speeds. The contraptions are often animated not by slots to peer through, but with perfectly calibrated strobe lights flickering onto their spinning surfaces. During my time working in the education department at New York's Museum of the Moving Image, I showed Gregory Barsamian's *Feral Font* (1996) to scores of schoolchildren. On display in the gallery, the sculpture's strobe shutter is on a timed loop. The artwork—a spinning column—remains in perpetual motion, but it is alternatingly bathed in full light, permitting visitors to watch it spin as a blur, and then plunged into darkness, illuminated by a timed strobe, which acts as a shutter mechanism and gives the illusion that the objects are moving. Similar zoetrope-inspired structures have been built to advertise tea, chocolate, beer, and more. In 2008, an enormous zoetrope was constructed in a city plaza in northern Italy for a commercial for Sony's Bravia televisions. Measuring 10 meters in diameter and capable of reaching speeds up to 50 miles per hour, Sony's BRAVIA-Drome is on record as the world's largest zoetrope (figure 7.2).[18]

Why advertise digital television using century-old moving-image technology? What cultural work does this recent zoetropic paradigm perform? It is no surprise that the oversized, 3D zoetrope's ascendance correlates with the years marking the definitive eclipse of celluloid motion picture distribution and exhibition (and, to an extent, production) by digital technologies.[19] The zoetrope's resurgence in contemporary art and advertising reflects an interest in the reinscription of materiality into the moving

Figure 7.2
Sony BRAVIA-Drome, 2008.

image—a response to anxieties about the digital image's ontology in relation to its indexical celluloid counterpart.[20] Animator George Griffin characterizes this kind of zoetropic-inspired work as "concrete animation," a contemporary animation form and practice, consisting, in one incarnation, of "physical moving objects arrested in synthetic time by strobe light or shuttering devices."[21] This "material turn" in moving-image media functions both to ground the image in a familiar frame and gestures to bustling production cultures where STEAM skills are of central relevance, thereby assuaging broader economic concerns. Here, as in the nineteenth century, children represent one population for whom the epistemic shift of the digital has potentially been less anxiety provoking. They are observers who, by virtue of their age, have never occupied a world when the digital was not already in circulation. However, this chronological overlap does not necessarily produce the skills or dispositions associated with the figure of the digital native. Those attitudes are cultivated through a range of experiences, including encounters with contemporary zoetropes.

Many contemporary displays of optical spectacle assert materiality through their size and site specificity. In galleries, the animation is rendered "live" for the viewer, framed by careful lighting conditions. Hans Polterauer's *Stroboskopscheibe #3* (1999) is installed mounted flush against the wall, where it spins as a strobe flashes at sixteen frames per second. Mat Collishaw's *Garden of Unearthly Delights* (2009) features a rotating disk 200 centimeters in diameter. A protective guard extends out an additional 185 centimeters beyond the spinning mechanism to protect both artwork and viewer.[22] Whereas nineteenth-century persistence-of-vision devices emphasized the virtual or immaterial quality of their animated images, twenty-first-century adaptations commonly underscore the image's material basis by animating three-dimensional objects. These sculptures play with light and circulate air as they spin, creating a multisensory embodied experience distinct from the screen-based moving images common to contemporary consumer media culture. Within the realm of children's playthings, the tactile qualities of optical toys are presented as an antidote to the ills of screen culture, while in large-scale displays, these sculptures seem to ground the moving image's immateriality in something tangible.

Just as recorded observations of persistence of vision in the nineteenth century were inspired by the technologies and movements of daily life, from wagon wheels to moving trains, many large-scale adaptations use movement and environmental attributes in their production of zoetropic sensation. Bill Brand's *Masstransciscope* (1980, restored 2008), an installation in the New York City subway system, depicts a motion sequence of shapes behind a slotted wall that appear to move as the train rapidly moves past. *Union Square in Motion* (2011) was a lenticular zoetrope, animated as commuters walked past it in the station. In a promotional spot for the racing game Forza Motorsport 5 (Microsoft Studios, 2013), San Francisco agency 215 McCann constructed perhaps the world's fastest zoetrope, requiring speeds of over 100 miles an hour. The agency printed a series of 680 oversized images (frames of in-game footage) onto aluminum panels and installed them along a racetrack. To capture and reanimate the images, a camera was mounted to the roof of a McLaren Supercar, capable of achieving these high speeds. The short film that resulted, *Forza Filmspeed*, oscillates between the zoetropic illusion captured by the camera racing along the track and long shots of the car as it captures those frames, moving back and forth between creating the special effect and revealing the underlying conditions responsible for its production.

  Loop (2018) is a public art installation designed by Olivier Girouard, Jonathan Villeveuve, and Ottoblix. It consists of thirteen wheel-like pods, each of which seats two people facing one another with a lever between them. Pumping the lever activates a fairy-tale–themed zoetropic animated sequence that runs in a circle around the pod's interior and exterior.[23] Comparisons between *Loop*'s person-pumped lever and railroad handcars extend longstanding connections between the speed and sensation of locomotive travel and the experience of the moving image.[24] *Loop* has toured several cities, installed in plazas and common spaces like Houston's Avenida, CityCenter in Washington, DC, Burnett Park in Fort Worth, and the pedestrian plazas in New York's Garment District. These sites are parts of larger urban redesign projects meant to renew interest in downtown spaces and rekindle a sense of public culture. Scaled up and moved from parlors to public plazas, installations like the BRAVIA-Drome and *Loop* attest to the continuing role that optical spectacle plays in the cultivation of individual and collective spectatorial identities.

  Despite their transformed contexts and design, contemporary zoetropic forms largely follow a familiar experiential pedagogy predicated on looking both the "right" and the "wrong" ways at the moving image. Much like children (then and now) peer over the top of a zoetrope to see only a blur before looking through the sides, strobe-activated sculptures like Barsamian's and Collishaw's commonly run on timers. They invite onlookers to behold their spectacular effects, but when the strobes shut off, they disclose their underlying optical principles. Although these sculptures cannot always be manually manipulated in museum galleries, their appeal still stems from their presentation alternating between spectacle and revelation. In this way, they retain a sense of Gaudreault and Dulac's player mode of engagement by inviting contemplation. Other large-scale zoetropes are destined for screen-based playback, often for commercials or short films. Instead of a strobe-as-shutter mechanism common to on-site installations, artists and cinematographers synchronize their camera's frame rate to the speed of the rotating object to act as a shutter. Jim Le Fevre's *Holy Flying Circus* Phonotrope (2011), for example, was designed to be filmed for the opening credit sequence of a BBC docudrama about Monty Python of the same name. It is over 2 meters tall and features over two thousand "frames" or images. The animated sequences are organized on circular bands stacked on top of one another in tiers like an enormous wedding cake. In order to fluidly capture the animation, the device spun at 45 rpm and was recorded with a camera shutter speed of twenty-five frames per second.[25] Another example, designed by London-based firm AIS for the EDF Energy Company, features a series of vignettes, each related to a tier of prizes given away by the company, including tickets to the 2012 London Olympics and rides on the London Eye.

Like the timed strobes that control the view of gallery-based zoetropic sculptures, the videos that capture these zoetropes also show the sculptures at rest and in motion, revealing their optical principles and then concealing them to spectacular effect. The promotional spot that showcases the EDF Energy zoetrope begins with a shot of the object at rest and cuts to close-ups of individual figures on their stationary tiers. The sculpture slowly begins to turn until it reaches its top speed, appearing as a blur. At last, the frame rate is adjusted and the animated figures snap into focus—a thrilling moment timed perfectly with the accompanying music: a-ha's "Take on Me."[26] The same strategy of beginning with stationary shots is used in the Monty Python phonotrope and two zoetropic installations made by London production company 1stAveMachine for Coca-Cola's Fuze Tea product and Stella Artois beer.[27] These sculptures conjure before the viewer an image that could not otherwise be seen and invite onlookers to engage in a playful

Conclusion 219

dynamic of belief and doubt.[28] Beginning with the sculpture at rest certifies its object status before the shutter brings it "to life," much as a magician invites the audience to inspect a top hat before producing a rabbit from inside of it. Through timed strobes or the techniques of cinematography and editing, these zoetropes advance a mode of spectatorship characterized by shifting attention, not unlike the performances of optical discernment in the nineteenth-century parlor.

The museum gallery, the city plaza, and the Internet form the new contexts for exhibiting large-scale optical displays. Unlike analogous nineteenth-century optical spectacles, these artworks, installations, and promotional materials do not principally serve as mechanisms for the performance of discernment. Instead, they infuse public life with a fresh sense of play, making art accessible and interactive for diverse audiences. Onlookers of all ages encounter these works while walking downtown or surfing the internet, enjoying a momentary experience of surprise and delight. Moreover, in scaling up and materializing familiar perceptual phenomena, these artworks and installations refashion the zoetrope as a twenty-first-century feat of creativity, ingenuity, and technical knowledge. In so doing, they speak to the same skill sets and patterns of thought that optical toys as children's STEM playthings do. The "play" that large-scale zoetropes encourage, then, is productive—a tangible instantiation of contemporary rational recreation.

Opportunities behind the Scenes

In materially grounding the moving image, these gigantic zoetropic forms also materialize a professional context where optical play holds both creative and economic potential. Like the gallery's timed strobe light that alternately dazzles onlookers and demystifies the zoetropic illusion, many commercially designed zoetropes are accompanied by behind-the-scenes spots and featurettes that chronicle the devices' design and construction. Attributed either to individuals or teams that include production companies, visual effects postproduction houses, and advertising agencies, the 3D zoetrope occupies the status of a cultural product or work of art. This status is reinforced through the concurrent production of behind-the-scenes and making-of paratexts that document the construction process and spotlight the individuals and collective units responsible for their creation. The critical utility of paratexts, Dorothee Birke and Birte Christ argue, is that they call attention to a text's "specific form, which is affected by historically and socially determined modes of production and reception."[29] In other words, paratexts can illuminate the particular values and connotations surrounding an artwork in a given historical moment. Such materials are thus especially helpful in the interpretation of media forms that have enjoyed long histories, such as the zoetrope. Such paratexts frame the economic value and cultural significance of zoetropes in contemporary contexts. Behind-the-scenes footage reveals not only a longstanding fascination with optical spectacle but also the human labor that makes such spectacular feats possible. The concrete objects that large-scale zoetropes set into motion, then, also concretize for the viewer a context where groups of people are being paid to engage in optical play. In this sense, these zoetropes are children's STEAM toys supersized and "all grown up," at least implicitly assuaging economic anxieties through the depiction of thriving skill-variant creative industries.

The video series made by ad agency 215 McCann about their zoetrope for Coca-Cola's line of Fuze Iced Teas exemplifies how making-of materials highlight the professional triumph of the 3D zoetrope. The final zoetrope consists of thirty-six rotating carousels, each featuring eighteen frames of animation.[30] In one video, art director Steve Couture beams: "When you have a project of this scale, the amount of people that are required to come together to pull this thing off is pretty awe-inspiring." He begins, "There is this aspect of humanity …" but then trails off as the inspirational music swells. The video alternates between footage of the zoetrope's construction, including several shots of silhouetted figures made for the device and shots of the production crew in silhouette. Unlike the distancing and abstracting effect of silhouetted figures on nineteenth-century optical media, however, these visual continuities between optical media and the people constructing it give way to fully lit shots of crew members, revealing a racially and gender-diverse workplace.[31] The down-to-earth human aspect that Couture conjures for viewers is reinforced by the zoetrope's content, which shows human figures dancing, drinking tea (of course), and ascending a ladder through the clouds—a perfect symbol of individual and collective mobility.

One video documenting the fabrication of Sony's BRAVIA-Drome in London and its installation near Turin reveals the range of manual skills required for its operation. We see shots of a masked welder framed in a shower of sparks, time lapses of the zoetrope's huge base moved into place with heavy machinery, and workers unpacking each of its sixty-four mammoth frames. When the installation is complete, onlookers gather in amazement, and video footage captures a full camera rig moving toward the device on a dolly—a kind of "making-of" mise en abyme.[32] These manual and material feats carried over to other Sony Bravia ads, including its Color Like No Other campaign, which featured equivalent labor-intensive stunts. In one long-form commercial, London agency Fallon arranged to drop a glorious rainbow of 250,000 bouncy balls down a steep San Francisco street. Accounts of preproduction and the shoot, which yielded about seven hours' worth of video footage, speak to the playful qualities of the process. The bouncy balls were procured from amusement vendors rather than directly from manufacturers, and director Nicolai Fuglsig joked that the playful commercial caused a market shortage—they had taken all the bouncy balls for themselves. The balls were fired from cannons, and crew members ducked under gear borrowed from San Francisco's riot police for safety.[33] In another Bravia ad, seventeen hundred paint bombs were arranged in an abandoned Glasgow apartment complex and detonated—producing an explosive rainbow visible from a distance. Another featured a series of two hundred plasticine rabbits occupying Manhattan streets, animated through stop-motion techniques. Rather than leveraging technology to produce digital swarms of hopping rabbits or bouncing balls, the complex logistics of actually setting real bouncy balls loose in the streets garners more capital as an authentic (and audacious) endeavor.

These examples demonstrate how paratexts "create scripts of value" surrounding the works to which they refer. There is a domino effect in these representational layers. Not only do behind-the-scenes features reveal the inner workings of the zoetropic device, but the 3D zoetrope itself—as an advertisement—lends a particularly affective weight to a broader brand or corporate identity. Jonathan Gray argues that "author, aura, and artistry—all qualities often said to be lacking in the age of big-budget blockbusters and for-profit art—are hailed and awarded to texts by their paratexts."[34] These layers of value are of clear benefit to the kinds of global corporations that commission zoetropes. The "awe-inspiring" collaboration behind the Fuze Tea zoetrope's production humanizes a Coca-Cola product, a brand that commonly epitomizes cultural imperialism. The decision to use traditional stop-motion animation techniques and a century-old optical toy to showcase Sony Bravia's MotionFlow technology (and the decision to erect the BRAVIA-Drome in a historic plaza) suggests the emotional charges garnered from appealing to the worlds of toys and play and from pairing old technologies with new. Gray argues that paratexts can be especially powerful in positioning the work of commercial entities as sharing philanthropic interests.[35] This is the case with the Stella Artois zoetrope, in which each "frame" is a single glass chalice (an icon of the brand) with an image painted onto it. The empty glasses were mounted on a spinning rack, their transparency stark against the room's white backdrop. This establishes a visual contrast with the African women in the animation, depicted in traditional clothing gathering water, in market scenes, with a blackboard and books (hallmarks of humanitarianism), and dancing with one another. At the end of the animation sequence, the women's raised hands morph into the Stella Artois logo. The video was a promotion for Stella's "Buy a Lady a Drink" campaign—a partnership with water.org to supply those in the developing world with clean water.[36]

The rationale of these 3D zoetropes within the context of advertising is clear. These objects bundle together a network of values such as playfulness, authenticity, and historical continuity in the form of connecting old and new media technologies. The behind-the-scenes materials accompanying these promotions circulate according to the same viral logics. They amplify these bundled values and additionally represent a professional world characterized by inclusivity, experimentation, problem solving, and play. Making-of materials are not expressly aimed at young people, but as they circulate online, these young audiences, their parents, and their educators undoubtedly see them. The commercials associated with them raise the question, "How did they do that?" The discourses circulating around contemporary zoetropes are thus not explicitly vocationally oriented, nor do they directly specify career paths in visual effects production or advertising. However, in presenting dynamic professional environments, these materials affirm that there's more than play to optical toys (or, conversely, that optical play can become one's livelihood—that the right kind of childhood curiosity and experimentation can turn into a career).

A wordless promotional video for another Coca-Cola commission, this one installed at the Dutch theme park Efteling, shows an artist making a digital sketch with a fanciful quill-themed stylus. Another sketches on traditional paper, juxtaposed with screenshots of specialized software where animated characters' armature systems and motion paths are carefully edited. The zoetrope's tiers are assembled and the apparatus is carefully moved and installed, with close-ups showing hands lovingly adjusting each detail.[37] By documenting process, the video (and countless others like it) also documents a range of professional possibilities running the full gamut of the STEAM fields. From the intern conscripted to sweep up bouncy balls or the welder connecting the joints of a massive zoetrope frame, to the 3D modeling whiz, the storyboard artist, and the director presumed to be at the creative helm, these campaigns pull together human labor with a range of skill sets. As these zoetropes make the moving image tactile, they thus also ground an aspirational orientation, celebrating individual ingenuity and creativity alongside teamwork and collaboration. These are the same problem-solving and out-of-the box critical thinking skills that STEAM initiatives for children aim to cultivate.

Old Media, New Media

This enormous range of contemporary zoetropes connected to billion-dollar industries would make it easy to proclaim that optical toys are not *just* child's play. However, it is precisely the contention of this book that the complex (and contested) designs over child's play—the hopes and fears that such play practices produce and reflect—are inseparably bound to broader media and technology cultures. Large-scale 3D zoetropes address anxieties of the digital image's ephemerality and substantiate the image of a healthy industry populated by laborers equipped with a range of STEAM skills. In so doing, they sustain a subject position that in many ways resembles the nineteenth-century viewer who originally played with optical toys. These two spectatorial subject positions share an outlook characterized by faith that the class-based meritocracies of rational recreation and STEAM education, respectively, are key developmental contexts for children faced with navigating complex social dynamics and the looming specter of economic insecurity. The knot of practices and literacies broadly collected under the rubric of optical discernment has given way to the related banner cry for children to be "makers," not just "consumers." As media forms combining visual and tactile engagement, optical toys remain central in this new formulation.

This project outlines a culture of children's media spectatorship that developed during the nineteenth century and in many ways has established the terms in which children's engagement with visual media is imagined and discussed today. Shifts in the perception of Western childhood in the nineteenth century occurred concurrently with the birth and growth of a range of optical technologies. These two intertwining developments shaped one another and the prevailing currents of thought variously charging that mass culture "bred passivity" or, conversely, that it helped cultivate discerning publics.[38] Optical toys circulated as parlor novelties and elements of rational recreation, popularizing a broad set of visual practices that today might be regarded as forms of media literacy. Some of these devices, like the stereoscope and color mixer, found formal application as educational apparatuses. New media formats, such as the chromolithographed movable toy book, helped bridge and extend patterns of spectatorship and narrative engagement at a time when moving-image technologies were in flux and in the process of institutionalization. Such formats were met with both celebratory and critical responses, which began to articulate a now centuries-old link between the figure of the child and the polarized discourses of media technology that continue to structure the public imagination.

Despite the wide pendulum swings of optimism and concern, optical toys—like any other media—do not unilaterally produce in their users the kind of spectatorial positions intended. In form, content, and context, each contains multiple contending potentials that are as multivalent and dynamic as the children who play with them. This project's wider applicability, then, is to model the forms of material and discursive analysis crucial to understanding how media technologies "work" and to assert the importance of understanding this before proclaiming judgment or approval. Contemporary children's toys and media might be regarded with the same kind of care. Despite the user's ability to resist, negotiate, or challenge the visual logics that such toys sought to impart, there is significant value in articulating the characteristics and parameters of this ideal subject position, which maintains a distinct class orientation and commonly inflects assumptions about gender and race. The viewing subject produced by optical media is largely constituted according to the perceived needs and sensibilities of the white middle-class child.

Ultimately, by extending and rereading theories of optical toys, this project has enabled the exploration of a range of domestic and institutional

Conclusion 225

contexts, and has opened up a broader consideration of what constitutes the categories both of precinema and children's media. Optical toys and related visual media initiated children into a visual culture marked by increasing velocity, the focalization of attention, and the need to possess and execute a variety of perceptual competencies. In this respect, this study revises and contributes to existing scholarship on nineteenth-century visual media. It does so first by insisting that there are additional things to see and say about these objects, and second by implicating them in a discussion of children's media and asserting that certain modalities related to their use have persisted well past the era of their initial invention into the present day.

Figure 7.3

Optical toys continue to emerge in the unlikeliest forms. Artists and amateurs create zoetropic imagery in embroidery, from hollowed-out pumpkins, and on the surfaces of pizzas.[39] Three-dimensional printing hubs such as thingiverse.com and shapeways.com feature numerous designs of zoetropes and related components for members of craft communities to replicate and remix at their leisure. One spring, licensed Power Rangers praxinoscopes were handed over the counter of countless McDonald's restaurants. While eating Froot Loops one morning, I noticed a thaumatrope printed on the cereal box (figure 7.3). The template is labeled "Frooty Fun Binoculars" and is thematized as Toucan Sam holding a pair of binoculars with exaggerated, large lenses. Each lens is an incomplete image. Youngsters are instructed to cut out the two circles, "tape or glue the disks back-to-back" with a string in the middle (color-coded lines facilitate proper alignment), and "watch as the two images appear as one!" Often labeled as "spinners," "binoculars," or other names, these trivial instantiations are difficult to find and track, but anyone looking—as I have learned—will see them everywhere. Nearly two hundred years after most of these toys were introduced, they persist as childhood ephemera. Today, the toys and their lengthy perceptual legacies are woven into everyday life.

Notes

Introduction: The Ludic Archive

1. David Bordwell and Kristin Thompson, *Film Art: An Introduction*, 8th ed. (New York: McGraw-Hill, 2008), 10; David Bordwell and Kristin Thompson, *Film History: An Introduction*, 7th ed. (New York: McGraw-Hill, 2003), 15.

2. Subsequent accounts have challenged the persistence of vision as a model, introducing phenomena such as flicker fusion, apparent motion, and phi phenomenon. See Bordwell and Thompson, *Film Art*, 10; Joseph Anderson and Barbara Anderson, "The Myth of Persistence of Vision Revisited," *Journal of Film and Video* 45, no. 1 (1993): 3–12.

3. Barbara Maria Stafford, *Artful Science: Enlightenment Entertainment and the Eclipse of Visual Education* (Cambridge, MA: MIT Press, 1996).

4. Vanessa Schwartz and Jeannene Przyblyski characterize "modernity" as "a set of political, economic, social, and cultural attributes that include such things as nationalism, democracy, imperialism, consumerism, and capitalism—all of which appear associated with the nineteenth century by virtue of their radical expansion during that period." Vanessa R. Schwartz and Jeannene M. Przyblyski, "Visual Culture's History: Twenty-First Century Interdisciplinarity and Its Nineteenth-Century Objects," in *The Nineteenth-Century Visual Culture Reader*, ed. Jeannene M. Przyblyski and Vanessa R. Schwartz (New York: Routledge, 2004), 3–14, 9.

5. Anna Mae Duane, ed., *The Children's Table: Childhood Studies and the Humanities* (Athens: University of Georgia Press, 2013), 11.

6. Erkki Huhtamo and Jussi Parikka, eds., *Media Archaeology: Approaches, Applications, and Implications* (Berkeley: University of California Press, 2011), 3.

7. Thomas Elsaesser, *Film History as Media Archaeology: Tracking Digital Cinema* (Amsterdam: Amsterdam University Press, 2016), 25.

8. Elsaesser, *Film History as Media Archaeology*, 23.

9. Tom Gunning, "The Whole Town's Gawking: Early Cinema and the Visual Experience of Modernity," *The Yale Journal of Criticism* 7, no. 2 (1994): 189–201, 189.

10. Karen Sánchez-Eppler, "In the Archives of Childhood," in *The Children's Table: Childhood Studies and the Humanities*, ed. Anna Mae Duane (Athens: University of Georgia Press, 2013), 213–237, 215; Elsaesser, *Film History as Media Archaeology*, 34–35.

11. Robin Bernstein, "Dances with Things: Material Culture and the Performance of Race," *Social Text* 27, no. 4 (Winter 2009): 67–94, 90.

12. London and New York: E. P. Dutton and Griffith & Farran, 1884.

13. For examples of this discourse, see Lindsay Daugherty, "Step Aside, 'Screen Time,'" *US News & World Report*, November 17, 2015, https://www.usnews.com/opinion/knowledge-bank/2015/11/17/quality-screen-time-serves-educational-purposes-for-young-kids; Beth Holland, "How Much Screen Time? That's the Wrong Question," *Edutopia*, January 30, 2017, https://www.edutopia.org/article/reframing-debate-screen-time-beth-holland; and Nicholas Kardaras, "Screens in Schools Are a $60 Billion Hoax," *Time*, August 31, 2016, http://time.com/4474496/screens-schools-hoax/.

14. T. William Erle, *Children's Toys, and Some Elementary Lessons in General Knowledge Which They Teach* (London: C. Kegan Paul, 1877), 3–4.

15. Erle, *Children's Toys*, 3.

16. Maria Edgeworth and Richard Lovell Edgeworth, *Practical Education*, vol. 1 (New York: G. F. Hopkins, 1801), 36–56.

17. Lisa Jacobson. *Raising Consumers: Children and the American Mass Market in the Early Twentieth Century* (New York: Columbia University Press, 2005), 8.

18. Henry Jenkins, "Introduction: Childhood Innocence and Other Modern Myths," in *The Children's Culture Reader*, ed. Henry Jenkins (New York: NYU Press, 1998), 1–40.

19. Teresa Michals, "Experiments before Breakfast: Toys, Education and Middle-Class Childhood," in *The Nineteenth-Century Child and Consumer Culture*, 2nd ed., ed. Dennis Denisoff (New York: Routledge, 2016), 32.

20. Marsha Kinder, "Kids' Media Culture: An Introduction," in *Kids' Media Culture*, ed. Marsha Kinder (Durham, NC: Duke University Press, 1999), 1–30; David Buckingham, *The Material Child: Growing Up in Consumer Culture* (London: Polity Press, 2011).

21. See, for instance, Hugo Münsterberg, "Peril to Childhood in the Movies," in *Münsterberg on Film: The Photoplay: A Psychological Study and Other Writings*, ed. Allan Langdale (New York: Routledge, 2002), 191–200; periodicals such as the *Educational*

Screen; Lynn Spigel, "Seducing the Innocent: Childhood and Television in Postwar America," in *The Children's Culture Reader*, ed. Henry Jenkins (New York: NYU Press, 1998), 110–135.

22. See, for example, Jackie Marsh, "Childhood in the Digital Age," in *An Introduction to Early Childhood Studies*, ed. Trisha Maynard and Sacha Powell (London: Sage, 2013), 60–72, 62.

23. See, for instance, Marleena Mustola, Merja Koivula, Leena Turja, and Marja-Leena Laakso, "Reconsidering Passivity and Activity in Children's Digital Play," *New Media and Society*, August 4, 2016, 1–18; Mizuko Ito, Sonja Baumer, Matteo Bittanti, danah boyd, Rachel Cody, Becky Herr Stephenson, Heather A. Horst, et al. *Hanging Out, Messing Around, and Geeking Out: Kids Living and Learning with New Media* (Cambridge, MA: MIT Press, 2009).

24. Allison James, "Giving Voice to Children's Voices: Practices and Problems, Pitfalls and Potentials," *American Anthropologist* 109, no. 2 (2007): 261–272; 262, 264–266.

25. Meryl Alper, Vikki S. Katz, and Lynn Schofield Clark, "Researching Children, Intersectionality, and Diversity in the Digital Age," *Journal of Children and Media* 10, no. 1 (2016): 107–114, 108.

26. Alper, Katz, and Clark, 109.

27. Erle, *Children's Toys*.

28. Erle, *Children's Toys*.

29. Ellen Wartella and Michael Robb, "Historical and Recurring Concerns about Children's Use of the Mass Media," in *The Handbook of Children, Media, and Development*, ed. Sandra L. Calvert and Barbara J. Wilson (West Sussex, UK: Wiley Blackwell, 2008), 7–25; Yariv Tsfati, "Media Effects—Communication," *Oxford Bibliographies*, October 27, 2017, http://www.oxfordbibliographies.com/view/document/obo-9780199756841/obo-9780199756841-0081.xml.

30. Erle, *Children's Toys*, 39.

31. AAP Council on Communications and Media, "Media and Young Minds," *Pediatrics* 138, no. 5 (2016).

32. Examples of this contradiction can be seen in the photographs of Lewis Hine, who powerfully juxtaposed the work of laboring children to produce Campbell Kids dolls with the play of privileged children who owned those dolls. Hine's insensitivity to race regarding black and white children picking cotton is explicated in Robin Bernstein, *Racial Innocence: Performing American Childhood from Slavery to Civil Rights* (New York: NYU Press, 2011).

33. Nicholas Mirzoeff, "The Right to Look," *Critical Inquiry* 37, no. 3 (2011): 473–496, 473.

34. Mirzoeff, "The Right to Look," 474.

35. Mirzoeff, "The Right to Look," 480–484.

36. Schwartz and Przyblyski, "Visual Culture's History," 9, and "Introduction to Part Seven," 287–289, 287.

37. Radiclani Clytus, "'Keep It before the People': The Pictorialization of American Abolitionism," in *Early African American Print Culture*, ed. Lara Langer Cohen and Jordan Alexander Stein (Philadelphia: University of Pennsylvania Press, 2012), 291–317, 297–298.

38. Clytus, "'Keep It before the People," 291–293.

39. Erica Ball, *To Live an Antislavery Life: Personal Politics and the Antebellum Black Middle Class* (Athens: University of Georgia Press, 2012), 7, 2–6.

40. Patricia Crain, *Reading Children: Literacy, Property, and the Dilemmas of Childhood in Nineteenth-Century America* (Philadelphia: University of Pennsylvania Press, 2016), 6.

41. Crain, *Reading Children*, 10.

42. Karen Halttunen, *Confidence Men and Painted Women: A Study of Middle-Class Culture in America, 1830–1870* (New Haven, CT: Yale University Press, 1982).

43. James Cook, *The Arts of Deception: Playing with Fraud in the Age of Barnum* (Cambridge, MA: Harvard University Press, 2001), 1–29.

44. Melanie Dawson, *Laboring to Play: Home Entertainment and the Spectacle of Middle-Class Cultural Life, 1850–1920* (Tuscaloosa: University of Alabama Press, 2005).

45. Wendy Bellion, *Citizen Spectator: Art, Illusion, and Visual Perception in Early National America* (Chapel Hill: UNC Press Books, 2011), 5.

46. Karen Sánchez-Eppler, *Dependent States: The Child's Part in Nineteenth-Century American Culture* (Chicago: University of Chicago Press, 2005), xviii.

47. Thomas Elsaesser, "Discipline through Diegesis: The Rube Film between 'Attractions' and 'Narrative Integration,'" in *The Cinema of Attractions Reloaded*, ed. Wanda Strauven (Amsterdam: Amsterdam University Press, 2006), 205–223, 213. See also Wanda Strauven, "Early Cinema's Touch(able) Screens: From *Uncle Josh* to *Ali Barbouyou*," *NECSUS: European Journal of Media Studies* (Autumn 2012), http://www.necsus-ejms.org/early-cinemas-touchable-screens-from-uncle-josh-to-ali-barbouyou/.

48. See Neil Arnott, *Elements of Physics, or Natural Philosophy* (London: Longman, Rees, Orme, Brown, and Green, 1829), 280, referenced in Erkki Huhtamo, "Toward a History of Peep Practice," in *A Companion to Early Cinema*, ed. Nicolas Dulac, André Gaudreault, and Santiago Hidalgo, 32–51 (Hoboken, NJ: Wiley Blackwell, 2012), 41.

49. Eric L. Tribunella "Children's Literature and the Child Flâneur," *Children's Literature* 38, no. 1 (2010): 67–68.

50. Thad Logan, *The Victorian Parlour: A Cultural Study* (Cambridge: Cambridge University Press, 2001).

51. See, for example, Charles Acland, ed., *Residual Media* (Minneapolis: University of Minnesota Press, 2007); Lisa Gitelman, *Always Already New: Media, History and the Data of Culture* (Cambridge, MA: MIT Press, 2008).

52. See, for example, Tom Gunning, "The Cinema of Attractions: Early Film, Its Spectator, and the Avant-Garde," *Wide Angle* 8, no. 3–4 (1986): 63–70; Charles Musser, *The Emergence of Cinema: The American Screen to 1907*, vol. 1 (Berkeley: University of California Press, 1994).

53. Donald Crafton, "The Veiled Genealogies of Animation and Cinema," *Animation* 6, no. 2 (2011): 93–110, 97.

54. Allison James and Alan Prout, "A New Paradigm for the Sociology of Childhood? Provenance, Promise and Problems," in *Constructing and Reconstructing Childhood: Contemporary Issues in the Sociological Study of Childhood*, ed. Allison James and Alan Prout (London: Falmer Press, 1997), 10–14; Jens Qvortrup, *Childhood Matters: Social Theory, Practice and Politics* (Beatty, NV: Avebury, 1994), 4.

55. Jonathan Crary, *Techniques of the Observer: On Vision and Modernity in the Nineteenth Century* (Cambridge, MA: MIT Press, 1992), 20.

56. Crary, *Techniques of the Observer*, 6.

57. Miriam Bratu Hansen, "Room-for-Play: Benjamin's Gamble with Cinema," *October* 109 (2004): 3–45.

58. Wolfgang Schivelbusch, *The Railway Journey: The Industrialization of Time and Space in the Nineteenth Century*, 3rd ed. (Berkeley: University of California Press, 2014); Stephen Kern, *The Culture of Time and Space: 1880–1918* (Cambridge, MA: Harvard University Press, 1983).

59. Wanda Strauven, "The Observer's Dilemma: To Touch or Not to Touch," in *Media Archaeology: Approaches, Applications, and Implications*, ed. Erkki Huhtamo and Jussi Parikka (Berkeley: University of California Press, 2011), 148–163, 150, 154.

60. André Gaudreault and Nicolas Dulac, "Circularity and Repetition at the Heart of the Attraction: Optical Toys and the Emergence of a New Cultural Series," in *Cinema of Attractions Reloaded*, ed. Wanda Strauven (Amsterdam: Amsterdam University Press, 2006), 227–244.

61. Marit Grøtta, *Baudelaire's Media Aesthetics: The Gaze of the Flâneur and 19th-Century Media* (New York: Bloomsbury, 2016), 14, 86.

62. Karen E. Wohlwend, "One Screen, Many Fingers: Young Children's Collaborative Literacy Play with Digital Puppetry Apps and Touchscreen Technologies," *Theory into Practice* 54, no. 2 (2015): 154–162, 157.

63. Elsaesser, *Film History as Media Archaeology*, 34.

64. Ian Christie, "Toys, Instruments, Machines: Why the Hardware Matters," in *Multimedia Histories: From the Magic Lantern to the Internet*, ed. James Lyons and John Plunkett (Chicago: University of Chicago Press, 2006), 3–17.

65. Elizabeth Stinson, "These Incredible Animated GIFs Are More Than 150 Years Old," *Wired*, December 11, 2013, https://www.wired.com/2013/12/these-150-year-old-gifs-are-insane/.

66. Robin Bernstein, *Racial Innocence: Performing American Childhood from Slavery to Civil Rights* (New York: NYU Press, 2011), 8.

67. Hansen, "Room-for-Play," 3–45, 6.

68. In this way, they are not simply material objects but "dispositifs," comprising material and discursive components. For work in this line, see Giorgio Agamben, *What Is an Apparatus? And Other Essays*, trans. David Kishik and Stefan Pedatella (Stanford: Stanford University Press, 2009), 2–3; François Albera and Maria Tortajada, eds., *Cinema beyond Film: Media Epistemology in the Modern Era* (Amsterdam: Amsterdam University Press, 2010), 11–12; Huhtamo and Parikka, *Media Archaeology*, 3.

69. Jutta Schickore, "Misperception, Illusion and Epistemological Optimism: Vision Studies in Early Nineteenth-Century Britain and Germany," *British Journal for the History of Science* 39, no. 3 (2006): 383–405.

70. Lorraine Daston and Peter Galison, *Objectivity* (Brooklyn: Zone Books, 2010).

71. This phrase comes from Deborah J. Coon, "Standardizing the Subject: Experimental Psychologists, Introspection, and the Quest for a Technoscientific Ideal," *Technology and Culture* 34, no. 4 (1993): 757–783.

72. Cindy Aron, "Evolution of the Middle Class," in *A Companion to 19th Century America*, ed. William L. Barney (Malden, MA; Oxford: Blackwell, 2001), 181.

73. Sánchez-Eppler, *Dependent States*, 151.

74. Sánchez-Eppler, 152.

75. See, for instance, Marc Prensky, "Digital Natives, Digital Immigrants Part 1," *On the Horizon* 9, no. 5 (2001): 1–6; Sue Bennett, Karl Maton, and Lisa Kervin, "The 'Digital Natives' Debate: A Critical Review of the Evidence," *British Journal of Educational Technology* 39, no. 5 (2008): 775–786, 778–779.

76. Tereza Spiloti, "Digital Discourses: A Critical Perspective," in *The Routledge Handbook of Language and Digital Communication*, ed. Alexandra Georgakopoulou and Tereza Spiloti (New York: Routledge, 2015), 133–148, 142.

Chapter 1: Templates, Toys, and Text

1. John Scoffern, "Optical Toy Sport," *Boy's Own Paper*, December 17, 1881, 190; "Optical Toy Sports Part II," *Boy's Own Paper*, December 31, 1881, 228–229.

2. Scoffern, "Optical Toy Sport," 190.

3. Jules David Prown, "Mind in Matter: An Introduction to Material Culture Theory and Method," *Winterthur Portfolio* 17, no. 1 (1982): 1–19, 6.

4. Robin Bernstein, *Racial Innocence: Performing American Childhood from Slavery to Civil Rights* (New York: NYU Press, 2011), 13.

5. John Scoffern, "Optical Toy Sport," 190.

6. Kirsten Drotner, *English Children and Their Magazines, 1751–1945* (New Haven, CT: Yale University Press, 1988), 115.

7. Cindy Aron, "Evolution of the Middle Class" in *A Companion to 19th Century America*, ed. William L. Barney (Malden, MA; Oxford: Blackwell, 2001), 178–194, 181. Also see Stuart M. Blumin, *The Emergence of the Middle Class: Social Experience in the American City, 1760–1900* (Cambridge: Cambridge University Press, 1989).

8. Viviana A. Rotman Zelizer, *Pricing the Priceless Child: The Changing Social Value of Children* (Princeton: Princeton University Press, 1985); Karen Sánchez-Eppler, *Dependent States: The Child's Part in Nineteenth-Century American Culture* (Chicago: University of Chicago Press, 2005), xviii.

9. Promotional examples include thaumatropes advertising Biscuits-Germain and Clark's Spool Cotton.

10. Richard Balzer, *Peepshows: A Visual History* (New York: Abrams, 1998), 42.

11. Laurent Mannoni, *The Great Art of Light and Shadow: Archaeology of the Cinema*, trans. Richard Crangle (Exeter: University of Exeter Press, 2000), 83.

12. Deac Rossell, *Laterna Magica—Magic Lantern* (Stuttgart: Füsslin, 2008), 1:106.

13. Mike Simkin, "The Magic Lantern and the Child," in *Realms of Light: Uses and Perceptions of the Magic Lantern from the 17th to the 21st Century*, ed. Richard Crangle, Mervyn Heard, and Ine Van Dooren (Ripon, UK: Magic Lantern Society of Great Britain, 2005), 25–33, 31–33.

14. Laurent Mannoni, "The Tomb of Robertson," in *Magic Images: The Art of Hand-Painted and Photographic Lantern Slides*, ed. Dennis Crompton, David Henry, and Stephen Herbert, trans. David Robinson (Exeter: Magic Lantern Society of Great Britain, 1990), 32–33; Mannoni, *The Great Art of Light and Shadow*, 150–151.

15. Gary Cross, *The Cute and the Cool: Wondrous Innocence and Modern American Children's Culture* (Oxford: Oxford University Press), 2004.

16. Jennifer F. Eisenhauer, "Next Slide Please: The Magical, Scientific, and Corporate Discourses of Visual Projection Technologies," *Studies in Art Education* 47, no. 3 (2006): 198–214.

17. "Ri Timeline," accessed July 15, 2017, http://www.rigb.org/our-history/timeline-of-the-ri.

18. Frank A. J. L. James, "'Never Talk about Science, Show It to Them': The Lecture Theatre of the Royal Institution," *Interdisciplinary Science Reviews* 27, no. 3 (2002): 225–229.

19. Mannoni, *The Great Art of Light and Shadow*, 207.

20. Richard J. Leskosky, "Phenakiscope [sic]: 19th Century Science Turned to Animation," *Film History* 5, no. 2 (1993): 176–189, 178.

21. "A 'Wallis's Wheel of Wonders Exhibiting the Most Amusing Optical Illusions' Phenakistoscope, With," The Saleroom, accessed May 15, 2019, https://www.the-saleroom.com/en-gb/auction-catalogues/special-auction-services/catalogue-id-srspe10161/lot-b4f053cd-2ad7-4fd0-8ba3-a62c00b896a1.

22. Joseph Plateau and Rudolf Ackermann, *Fantascope* (London, 1833), Cotsen Children's Library, Department of Rare Books and Special Collections, Princeton University Library.

23. Chris Lane, "Ackerman's Repository of Arts," *Antique Prints* (blog), January 12, 2010, http://antiqueprintsblog.blogspot.com/2010/01/ackermans-repository-of-arts.html.

24. Mannoni, *The Great Art of Light and Shadow*, 219–220.

25. "Advertisement, Ackermann and Co," in *The Literary Gazette; and Journal of Belles Lettres, Arts, Sciences, Etc. for the Year 1833*, vol. 874 (London: Literary Gazette, 1833), 672.

26. *Evening Telegraph* (Philadelphia, PA), December 23, 1867, http://chroniclingamerica.loc.gov/lccn/sn83025925/1867-12-23/ed-1/seq-6/.

27. Mannoni, *The Great Art of Light and Shadow*, 218.

28. *Daily (Columbus) Ohio Statesman*, December 17, 1866, http://chroniclingamerica.loc.gov/lccn/sn84028645/1866-12-17/ed-1/seq-2/; Machiko Kusahara, "The 'Baby Talkie,' Domestic Media, and the Japanese Modern," in *Media Archaeology: Approaches, Applications, and Implications*, ed. Erkki Huhtamo and Jussi Parikka (Berkeley: University of California Press, 2011), 123–147, 142.

29. Stephen Herbert, "Wheel of Life Zoetrope," accessed July 15, 2017, http://www.stephenherbert.co.uk/wheelContents.htm.

30. See also Margaret Hofer, *The Games We Played: The Golden Age of Board and Table Games* (Princeton: Princeton Architectural Press, 2003).

31. *Burlington (VT) Weekly Free Press*, January 3, 1868, http://chroniclingamerica.loc.gov/lccn/sn86072143/1868-01-03/ed-1/seq-4/; *Kansas City (MO) Journal*, December 8, 1898, http://chroniclingamerica.loc.gov/lccn/sn86063615/1898-12-08/ed-1/seq-12/; *Record-Union* (Sacramento, CA), December 14, 1895, http://chroniclingamerica.loc.gov/lccn/sn82015104/1895-12-14/ed-1/seq-3/; *Saint Paul(MN) Globe*, December 1, 1901, http://chroniclingamerica.loc.gov/lccn/sn90059523/1901-12-01/ed-1/seq-14/; *Wheeling (WV) Daily Intelligencer*, December 25, 1868, http://chroniclingamerica.loc.gov/lccn/sn84026844/1868-12-25/ed-1/seq-4/, and December 13, 1900, http://chroniclingamerica.loc.gov/lccn/sn84026844/1900-12-13/ed-1/seq-8/.

32. *Regular New York Trade Sale of Books, Stereotype Plates, and Stationery* (New York: J. E. Cooley, 1865), as "phenikisticscope."

33. *Topeka (KS) State Journal*, December 20, 1900, http://chroniclingamerica.loc.gov/lccn/sn82016014/1900-12-20/ed-1/seq-8/.

34. *Neal's Penny Games: Shadows, Models, Dissected Puzzles &c: Wheel of Life*, ca. 1860s, Graphic Arts Collection, Department of Rare Books and Special Collections, Princeton University Library.

35. Edwin A. Perry, *The Boston Herald and Its History: How, When and Where It Was Founded. Its Early Struggles and Hard-Won Successes* … (Boston, 1878), 59–60.

36. Peter Bailey, *Leisure and Class in Victorian England: Rational Recreation and the Contest for Control, 1830–1885* (New York: Routledge, 2014), 4.

37. Hugh Cunningham, *Leisure in the Industrial Revolution: c. 1780–c. 1880* (New York: Routledge, 2016), 90.

38. John Henry Anderson, *The Fashionable Science of Parlour Magic*, 108th ed. (London: R. S. Francis, 1855), iv.

39. Joakim Landahl, "The Eye of Power(-Lessness): On the Emergence of the Panoptical and Synoptical Classroom," *History of Education* 42, no. 6 (2013): 803–821, 810.

40. Barbara Beatty, *Preschool Education in America: The Culture of Young Children from the Colonial Era to the Present* (New Haven, CT: Yale University Press, 1997), 6–9.

41. Barbara Maria Stafford, *Artful Science: Enlightenment Entertainment and the Eclipse of Visual Education* (Cambridge, MA: MIT Press, 1994), 58.

42. Wendy Bellion, *Citizen Spectator: Art, Illusion, and Visual Perception in Early National America* (Durham, NC: UNC Press Books, 2011), 33.

43. Jordan Bear, *Disillusioned: Victorian Photography and the Discerning Subject* (University Park: Pennsylvania State University Press, 2016), 2.

44. John Locke, *Some Thoughts Concerning Education: By John Locke, Esq* (London: J. and R. Tonson, 1779), 221.

45. Locke, *Some Thoughts Concerning Education*, 223.

46. Anderson, *The Fashionable Science of Parlour Magic*, 1855, iii.

47. Paul B. Ringel, *Commercializing Childhood: Children's Magazines, Urban Gentility, and the Ideal of the American Child, 1823–1918* (Amherst: University of Massachusetts Press, 2015), 7.

48. Noah W. Sobe, "Concentration and Civilisation: Producing the Attentive Child in the Age of Enlightenment," *Paedagogica Historica* 46, no. 1–2 (2010): 149–160, 157.

49. Maria Edgeworth and Richard Lovell Edgeworth, *Practical Education*, vol. 1 (New York: G. F. Hopkins, 1801), 2.

50. Edgeworth and Edgeworth, *Practical Education*, 5.

51. Edgeworth and Edgeworth, *Practical Education*, 3.

52. Melanie Dawson, *Laboring to Play: Home Entertainment and the Spectacle of Middle-Class Cultural Life, 1850–1920* (Tuscaloosa: University of Alabama Press, 2005), 11.

53. T. William Erle, *Children's Toys, and Some Elementary Lessons in General Knowledge Which They Teach* (London: C. Kegan Paul, 1877), 6.

54. John Ayrton Paris, *Philosophy in Sport Made Science in Earnest: Being an Attempt to Implant in the Young Mind the First Principles of Natural Philosophy by the Aid of the Popular Toys and Sports of Youth*, 5th ed. (London: John Murray, 1842), viii.

55. Teresa Michals, "Experiments before Breakfast: Toys, Education and Middle-Class Childhood," in *The Nineteenth-Century Child and Consumer Culture*, 2nd ed., ed. Dennis Denisoff (New York: Routledge, 2016), 29–42, 30.

56. David Buckingham, *The Material Child: Growing Up in Consumer Culture* (London: Polity Press, 2011).

57. Lawrence A. Cremin, *The Transformation of the School: Progressivism in American Education 1876–1957* (New York: Knopf, 1961), 13; Barbara Finkelstein and Kathy Vandell, "The Schooling of American Childhood: The Emergence of Learning Communities, 1820–1920," in *A Century of Childhood, 1820–1920* (Rochester, NY: Margaret Woodbury Strong Museum, 1984), 65–95, 80.

58. Johann N. Neem, *Democracy's Schools: The Rise of Public Education in America* (Baltimore: Johns Hopkins University Press, 2017), 162–163.

59. Neem, *Democracy's Schools*.

60. Valentina K. Tikoff, "A Role Model for African American Children: Abigail Field Mott's Life and Adventures of Olaudah Equiano and White Northern Abolitionism," in *Who Writes for Black Children? African American Children's Literature before 1900*,

ed. Katharine Capshaw and Anna Mae Duane (Minneapolis: University of Minnesota Press, 2017).

61. Carl F. Kaestle, "Introduction," in *School: The Story of American Public Education*, ed. Sarah Mondale and David Tyack (New York: Beacon Press, 2001), 11–17, 16.

62. Cremin, *The Transformation of the School*, ix.

63. Pierre Bourdieu, *The Logic of Practice*, trans. Richard Nice (Stanford: Stanford University Press, 1990), 60.

64. Caroline L. Smith, *Popular Pastimes for Field and Fireside; Or, Amusements for Young and Old* (Springfield, MA: Milton Bradley, 1867), 4.

65. *Parlour Magic: A Manual of Amusing Experiments, Transmutations, Sleights and Subtleties, Legerdemain, &c., for the Instruction and Amusement of Youth*, 4th ed. (London: W. Kent, 1858), preface.

66. Smith, *Popular Pastimes*, iv.

67. See, for instance, Stephen Kern, *The Culture of Time and Space: 1880–1918* (Cambridge, MA: Harvard University Press, 1983).

68. See, for instance, Nicholas Kardaras, *Glow Kids: How Screen Addiction Is Hijacking Our Kids—and How to Break the Trance* (New York: Macmillan, 2016); Martin L. Kutscher, *Digital Kids: How to Balance Screen Time, and Why It Matters* (London: Jessica Kingsley, 2016).

69. Ebenezer Landells, *The Boy's Own Toy-Maker: A Practical Illustrated Guide to the Useful Employment of Leisure Hours*, 3rd ed. (London: Griffith and Farran, 1860), vi.

70. Landells, *The Boy's Own Toy-Maker*, vi.

71. Marc Prensky, "Digital Natives, Digital Immigrants Part 1," *On the Horizon* 9, no. 5 (2001): 1–6, 4.

72. Alexander S. Galt, ed., *Cassell's Popular Science*, vol. 1, part 1 (London: Cassell and Company, 1904), xi.

73. Archibald Montgomery Low, *Popular Scientific Recreations, Tr. and Enlarged from "Les Récréations Scientifiques"* (London: Ward, Lock, and Co., 1949), 104–105.

74. A. Castillon, *Récréations Physique*, 7th ed. (Paris: Libraire Hachette, 1881), 300.

75. John Ayrton Paris, *Philosophy in Sport Made Science in Earnest: Being an Attempt to Implant in the Young Mind the First Principles of Natural Philosophy by the Aid of the Popular Toys and Sports of Youth*, 7th ed. (London: John Murray, 1853), 12–13.

76. Paris, *Philosophy in Sport Made Science in Earnest*, 381.

77. Paris, *Philosophy in Sport Made Science in Earnest*, 389–393.

78. Tom Gunning, for instance, suggests that the thaumatrope may have helped interest children in the classics: Tom Gunning, "Hand and Eye: Excavating a New Technology of the Image in the Victorian Era," *Victorian Studies* 54, no. 3 (2012): 495–516, 503.

79. Katharine Morrison McClinton, *Antiques of American Childhood* (New York: Bramhall House, 1970), 112.

80. Sánchez-Eppler, *Dependent States*, 29.

81. *The Boy's Treasury of Sports, Pastimes, and Recreations*, 2nd American ed. (Boston: John P. Hill, 1847), https://hdl.handle.net/2027/hvd.hn2ggl; Ebenezer Landells, *The Boy's Own Toy-Maker* (London: Griffith and Farran, ca. 1892), http://ufdc.ufl.edu/UF00081179/00001; *Nice Games for Little Parties* (London: Dean & Son, 1865), http://ufdc.ufl.edu/UF00005008/00001.

82. Drotner, *English Children and Their Magazines*, 73, 91.

83. *The Boy's Own Book: A Complete Encyclopedia of All Athletic, Scientific, Recreative, Outdoor and Indoor Exercises and Diversions*, 5th ed. (New York: Allen Brothers, 1869), prelude, n.p.

84. *Parlour Magic*, vii.

85. *Children's Toys, and Some Elementary Lessons in General Knowledge Which They Teach*, 2.

86. John Denison Champlin and Arthur E. Bostwick, *The Young Folks' Cyclopaedia of Games and Sports*. 2nd ed. (New York: Holt, 1899), iii; *Children's Toys*, 7.

87. Dawson, *Laboring to Play*, 9.

88. *The Boy's Own Book; A Complete Encyclopedia of All the Diversions, Athletic, Scientific, and Recreative, of Boyhood and Youth*, 1st American ed. (Boston: Monroe and Francis, 1829).

89. Robin Carver, *The Book of Sports* (Boston: Lily, Wait, Colman and Holden, 1834).

90. Champlin and Bostwick, *The Young Folk's Cyclopædia*.

91. See, for instance, Kate Flint, *The Victorians and the Visual Imagination* (Cambridge: Cambridge University Press, 2000).

92. Horace Mann and Felix Pécant, *Life and Works of Horace Mann* (Boston: Lee and Shepard, 1891), 2:56.

93. Mann and Pécant, *Life and Works of Horace Mann*, 2:59.

94. Mann and Pécant, *Life and Works of Horace Mann*, 2:57.

95. Uncle Charles, *The Little Boy's Own Book* (London: Henry Allman, 1850), 12–13.

96. Michals, "Experiments before Breakfast," 37.

Notes

Chapter 2: Language in Motion

1. Twelve Thaumotropes for the Flirtation Game, England, before 1900, Cotsen Children's Library, Department of Rare Books and Special Collections, Princeton University Library.

2. Tom Gunning, "Hand and Eye: Excavating a New Technology of the Image in the Victorian Era," *Victorian Studies* 54, no. 3 (2012): 495–516, 502.

3. Elizabeth White Nelson, *Market Sentiments: Middle-Class Market Culture in 19th-Century America* (Washington, DC: Smithsonian Institution Press, 2010), 179.

4. Nelson, *Market Sentiments*, 177.

5. Barbara Maria Stafford, *Artful Science: Enlightenment Entertainment and the Eclipse of Visual Education* (Cambridge, MA: MIT Press, 1994), xxii.

6. Karen Sánchez-Eppler, *Dependent States: The Child's Part in Nineteenth-Century American Culture* (Chicago: University of Chicago Press, 2005), 5.

7. Martin Quigley Jr., *Magic Shadows: The Story of the Origin of Motion Pictures* (Washington, DC: Georgetown University Press, 1948), 83.

8. See, for instance, Richard Leskosky, "Two-State Animation: The Thaumatrope and Its Spin-Offs," *Animation* 2, no. 1 (1993): 20–34, 22–23; John Barnes. *Dr. Paris's Thaumatrope or Wonder-Turner* (London: Projection Box, 1995), 11–14; Gunning "Hand and Eye," 498–499, Laurent Mannoni, *The Great Art of Light and Shadow: Archaeology of the Cinema*, trans. Richard Crangle (Exeter: University of Exeter Press, 2000), 205–207, among others.

9. Mannoni, *The Great Art of Light and Shadow*, 207.

10. Jonathan Crary, *Techniques of the Observer: On Vision and Modernity in the Nineteenth Century* (Cambridge, MA: MIT Press, 1992), 106, quoted in Gunning, "Hand and Eye," 499.

11. *The Magician's Own Book* (New York: Dick and Fitzgerald, 1857), 168.

12. Mary Mapes Dodge, "Holiday Whispers Concerning Games and Toys," *Riverside Magazine for Young People* 2, no. 13 (January 1868): 41.

13. "Literary Report," *New Monthly Magazine and Universal Register* Part III (London: Henry Colburn, 1825), 177.

14. Samuel Williams, *The Boy's Treasury of Sports, Pastimes, and Recreations* (London: D. Bouge, 1844), 368.

15. Gunning, "Hand and Eye," 506.

16. Stephen Herbert, "Paris' Thaumatrope," accessed July 20, 2017, http://stephenherbert.co.uk/ParisThauma.htm.

17. Barbara Finkelstein and Kathy Vandell, "The Schooling of American Childhood: The Emergence of Learning Communities, 1820–1920," in *A Century of Childhood, 1820–1920* (Rochester, NY: Margaret Woodbury Strong Museum, 1984), 65–95, 74.

18. Katharine Morrison McClinton, *Antiques of American Childhood* (New York: Bramhall House, 1970), 79.

19. Annette Joyce Patterson, Phillip Anton Cormack, and William Charles Green, "The Child, the Text and the Teacher: Reading Primers and Reading Instruction," *Paedagogica Historica* 48, no. 2 (2012): 185–196, 190.

20. Horace Mann and Felix Pécant, *Life and Works of Horace Mann* (Boston: Lee and Shepard, 1891), 2:524.

21. Josiah Freeman Bumstead, *Spelling and Thinking Combined, Or The Spelling-Book Made a Medium of Thought* (Boston: T. R. Marvin, 1845), 3.

22. "Spelling," *Common School Journal* 1, no. 23 (1839): 355.

23. McClinton, *Antiques of American Childhood*, 115, 120–122.

24. *Rebus, ABC* (New York: McLoughlin Brothers, 1875), n.p.

25. *Rebus, ABC*.

26. Tom Getton, "Not the Flâneur Again: Reading Magazines and Living the Metropolis around 1880," in *The Invisible Flâneuse? Gender, Public Space, and Visual Culture in Nineteenth-Century Paris*, ed. Aruna D'Souza and Tom McDonough (Manchester, UK: Manchester University Press, 2006), 94–112, 98.

27. Olive Cook, *Movement in Two Dimensions* (London: Hutchinson, 1963), facing 117, quoted in Herbert, "Paris' Thaumatrope," http://www.stephenherbert.co.uk/thaumatropeTEXT1.htm#ref43.

28. Gunning, "Hand and Eye," 499–500.

29. Lynda Nead, *The Haunted Gallery: Painting, Photography, Film C.1900* (New Haven, CT: Yale University Press, 2007), 30.

30. Herbert Spencer, *The Principles of Psychology* (London: Williams and Norgate, 1870), 1:169.

31. Crary, *Techniques of the Observer*, 69.

32. Melanie Dawson, *Laboring to Play: Home Entertainment and the Spectacle of Middle-Class Cultural Life, 1850–1920* (Tuscaloosa: University of Alabama Press, 2005), 27–28.

33. Nead, *The Haunted Gallery*, 30.

34. Sharrona Pearl, *About Faces: Physiognomy in Nineteenth-Century Britain* (Cambridge, MA: Harvard University Press, 2010), 26–27.

Notes

35. Linda Hannas, *The English Jigsaw Puzzle, 1760–1890: With a Descriptive Check-List of Puzzles in the Museums of Great Britain and the Author's Collection* (London: Wayland, 1972), 14.

36. Alvaro Aleman, "Paraliterary Immersion and the Puzzleform: An Essay in Social Restitution," *ImageTexT: Interdisciplinary Comics Studies* 2, no. 1 (2005), para. 15, http://www.english.ufl.edu/imagetext/archives/v2_1/aleman/.

37. Hannas, *The English Jigsaw Puzzle*, 75.

38. "Changeable Ladies and Gentlemen," *The Repository of Arts, Literature, Fashions, Manufactures, &c.* 7, no. 37 (1819), 62.

39. Lina Beard and Adelia Belle Beard, *The American Girl's Handy Book: How to Amuse Yourself and Others* (New York: Charles Scribner's Sons, 1898), 380–400, 397.

40. Rebus Puzzle, *Mother [Goose] in Hieroglyphics* (New York: Sherman and Co., 1855), 37, Cotsen Children's Library, Department of Rare Books and Special Collections, Princeton University Library.

41. "The Thaumatrope," *Cincinnati Literary Gazette*, June 11, 1825, 188.

42. Martina Lauster, *Sketches of the Nineteenth Century* (New York: Palgrave Macmillan, 2007), 13, 48.

43. Herbert, "Paris' Thaumatrope."

44. Cook, *Movement in Two Dimensions*, 122. See also Richard Balzer, "Dick Balzer's Website: Thaumatropes," accessed January 30, 2019, https://www.dickbalzer.com/Thaumatropes.602.0.html.

45. Katherine C. Grier, *Pets in America: A History* (Chapel Hill: University of North Carolina Press, 2006), 46.

46. Monica Flegel, *Conceptualizing Cruelty to Children in Nineteenth-Century England: Literature, Representation, and the NSPCC* (Farnham, UK: Ashgate, 2013), 43.

47. Grier, *Pets in America*, 226.

48. Mrs. Fenwick. *Lessons for Children*, new ed. (London: Baldwin and Cradock, 1828), 44.

49. Lydia Maria Child, *Flowers for Children* (New York: C. S. Francis and Co., 1854), 175–176.

50. Flegel, *Conceptualizing Cruelty to Children in Nineteenth-Century England*, 44–45; Susan J. Pearson. *The Rights of the Defenseless: Protecting Animals and Children in Gilded Age America* (Chicago: University of Chicago Press, 2011), 23.

51. "Le prisonnier" bird-and-cage thaumatrope, Thaumatrope Cards, France, c. 1850. Cotsen Children's Library, Department of Rare Books and Special Collections,

Princeton University Library. Leonida Valerio. *1200 Gioche de Scienza Dilettevole*, 5th ed. (Milan: Ulrico Hoepli, 1929), 214.

52. Pearson, *The Rights of the Defenseless*, 22.

53. Henry Jenkins, "Introduction: Childhood Innocence and Other Modern Myths," in *The Children's Culture Reader*, ed. Henry Jenkins (New York: NYU Press, 1998), 1–40, 1.

54. Robin Bernstein, "Dances with Things: Material Culture and the Performance of Race," *Social Text* 27, no. 4 (Winter 2009): 67–94, 71.

55. Robin Bernstein, *Racial Innocence: Performing American Childhood from Slavery to Civil Rights* (New York: NYU Press, 2011), 76.

56. Gary Cross, *Kids' Stuff: Toys and the Changing World of American Childhood* (Cambridge, MA: Harvard University Press, 2009), 98.

57. T. William Erle, *Children's Toys, and Some Elementary Lessons in General Knowledge Which They Teach* (London: C. Kegan Paul, 1877, 32.

58. McLoughlin Brothers, *Catalogue of McLoughlin Bros. Toy Books, Games, ABC Blocks, &c.* (New York: McLoughlin Brothers, 1882), https://www.americanantiquarian.org/mcloughlin/001129.pdf.

59. Barbara Rusch, "The Secret Life of Victorian Cards," *Ephemera Society of America*, February 13, 2013, http://www.ephemerasociety.org/blog/?p=244.

60. Linton Weeks, "When 'Flirtation Cards' Were All the Rage," *NPR*, July 31, 2015, http://www.npr.org/sections/npr-history-dept/2015/07/31/427707613/when-flirtation-cards-were-all-the-rage.

61. Karen Halttunen, *Confidence Men and Painted Women: A Study of Middle-Class Culture in America, 1830–1870* (New Haven, CT: Yale University Press, 1982), xv.

62. Nelson, *Market Sentiments*, 201.

63. Annabella Pollen, "'The Valentine Has Fallen upon Evil Days': Mocking Victorian Valentines and the Ambivalent Laughter of the Carnivalesque," *Early Popular Visual Culture* 12, no. 2 (2014): 127–173.

64. Nelson, *Market Sentiments*, 183.

65. Nelson, 208.

66. John Ayrton Paris, *Philosophy in Sport Made Science in Earnest* (London: Longman, Rees, Orme, Brown, and Green, 1827), 3:4–5.

67. Paris, *Philosophy in Sport Made Science in Earnest*, new ed. (London: Sherwood, Gilbert, and Piper, 1833), 343.

Chapter 3: Seeing Things

1. Annie van den Oever and Andreas Fickers, "Doing Experimental Media Archaeology: Epistemological and Methodological Reflections of Experiments with Historical Objects of Media Technologies," in *New Media Archaeologies*, ed. Mark Goodall and Ben Roberts (Amsterdam: Amsterdam University Press, 2019), 45–68, 62.

2. John Plunkett, "From Optical to Digital (and Back Again)," *19: Interdisciplinary Studies in the Long Nineteenth Century* 6 (2008), 1–4, http://www.19.bbk.ac.uk.

3. Kevin Crowley and Jodi Galco, "Everyday Activity and the Development of Scientific Thinking" in *Designing for Science: Implications from Everyday, Classroom, and Professional Settings*, ed. Kevin Crowley, Christian D. Schunn, and Takeshi Okada (London: Psychology Press, 2001), 349–368.

4. T. William Erle, *Children's Toys, and Some Elementary Lessons in General Knowledge Which They Teach* (London: C. Kegan Paul, 1877), 37.

5. Jordan Bear introduces an almost identical notion of "visual discernment" as a consummate characteristic of liberal subjectivity in the nineteenth century, arguing that this position was most centrally cultivated and refined through photography. Jordan Bear, *Disillusioned: Victorian Photography and the Discerning Subject* (University Park: Pennsylvania State University Press, 2016), 4.

6. Pamela Cole, "The Definitions of Persistence of Vision by Pamela Cole" (Fall 2001), http://www.pamcole.com/DOCS/POV.html.

7. Joseph Anderson and Barbara Anderson, "The Myth of Persistence of Vision Revisited," *Journal of Film and Video* 45, no. 1 (1993): 3–12, 3–4.

8. Jonathan Crary. *Techniques of the Observer: On Vision and Modernity in the Nineteenth Century* (Cambridge, MA: MIT Press, 1992).

9. Miriam Bratu Hansen, *Cinema and Experience: Siegfried Kracauer, Walter Benjamin, and Theodor W. Adorno* (Berkeley: University of California Press, 2012), 183. Although film was central to Benjamin in this project, the perceptual basis for the possibility for play and resistance suggests the concept's applicability to optical toys and the images they produced.

10. Robin Bernstein, *Racial Innocence: Performing American Childhood from Slavery to Civil Rights* (New York: NYU Press, 2011), 12.

11. Bear, *Disillusioned*, 3–4.

12. Erica Armstrong Dunbar, *A Fragile Freedom: African American Women and Emancipation in the Antebellum City* (New Haven, CT: Yale University Press, 2008), 121.

13. Katherine C. Grier, *Culture and Comfort: Parlor Making and Middle-Class Identity, 1850–1930* (Washington, DC: Smithsonian Books, 2010, 5.

14. For example, Kate Flint's *The Victorians and the Visual Imagination* (Cambridge: Cambridge University Press, 2000) explores the characterization of an invisible world of germ threats as one of the central anxieties produced by the widespread use of the microscope. Isobel Armstrong. *Victorian Glassworlds: Glass Culture and the Imagination 1830–1880* (Oxford: Oxford University Press, 2008), 254.

15. Nicholas Mirzoeff, "The Right to Look," *Critical Inquiry* 37, no. 3 (2011): 473–496, 480.

16. Britt Rusert, *Fugitive Science: Empiricism and Freedom in Early African American Culture* (New York: NYU Press, 2017), 99.

17. Adam Gurowski, *America and Europe* (New York: D. Appleton, 1857), 182.

18. According to Lorraine Daston and Peter Galison, objectivity, as an "epistemic virtue," came to dominate the empirical sciences around 1850. See Lorraine Daston and Peter Galison, *Objectivity* (Brooklyn: Zone Books, 2010).

19. Gaston Tissandier, *Popular Scientific Recreations* (London: Ward, Lock, and Co., ca. 1890), 134.

20. Mary Ann Doane, *The Emergence of Cinematic Time: Modernity, Contingency, the Archive* (Cambridge, MA: Harvard University Press, 2002), 72, 80.

21. Susan R. Horton, "Were They Having Fun Yet? Victorian Optical Gadgetry, Modernist Selves," in *Victorian Literature and the Victorian Visual Imagination*, ed. Carol T. Christ and John O. Jordan (Berkeley: University of California Press, 1995), 1–26, 2.

22. Stuart M. Blumin, *The Emergence of the Middle Class: Social Experience in the American City, 1760–1900* (Cambridge: Cambridge University Press, 1989), 115.

23. Karen Halttunen, *Confidence Men and Painted Women: A Study of Middle-Class Culture in America, 1830–1870* (New Haven, CT: Yale University Press, 1982), 29.

24. Pierre Bourdieu, *The Logic of Practice*, trans. Richard Nice (Stanford: Stanford University Press, 1990), 54.

25. Helen Groth, "Domestic Phantasmagoria: The Victorian Literary Domestic and Experimental Visuality," *South Atlantic Quarterly* 108, no. 1 (2009): 147–169, 167.

26. Bourdieu, *The Logic of Practice*, 60–61. See also Bernstein, *Racial Innocence*, 80: "By reading things' scripts within historically located traditions of performance, we can make well-supported claims about normative aggregate behavior."

27. Susan Prentiss, *Little Susy's Little Servants* (New York: Anson D. F. Randolf & Co., 1883), 12–13.

28. Prentiss, *Little Susy's Little Servants*, 60.

29. Prentiss, 78.

Notes

30. Prentiss, *Little Susy's Little Servants*, series 2, 21–23.

31. Prentiss, 54–55.

32. Cecil H. Bullivant, *Home Fun* (London: T. C. & E. C. Jack, 1910), 524.

33. Maaike Lauwaert, *The Place of Play: Toys and Digital Cultures* (Amsterdam: Amsterdam University Press, 2009), 34.

34. Mirzoeff, "The Right to Look," 474.

35. Ning De Coninck-Smith, "Geography and the Environment," in *A Cultural History of Childhood and Family in the Age of Empire*, ed. Colin Heywood (London: Bloomsbury Academic, 2014), 90; Bengt Sandin, "Education," in *A Cultural History of Childhood and Family in the Age of Empire*, ed. Colin Heywood (London: Bloomsbury, 2012), 95.

36. van den Oever and Fickers, "Doing Experimental Media Archaeology," 59.

37. Ann C. Colley, "Bodies and Mirrors: The Childhood Interiors of Ruskin, Pater and Stephenson," in *Domestic Space: Reading the Nineteenth-Century Interior*, ed. Inga Bryden and Janet Floyd (Manchester, UK: Manchester University Press, 1999), 40–57.

38. Bear, *Disillusioned*, 13.

39. See, for example, "To the Amateur Conjuror," in John H. Anderson, *Twenty-Five Cents' Worth of Magic and Mystery: Or Parlor Magic for the Amateur Conjurer* (New York: Wyncoop, Hallenbeck & Thomas, 1860). For more on the relationship between science and showmanship, see Iwan Rhys Morus, "Seeing and Believing Science," *Isis* 97, no. 1 (2006): 101–110.

40. William Ackroyd, "Scientific Deceptions," in *Cassell's Popular Science*, ed. Alexander S. Galt (London: Cassell, 1904), 400.

41. Fulgence Marion, *The Wonders of Optics*, trans. Charles Quin (New York: Charles Scribner, 1871), 173.

42. Oliver Grau, *Virtual Art: From Illusion to Immersion* (Cambridge, MA: MIT Press, 2003), 13.

43. Grier, *Culture and Comfort*.

44. Thad Logan, *The Victorian Parlour: A Cultural Study* (Cambridge: Cambridge University Press, 2001), 92.

45. Even as many scholars note that such displays tended to be culturally conservative. For more, see Lynne Walker and Vron Ware, "Political Pincushions: Decorating the Abolitionist Interior 1787–1865," in *Domestic Space: Reading the Nineteenth-Century Interior*, ed. Inga Bryden and Janet Floyd (Manchester, UK: Manchester University Press, 1999), 58–83; David Jaffee, "John Rogers Takes His Place in the Parlor,"

in *John Rogers: American Stories*, ed. Kimberly Orcutt (New York: New-York Historical Society, 2010), 167–180; Radiclani Clytus, "'Keep It before the People': The Pictorialization of American Abolitionism," in *Early African American Print Culture*, ed. Lara Langer Cohen and Jordan Alexander Stein (Philadelphia: University of Pennsylvania Press, 2012), 291–317, 315.

46. Groth, "Domestic Phantasmagoria," 167.

47. Some examples include "Nancy Naumburg [Domestic Interior with Table, Loveseat, and Rocking Chair] The Met," Metropolitan Museum of Art, accessed January 23, 2019, https://www.metmuseum.org/art/collection/search/282259; "Attributed to John H. Belter, Tête-à-Tête—American—The Met," Metropolitan Museum of Art, accessed January 23, 2019, https://www.metmuseum.org/art/collection/search/8489.

48. Richard Balzer collection online, Optische Belustigungen, colored lithographs, Germany. ca. 1835. Disks: 7" diameter. Box contains seven double-sided disks, handle and disk with instructions in English, German, and French, http://www.dickbalzer.com/Phenakistascopes.604.0.html.

49. Wolfgang Schivelbusch, *Disenchanted Night: The Industrialization of Light in the Nineteenth Century* (Berkeley: University of California Press, 1995), 158–162.

50. Caroline L. Smith, *Popular Pastimes for Field and Fireside; Or, Amusements for Young and Old* (Springfield, MA: Milton Bradley, 1867), 230.

51. Smith, *Popular Pastimes for Field and Fireside*.

52. Mary Hartwell, "The Firm of Pixie and Prog. Chapter VII: Kate Lane," in *Golden Hours: A Magazine for Boys and Girls* 8 (1876), 301–305, 302–303.

53. Hartwell, "The Firm of Pixie and Prog," 303.

54. For more on these performances in the context of toy magic lanterns, see Meredith A. Bak, "'Ten Dollars' Worth of Fun': The Obscured History of the Toy Magic Lantern and Early Children's Media Spectatorship," *Film History* 27, no. 1 (2015): 111–134.

55. Gaston Tissandier, *Popular Scientific Recreations*, trans. and enl. from "Les récréations scientifiques" (London: Ward, Lock, and Co., 1882), 126–127.

56. André Gaudreault and Nicolas Dulac, "Circularity and Repetition at the Heart of the Attraction: Optical Toys and the Emergence of a New Cultural Series," in *Cinema of Attractions Reloaded*, ed. Wanda Strauven (Amsterdam: Amsterdam University Press, 2006), 227–244, 233, 238.

57. Erkki Huhtamo, "Toward a History of Peep Practice," in *A Companion to Early Cinema*, ed. Nicolas Dulac, André Gaudreault, and Santiago Hidalgo (Hoboken, NJ: Wiley Blackwell, 2012), 32–51, 38, 39–40.

58. Alison Griffiths, *Shivers Down Your Spine: Cinema, Museums, and the Immersive View* (New York: Columbia University Press, 2008), 2.

59. Sara Danius, "Novel Visions and the Crisis of Culture: Visual Technology, Modernism, and Death in 'The Magic Mountain,'" *Boundary* 27, no. 2 (2000), 187.

60. This was one feature that distinguished home recreation books of the nineteenth century from the eighteenth; see Barbara Maria Stafford, *Artful Science: Enlightenment Entertainment and the Eclipse of Visual Education* (Cambridge, MA: MIT Press, 1994), 70.

61. Iwan Rhys Morus, "Seeing and Believing Science," *Isis* 97, no. 1 (2006): 101–110, 102.

62. Tom Gunning, "The Play between Still and Moving Images: Nineteenth-Century 'Philosophical Toys' and Their Discourse," in *Between Stillness and Motion: Film, Photography, Algorithms*, ed. Eivind Røssaak (Amsterdam: Amsterdam University Press, 2011), 27–44, 28–29.

63. Edward Bradford Titchener, *An Outline of Psychology* (New York: Macmillan, 1916), 197.

64. Stephen Herbert, "ZOETROPE 1," accessed December 10, 2018, https://www.stephenherbert.co.uk/wheelZOETROPEpart1.htm.

65. Michelle Dacus Carr, *Black and White and Read in Profile: The Silhouette as Race Manirhetoric in Flannery O'Connor and Kara Walker* (Clemson, SC: Clemson University, 2010), 26, 25.

66. Carr, *Black and White and Read in Profile*, 26.

67. Adaptations of the same story appear in a range of titles, such as McLoughlin Brothers' 1860s compilation *Little Miss Consequence*, where the story features a little girl who stains herself with ink, gesturing to racially caricatured blotters, such as Miss Dinah Pen-Wiper. See Bernstein, *Racial Innocence*, 224, 206–207.

68. Heinrich Hoffmann, *The English Struwwelpeter, Or, Pretty Stories and Funny Pictures for Little Children*, 31st ed. (London: A. N. Myers & Co., 1885), 11.

69. David Robinson, *Masterpieces of Animation: 1833–1908*, Griffithiana 43 (Gemona del Friuli, Italy: La cineteca del Friuli, 1991), 10.

70. Gaudreault and Dulac, "Circularity and Repetition," 232.

71. Gaudreault and Dulac, "Circularity and Repetition."

72. Gaudreault and Dulac, 238–239.

73. Peter-Paul Bänziger, Mischa Suter, and Marcel Streng, "Histories of Productivity: An Introduction," in *Histories of Productivity: Genealogical Perspectives on the Body and*

Modern Economy, ed. Peter-Paul Bänziger and Mischa Suter (New York: Routledge, 2016), 1–202.

74. Joseph Bizup, *Manufacturing Culture: Vindications of Early Victorian Industry* (Charlottesville: University of Virginia Press, 2003), 22.

75. Hannah Field, *Playing with the Book: Victorian Movable Picture Books and the Child Reader* (Minneapolis: University of Minnesota Press, 2019), 165.

76. "Mechanical Toys as a Means of Practical Instruction," *Scientific American* 20, no. 14 (1869): 217.

77. Anson Rabinbach, *The Human Motor: Energy, Fatigue, and the Origins of Modernity* (Berkeley: University of California Press, 1992).

78. Charles Musser, *Before the Nickelodeon: Edwin S. Porter and the Edison Manufacturing Company* (Berkeley: University of California Press, 1991), 34.

79. John Clark Murray, *A Handbook of Psychology*, 2nd ed. (Boston: DeWolfe, Fiske & Co., 1890), 107.

80. Murray, *A Handbook of Psychology*.

81. Hugo Münsterberg, *Psychological Laboratory of Harvard University* (Cambridge, MA: Harvard University Press, 1893), 10, 14.

82. Edward Bradford Titchener, "The Equipment of a Psychological Laboratory," *American Journal of Psychology* 11, no. 2 (1900): 257–258.

83. See Erwin Feyersinger, "Diegetic Short Circuits: Metalepsis in Animation," *Animation* 5, no. 3 (2010): 279–294.

84. Marit Grøtta, *Baudelaire's Media Aesthetics: The Gaze of the Flâneur and 19th-Century Media* (New York: Bloomsbury, 2016), 17.

85. Pierre Bourdieu, *The Logic of Practice*, 55.

Chapter 4: Movable Toy Books and the Culture of Independent Play

1. *Dean's New Book of Parlor Magic, or, Tricks for the Drawing Room* (London: Dean & Son, 1862), n.p. Cotsen Children's Library, Department of Rare Books and Special Collections, Princeton University Library.

2. Ann Montanaro, *Pop-Up and Movable Books: A Bibliography* (Metuchen, NJ: Scarecrow Press, 1993), 1:ix.

3. John Locke, *Some Thoughts Concerning Education: By John Locke, Esq* (London: J. and R. Tonson, 1779), 220–222.

4. Karin Lee Fishbeck Calvert, *Children in the House: The Material Culture of Early Childhood, 1600–1900* (Boston: Northeastern University Press, 1992), 124–125.

Notes

5. William Livingston Alden, *Domestic Explosives and Other Sixth Column Fancies: (From the* New York Times*)* (New York: Lovell, Adam, Wesson, 1877), 75.

6. Alden, *Domestic Explosives*, 76.

7. "Little Children Should Not Be Annoyed by Older Ones," *Our Home Magazine and Mothers' Journal*, 1842, 132.

8. "Jessie Elder Ringwalt (1835–1917)—Find a Grave … ," accessed October 28, 2018, https://www.findagrave.com/memorial/108595040/jessie-ringwalt; Family bonds and sentiment feature across Ringwalt's work. She is known for her 1863 adaptation of James Cobb's play *Paul and Virginia: or, The Runaway Slave*, in which she notably rewrote the part of a defiant runaway slave, Zabi, into a "benign, unthreatening" patriarch whose heart is broken when he is sold apart from his family. See Melinda Lawson, "Imagining Slavery: Representations of the Peculiar Institution on the Northern Stage, 1776–1860," *Journal of the Civil War Era* 1, no. 1 (2011): 25–55, 47.

9. Jessie E. Ringwalt, "Fun for the Fireside: A Help to Mothers. Playing at Optics—No. 1," in *Godey's Lady's Book*, ed. J. Hannum Jones, A. E. Brown, and S. Annie Frost (Philadelphia: Godey's Lady's Book, 1879), 98:65–66, 65.

10. Jessie E. Ringwalt, "Fun for the Fireside: A Help to Mothers. Playing at Optics—No. 1," 65.

11. Ringwalt, "Fun for the Fireside–No. 1."

12. *Dean's New Book of Parlor Magic* (London: Dean and Son, 1862), 5.

13. Jessie E. Ringwalt, "Fun for the Fireside: A Help to Mothers. Playing at Optics, No. 2," *Godey's Lady's Book and Magazine* (February 1879): 144.

14. Ringwalt, "Fun for the Fireside—No. 2," 145.

15. Ringwalt, 145–146.

16. Ringwalt, 146.

17. Hannah Field, *Playing with the Book: Victorian Movable Picture Books and the Child Reader* (Minneapolis: University of Minnesota Press, 2019), 38, 40.

18. Field, *Playing with the Book*, 159.

19. "Brief Comment," *Literary News: A Monthly Journal of Current Literature* (October 1880) 251; Frederick Warne & Co., "Ad for Frederick Warne & Co's Picture Puzzle Toy Books, New Books, Season 1873–74," *Athenaeum* no. 2408, December 20, 1873, 798.

20. George Routledge and Sons, "Ad for Walter Crane's New Toy Books," *Athenaeum* no. 2458, December 5, 1874, 736.

21. Montanaro, *Pop-Up and Movable Books*, xi–xiii.

22. *Bookman* 5 (October 1893–March 1894): 100; *Spectator* 71, December 9, 1893, 844.

23. "Nursery Picture Books," *Literary World* (London: James Clarke and Co., 1893), 48:507.

24. Kayla Haveles Hopper, Lauren B. Hewes, and Laura Wasowicz, eds., *Radiant with Color and Art: Mcloughlin Brothers and the Business of Picture* (Worcester, MA: American Antiquarian Society, 2017), 22, 42.

25. Hopper, Hewes, and Wasowicz, *Radiant with Color*, 19.

26. Hopper, Hewes, and Wasowicz, 105.

27. Locke, *Some Thoughts Concerning Education*, 220–223.

28. Robin Bernstein, "Toys Are Good for Us: Why We Should Embrace the Historical Integration of Children's Literature, Material Culture, and Play," *Children's Literature Association Quarterly*, no. 4 (2013): 458–463, 458–459.

29. Katharine Morrison McClinton, *Antiques of American Childhood* (New York: Bramhall House, 1970), 75–78.

30. Gillian Brown, "The Metamorphic Book: Children's Print Culture in the Eighteenth Century," *Eighteenth-Century Studies* 39, no. 3 (2006): 351–362, 358–359.

31. Bernstein, "Toys Are Good for Us," 461.

32. Jacqueline Reid-Walsh, *Interactive Books: Playful Media before Pop-Ups* (New York: Routledge, 2017), 62.

33. Benjamin Sands, *Metamorphosis, or A Transformation of Pictures, with Poetical Explanations: For the Amusement of Young Persons*, illustrated by H. Anderson (Cadiz, OH: H. Anderson, 1836).

34. John Bunyan, *The Pilgrim's Progress, Exhibited in a Metamorphosis, or a Transformation of Pictures* (Hartford, CT: J. W. Barber, 1819).

35. Jacqueline Reid-Walsh, "Activity and Agency in Historical 'Playable Media,'" *Journal of Children and Media* 6, no. 2 (2012): 164–181, 170.

36. Reid-Walsh, "Activity and Agency," 177.

37. Reid-Walsh, 174.

38. André Gaudreault and Nicolas Dulac, "Circularity and Repetition at the Heart of the Attraction: Optical Toys and the Emergence of a New Cultural Series," in *Cinema of Attractions Reloaded*, ed. Wanda Strauven (Amsterdam: Amsterdam University Press, 2006), 227–244, 233.

39. Gaudreault and Dulac, "Circularity and Repetition," 237.

Notes

40. Karen Sánchez-Eppler, *Dependent States: The Child's Part in Nineteenth-Century American Culture* (Chicago: University of Chicago Press, 2005), 4–5

41. Marah Gubar, "Entertaining Children of All Ages: Nineteenth-Century Popular Theater as Children's Theater," *American Quarterly* 66, no. 1 (2014): 1–34, 6; Reid-Walsh, *Interactive Books*, 190–191.

42. John Plunkett, "Moving Books/Moving Images: Optical Recreations and Children's Publishing 1800–1900," *Interdisciplinary Studies in the Long Nineteenth Century* 1, no. 5 (2007): 1–27, 17.

43. Field, *Playing with the Book*, 60.

44. Endpapers on *Dean's New Book of Magic Illuminations* (London: Dean and Son, ca. 1862).

45. See the American Antiquarian Society Catalog Record: https://catalog.mwa.org/vwebv/holdingsInfo?&bibId=221147&searchId=525&recPointer=0&recCount=10.

46. "Brief Comment," *Literary News: A Monthly Journal of Current Literature* (October 1880): 251.

47. *Catalogue of McLoughlin Brothers Toy Books Games, A B C Blocks, &c.* (1882–1883), n.p., available from the American Antiquarian Society: http://www.americanantiquarian.org/mcloughlin/001129.pdf.

48. Eric Faden, "Movables, Movies, Mobility: Nineteenth-Century Looking and Reading," *Early Popular Visual Culture* 5 (2007): 71–89, 79, 82, 74.

49. Advertisement for Pantomime Toy Book series on the back of *Mother Goose Magic Transformations* (New York: McLoughlin Brothers, ca. 1890).

50. Marah Gubar, "Entertaining Children of All Ages," 3.

51. Jeffrey Richards, *The Golden Age of Pantomime: Slapstick, Spectacle and Subversion in Victorian England* (London: I. B. Tauris, 2014), 319–320.

52. Field, *Playing with the Book*, 107.

53. Sánchez-Eppler, *Dependent States*, 23.

54. The copy of this title in the American Antiquarian Society's collection appears torn; the right half of the seesaw and the child riding it are missing.

55. Jessie Ringwalt's ninth "Fun for the Fireside" column was on "Playing at Physics." Of the seesaw, Ringwalt noted, "Every child who manufactures this toy is really a mechanic making a machine." Jessie E. Ringwalt, "Fun for the Fireside: A Help to Mothers. Playing at Physics, No. 9," *Godey's Lady's Book and Magazine* (September 1879): 263. The seesaw was commonly framed in this way. In Norman Calkins's 1882 book of object lessons for experiments concerning gravity, he notes its utility

to "furnish practical illustrations of the importance of giving attention to the centre of gravity." Norman Allison Calkins, *Manual of Object-Teaching: With Illustrative Lessons in Methods and the Science of Education* (New York: Harper, 1882), 338.

56. Advertisement for McLoughlin Bros.'s Little Showman's series. Back cover of George W. Mooney, *Cinderella, Or, The Little Glass Slipper: An Entertainment for the Parlor: With Full Stage Directions, and Hints for Costumes, and Decorations* (New York: McLoughlin Bros., 1883).

57. Mooney, *Cinderella*.

58. Although some "Circassian Beauties" performed with snakes, their most notable feature was exaggerated, teased-up hair, which the McLoughlin Brothers' image does not reference.

59. *Spectator*, May 21, 1853, 485, quoted in Bernth Lindfors, "Hottentot, Bushman, Kaffir: The Making of Racist Stereotypes in 19th-Century Britain," in *Encounter Images in the Meetings between Africa and Europe*, ed. Mai Palmberg (Uppsala: Nordic Africa Institute, 2001), 54–75, 67.

60. Lindfors, "Hottentot, Bushman, Kaffir," 66–71.

61. Field, *Playing with the Book*, 86.

62. Advertisement for Pantomime Toy Books series on the back of *Mother Goose Magic Transformations* (New York: McLoughlin Brothers, ca. 1890).

63. *Aunt Louisa's Fairy Legends* (New York: McLoughlin Brothers, 1875); *Puss in Boots*, Pantomime Toy Books series (New York: McLoughlin Brothers, 1882).

64. Although nineteenth-century publishers did not construct proto-transmedia worlds with a specific aim to add depth to those worlds as twenty-first-century media franchises do, historical publishers nevertheless produced variations of the same stories as an economic strategy, inadvertently creating layered and more complex representations of the worlds in which these stories took place. See David Buckingham and Julian Sefton-Green, "Gotta Catch 'em All: Structure, Agency and Pedagogy in Children's Media Culture," *Media, Culture and Society* 25, no. 3 (2003): 379–399.

65. Laura Wasowicz notes that McLoughlin alone "published over a thousand titles in about 150 series between 1860 and 1890," Hopper, Hewes, and Wasowicz, *Radiant with Color*, 11.

66. Maria Tatar, *Off with Their Heads!: Fairy Tales and the Culture of Childhood* (Princeton: Princeton University Press, 1993), 30.

67. Walter Sauer, "Struwwelpeter Naturalized: McLoughlin Imprints of Slovenly Peter and Related Books," *Princeton University Library Chronicle* 62, no. 1 (2000): 16–30, 16.

68. Lothar Meggendorfer, *Dean's Living Strewelpeter* (London: Dean and Son, 1890).

69. Hopper, Hewes, and Wasowicz, *Radiant with Color*, 18.

70. See the Yale Catalog record: https://brbl-dl.library.yale.edu/vufind/Record/4103364.

71. Charles W. Wendte, "Good Gifts to Children," *Unity*, December 16, 1884, 400–401, 401.

72. Field, *Playing with the Book*, 27.

73. Field, *Playing with the Book*, 31.

74. George Washington Doane, Palmer Dyer, William Croswell, and Samuel Fuller, eds., "Toy Books," *Episcopal Watchman* 4, no. 15 (1830): 116.

75. Doane et al., "Toy Books."

76. *Panorama of Juvenile Sports and Occupations* (Hartford, CT: Brockett, Hutchinson & Co., ca. 1853–1855), n.p.

77. In the following titles, for instance, while not exclusively critiques of technology and screen culture, these concerns factor strongly into their commentary. Scott D. Sampson, *How to Raise a Wild Child: The Art and Science of Falling in Love with Nature* (New York: Houghton Mifflin Harcourt, 2015); Angela J. Hanscom, *Balanced and Barefoot: How Unrestricted Outdoor Play Makes for Strong, Confident, and Capable Children* (Oakland, CA: New Harbinger, 2016); Richard Louv, *Last Child in the Woods: Saving Our Children from Nature-Deficit Disorder* (Chapel Hill, NC: Algonquin Books, 2008).

78. Ann E. Porter, *Uncle Jerry's Letters to Young Mothers* (Boston: J. P. Jewett, 1854), 32–33.

79. Mrs. C. A. Hopkinson, *Hints for the Nursery: The Young Mother's Guide* (Boston: Little, Brown, 1863), 150–151.

80. Sampson, *How to Raise a Wild Child*, 6.

81. "Art for the Nursery," *Athenaeum*, November 29, 1873, 702.

82. "Art for the Nursery."

83. "Art for the Nursery," *Athenaeum*, December 9, 1893, 812–813, 813.

84. Wendte, "Good Gifts to Children," 400.

85. Wendte, 400.

86. Gary Cross, *Kids' Stuff: Toys and the Changing World of American Childhood* (Cambridge, MA: Harvard University Press, 2009).

87. *Motograph Moving Picture Book*, illustrated by F. J. Vernay, Yorick, &c, cover design specially drawn for the book by H. de Toulouse-Lautrec (London: Bliss, Sands

and Co., 1898). Cotsen Children's Library, Department of Rare Books and Special Collections, Princeton University Library. The Met catalog record notes printing methods. http://www.metmuseum.org/collection/the-collection-online/search/334265.

88. The Edison (Dickson and Heise) version was made in 1895, the Lumière version in 1896.

89. Instructions for "The Mortar Mill," *The Motograph Moving Picture Book* (London: Bliss Sands, 1898).

90. "Advertisement for The Motograph Moving Picture Book," *Publishers' Circular* no. 1642, December 18, 1897, 706.

91. Nancy Mowll Mathews, Charles Musser, and Marta Braun, *Moving Pictures: American Art and Early Film, 1880–1910* (Manchester, VT: Hudson Hills, 2005), 5.

92. Perry Nodelman, "Decoding the Images: Illustration and Picture Books," in *Understanding Children's Literature*, ed. Peter Hunt (London: Routledge, 1999), 69–80, 73.

Chapter 5: Color Education

1. *Bradley's Game and Toy Catalogue* (Springfield, MA: Milton Bradley, 1889), 39.

2. Erkki Huhtamo, "'All the World's a Kaleidoscope': A Media Archaeological Perspective to the Incubation Era of Media Culture," *Rivista Di Estetica*, no. 55 (2014): 139–153.

3. Huhtamo, "All the World's a Kaleidoscope," 141.

4. David Brewster, *A Treatise on the Kaleidoscope* (Edinburgh: Archibald Constable & Company, 1819), 7.

5. Jonathan Crary, *Techniques of the Observer: On Vision and Modernity in the Nineteenth Century* (Cambridge, MA: MIT Press, 1990), 116.

6. Helen Groth, "Kaleidoscopic Vision and Literary Invention in an 'Age of Things': David Brewster, Don Juan, and 'A Lady's Kaleidoscope,'" *English Literary History* 74 (2007) 217–237, 221.

7. Groth, "Kaleidoscopic Vision," 218.

8. See, for instance, Catherine Sinclair, *The Kaleidoscope of Anecdotes and Aphorisms* (London: Richard Bentley, 1851); S. G. Goodrich, *Peter Parley's Kaleidoscope, or Parlor Pleasure Book* (Cincinnati: Mack R. Barnitz, 1859), which is described as "gleanings from many fields of the curious, the beautiful, and the wonderful."

9. Louisa Parsons Stone Hopkins, *How Shall My Child Be Taught? Practical Pedagogy, or, The Science of Teaching Illustrated* (Boston: Lee and Shepard, 1887), 199.

10. Hopkins, *How Shall My Child Be Taught?*, 200.

11. Erkki Huhtamo, "From Kaleidoscomaniac to Cybernerd: Notes toward an Archaeology of the Media," *Leonardo* 30:3 (1997): 221–224, 222.

12. Jason Farman, "The Forgotten Kaleidoscope Craze in Victorian England," *Atlas Obscura*, November 9, 2015, http://www.atlasobscura.com/articles/the-forgotten-kaleidoscope-craze-in-victorian-england.

13. CBS's *The Early Show*'s coverage is here: https://youtu.be/ZXYY_ep5Nh0, and ABC's *America This Morning* here: https://youtu.be/bGpVpsaItpU.

14. Clyde Haberman, "Opinion: Do Not Read This Editorial While Walking," *New York Times*, March 22, 2018, https://nyti.ms/2GBOLc0; Tiffany May, "For Chinese Pedestrians Glued to Their Phones, a Middle Path Emerges," *New York Times*, August 7, 2018, https://nyti.ms/2Hv8OaR; Roni Caryn Rabin, "Cellphones and Crosswalks: A Hazardous Mix," *New York Times*, August 7, 2018, https://nyti.ms/2O1lk5J.

15. William James, *Psychology* (New York: Henry Holt, 1920), 221–222.

16. George Luckey, "Comparative Observations on the Indirect Color Range of Children, Adults, and Adults Trained in Color," in *The American Journal of Psychology*, ed. G. Stanley Hall (Worcester, MA: J. H. Orpha, 1893), 6:489–504.

17. Luckey, "Comparative Observations on the Indirect Color Range of Children," 491, 494.

18. Huhtamo, "'All the World's a Kaleidoscope,'" 151.

19. Charles G. Bush, "Improvement in Objects for Kaleidoscope," US Patent 143,271, September 30, 1873; Charles G. Bush, "Improvement in Object-Boxes for Kaleidoscopes," US Patent 151,006, May 19, 1874.

20. Charles G. Bush, "Improvement in Kaleidoscope Stands," US Patent 156,875, November 17, 1874.

21. Farman, "The Forgotten Kaleidoscope Craze in Victorian England."

22. David Brewster, *The Kaleidoscope, Its History, Theory and Construction: With Its Application to the Fine and Useful Arts*, 3rd ed. (London: John Camden Hotten, 1870), 71.

23. "The Single Kaleidoscope. Its Construction and Use," and "Objects for the Kaleidoscope," *Magazine of Science and School of Arts*, First Part, no. 67, July 11, 1840, 116–118; Second Part no. 70, August 1, 1840, 139–141.

24. "Piano Kaleidoscope," *American Agriculturist* (May 1877): 186.

25. Huhtamo, "'All the World's a Kaleidoscope,'" 143–144.

26. Charles G. Bush, "Improvement in Kaleidoscopes," US Patent 151,005, May 19, 1874.

27. Robert F. Macy, "Improvement in Kaleidoscopes," US Patent 174,690, May 14, 1876.

28. *The Boy's Own Conjuring Book: Being a Complete Handbook of Parlour-Magic, Etc.* (New York: Dick and Fitzgerald, 1860), 297.

29. Thomas De Witt Talmage, "The Dumb Prayer Answered," *Frank Leslie's Sunday Magazine* (December 1884): 532–534, 532.

30. Martin Farquhar Tupper, *The Complete Works of Martin F. Tupper in Four Volumes*, vol. 2: *An Author's Mind, Essay's Probabilities* (Philadelphia: E. H. Butler, 1851), 32, 31.

31. Wolfgang Schivelbusch, *The Railway Journey: The Industrialization of Time and Space in the Nineteenth Century*, 3rd ed. (Berkeley: University of California Press, 2014), 57.

32. *Children's Toys, and Some Elementary Lessons in General Knowledge Which They Teach* (London: C. Kegan Paul & Co., 1877), 234.

33. Parlor Kaleidoscope advertisement, in Benjamin Leopold Farjeon, *Widow Cherry: Or, The Mystery of Roaring Meg. A Novel* (New York: G. W. Carleton, 1878), 99.

34. Maria Edgeworth, *Practical Education*, 2 vols. (New York: G. F. Hopkins, 1801), 1:2.

35. Regina Lee Blaszczyk, *The Color Revolution* (Cambridge, MA: MIT Press, 2012), 3.

36. Milton Bradley, *Color in the School-Room: A Manual for Teachers* (Springfield, MA: Milton Bradley, 1890), 64.

37. Nicholas Gaskill, "Learning to See with Milton Bradley," in *Bright Modernity: Color, Commerce, and Consumer Culture*, ed. Regina Lee Blaszczyk and Uwe Spiekermann (Cham, Switzerland: Springer, 2017), 55–76, 65.

38. Schivelbusch, *The Railway Journey*, 129–130.

39. Ogden Nicholas Rood, *Students' Text-Book of Color: or, Modern Chromatics, with Applications to Art and Industry* (New York: D. Appleton, 1881), 99.

40. J. D. Mollon and L. R. Cavonius, "The Lagerlunda Collision and the Introduction of Color Vision Testing," *Survey of Ophthalmology* 57, no. 2 (2012): 178–194.

41. "Toys for the Holidays" *Brooklyn Daily Eagle*, December 5, 1886, 11.

42. Walter Benjamin, "Toys and Play: Marginal Notes on a Monumental Work," in *Walter Benjamin: Selected Writings, 1927–1930*, ed. Michael W. Jennings, Howard Eiland, and Gary Smith (Cambridge, MA: Harvard University Press, 1999), 2:117–121, 119.

43. Benjamin Joy Jeffries, *Report of the Examination of 27,927 School Children for Color-Blindness*, school document no. 13 (Boston: Rockwell and Churchill, City Printers, 1880).

44. Benjamin Joy Jeffries, *Our Eyes and Our Industries* (Boston: Franklin Press, 1883), 4.

45. Benjamin Joy Jeffries, *Color-Names, Color-Blindness, and the Education of the Color-Sense in Our Schools* (Boston: L. Prang & Company, 1882), 5.

46. Bradley, *Color in the School Room*, 25.

47. Benjamin Joy Jeffries, *Report of the Examination of 27,927 School Children for Color-Blindness* (Boston: Houghton, Osgood, 1880), 6.

48. Ogden Nicholas Rood, *Students' Text-Book of Color: or, Modern Chromatics, with Applications to Art and Industry* (New York: D. Appleton, 1881), 96.

49. Jeffries, *Color-Names, Color-Blindness*, 5.

50. Jeffries, 76, 68.

51. Daniel M. Albert and Sarah L. Atzen, "Swan M. Burnett, MD, PhD: The Forgotten Father of Little Lord Fauntleroy," *Archives of Ophthalmology* 127, no. 12 (2009): 1664–1671, 1664.

52. Sally Cochrane, "The Munsell Color System: A Scientific Compromise from the World of Art," *Studies in History and Philosophy of Science* 47 (2014): 26–41, 29–30.

53. Edith Goodyear, "Color in Primary Occupations," *Primary Education* 2, no. 6 (1894): 201–202, 201.

54. Goodyear, "Color in Primary Occupations," 201.

55. Patrick Feaster, "Edith Goodyear Alger: Lyricist of 'Happy Birthday to You'? Griffonage-Dot-Com," June 20, 2014, https://griffonagedotcom.wordpress.com/2014/06/20/edith-goodyear-alger-lyricist-of-happy-birthday-to-you/.

56. Milton Bradley, "Colored Standards Necessary for Logical Color Teaching (II)," *Journal of Education* 35, no. 6 (1892): 84–85.

57. Jennie G. Paine, "Wall Finish of Schoolrooms," *School Board Journal* 36, no. 5 (1908): 26.

58. Vermont Department of Education and Mason S. Stone, *Teacher's Manual for Use in the Elementary Schools State of Vermont* (Bradford, VT: Opinion Press, 1907), 155.

59. Prang Educational Company, "Color Schemes for School Interiors," *School Education* 22, no. 5 (May 1903): 27.

60. Chas M. Carter, "School-Room Decoration," *Colorado School Journal* 14 (September 1898): 6–8; Prang Educational Company, "Color Schemes for School Interiors," 27.

61. Cochrane, "The Munsell Color System," 32.

62. Cochrane, 36, 39.

63. Bradley, *Color in the School-Room*, 1.

64. Milton Bradley, *Elementary Color* (Springfield, MA: Milton Bradley, 1895), 5.

65. Jimena Canales, *A Tenth of a Second: A History* (Chicago: University of Chicago Press, 2010), 5–7.

66. Fairfield M. Caudle, "The Developing Technology of Apparatus in Psychology's Early Laboratories," *Annals of the New York Academy of Sciences* 412 (1983): 19–55, 37.

67. Herbert Nichols, "The Psychological Laboratory at Harvard," *McClure's Magazine* 1, no. 5 (1893), 402.

68. Nichols, "The Psychological Laboratory at Harvard," 401.

69. Edward Wheeler Scripture, *Thinking, Feeling, Doing* (Meadville, PA: Flood and Vincent, 1895), 189–193.

70. Bradley, *Elementary Color*, 45.

71. Edith Goodyear, "Color in Primary Occupations," *Primary Education* 2, no. 6 (1894): 201–202, 202; Bradley, *Color in the School-Room*, 14.

72. Norman A. Calkins, *Primary Object Lessons, for Training the Senses and Developing the Faculties of Children: A Manual of Elementary Instruction for Parents and Teachers* (New York: Harper and Brothers, 1874), title page.

73. Louis Prang, Mary Dana Hicks, and John S. Clark, *Color Instruction: Suggestions for a Course of Instruction in Color for Public Schools* (Boston: Prang Educational Company, 1893), 1.

74. Prang et al., *Color Instruction*, 31–33.

75. Bradley, *Elementary Color*, 78–79.

76. Prang et al., *Color Instruction*, 34–37.

77. Prang et al., iv, 39.

78. Lewis Campbell and William Garnett, *The Life of James Clerk Maxwell* (New York: Johnson Reprint, 1969), 469–470.

79. Bradley, *Color in the School-Room*, 58.

80. Joseph Wachelder, "Toys as Mediators," *Icon* 13 (2007): 135–169, 151–152; 158.

81. Wachelder, "Toys as Mediators," 165.

82. Campbell and Garnett, *The Life of James Clerk Maxwell*, 36–38.

Notes

83. Campbell and Garnett, 484–485.

84. Daniel Brown, *The Poetry of Victorian Scientists: Style, Science and Nonsense* (Cambridge: Cambridge University Press, 2013), 32–36.

85. Bradley, *Color in the School-Room*, 52–53.

86. Bradley, 58.

87. Edward Wiebé, and Henry Wolcott Blake, *Quarter Century Edition of The Paradise of Childhood: A Practical Guide to Kindergartners* (Springfield, MA: Milton Bradley, 1907), 223.

88. Bradley, *Elementary Color*, 83.

89. "Advertisement for the Bradley Color Top," *Primary Education* 2, no. 6 (1894): 221.

90. Bradley, *Elementary Color*, 83.

91. E. W. Scripture, "New Materials for Color Teaching," *Educational Review* 7:382–383, 383.

92. Joshua Yumibe, *Moving Color: Early Film, Mass Culture, Modernism* (New Brunswick, NJ: Rutgers University Press, 2012), 17.

93. Bradley, *Elementary Color*, 43.

94. Michael Keevak, *Becoming Yellow: A Short History of Racial Thinking* (Princeton, NJ: Princeton University Press, 2011), 90. See also Werner Sollors, *Neither Black nor White yet Both: Thematic Explorations of Interracial Literature* (Cambridge, MA: Harvard University Press, 1999).

95. Keevak, *Becoming Yellow*, 98.

96. Bradley, *Elementary Color*, 18–19.

97. Yumibe, *Moving Color*, 24.

98. Prang, *Color Instruction*, 14.

99. Bradley, *Color in the School-Room*, 5.

100. Bradley, 40.

Chapter 6: Democracy and Discipline

1. The New York Public Library has produced a helpful tool, the stereograminator, which uses the animated .gif format to simulate the stereograph's depth. https://stereo.nypl.org/.

2. Jonathan Crary, *Techniques of the Observer* (Cambridge, MA: MIT Press, 1992), 125.

3. Frank McMurry, *The World Visualized for the Classroom* (New York: Underwood & Underwood, 1915), 20, 446, 442.

4. Edward Scripture, "Education as a Science," *Pedagogical Seminary* 2 (1892): 114.

5. Mona Gleason, "Metaphor, Materiality, and Method: The Central Role of Embodiment in the History of Education," *Paedagogica Historica* 54, no. 1–2 (2018): 4–19, 5.

6. Gleason, "Metaphor, Materiality, and Method," 10.

7. Laura Burd Schiavo, "From Phantom Image to Perfect Vision: Physiological Optics, Commercial Photography, and the Popularization of the Stereoscope," in *New Media: 1715–1915*, ed. Lisa Gitelman and Geoffrey B. Pingree (Cambridge, MA: MIT Press, 2004), 114–115.

8. David Brewster, *The Stereoscope; Its History, Theory, and Construction, with Its Application to the Fine and Useful Arts and to Education: With Fifty Wood Engravings* (London: John Murray, 1856), 31.

9. Brewster, *The Stereoscope*, 36.

10. William Culp Darrah, *Stereo Views. A History of Stereographs in America and their Collection* (Gettysburg, PA: Times and News Publishing, 1962), 41–43.

11. "Foreword," *Visual Education* 1, no. 1 (January 1920): 2–6, 4.

12. Wendell G. Johnson, "'Making Learning Easy and Enjoyable': Anna Verona Dorris and the Visual Instruction Movement, 1918–1928," *Tech Trends* 52, no 4 (July–August 2008), 51–58.

13. Sarah Carter, *Object Lessons: How Nineteenth-Century Americans Learned to Make Sense of the Material World* (Oxford: Oxford University Press, 2018), 1.

14. Carter, *Object Lessons*, 1–2.

15. Carter, 16–17.

16. Carter, 57.

17. Carter, 30.

18. Adonijah Strong Welch, *Object Lessons: Prepared for Teachers of Primary Schools and Primary Classes* (New York: A. S. Barnes, 1890), iii.

19. Leon Sachs, *The Pedagogical Imagination: The Republican Legacy in Twenty-First-Century French Literature and Film* (Lincoln: University of Nebraska Press, 2014), 29.

20. Carter, *Object Lessons*, 121. See also Brenton J. Malin, *Feeling Mediated: A History of Media Technology and Emotion in America* (New York: NYU Press, 2014), 105.

21. "Discussion of Miss Kee'er's Paper on Object Lessons," *National Teacher* 2, no. 9 (1872): 329.

22. William Hailmann, *Kindergarten Culture in the Family and Kindergarten* (Cincinnati, OH: Van Antwerp, Bragg, 1873), 103.

23. For instance, object lessons played a secularizing role when materials were exported to India (Carter, *Object Lessons*, 18); in lessons about "civilizing" Native Americans (Carter, 111–113), and in cultivating "the bodily conceptions of the labor necessary for service" for future servants (Carter, 105).

24. Carter, 61–63.

25. Carter, 121–122.

26. Brewster, *The Stereoscope*, 193–194.

27. Carter, *Object Lessons*, 49.

28. For more, see Fairfield M. Caudle, "The Developing Technology of Apparatus in Psychology's Early Laboratories," *Annals of the New York Academy of Sciences* 412 (1983): 20–21; James Sully, *Teacher's Handbook of Psychology on the Basis of the "Outlines of Psychology"* (New York: D. Appleton, 1888), 127–129.

29. Rand B. Evans, "Brass Instrument Psychology: Timing—1840–1940," Max Planck Institute for the History of Science, accessed January 26, 2019, https://www.mpiwg-berlin.mpg.de/research/projects/DepIII_Rand_B_Evans.

30. Herbert Spencer, *Principles of Psychology* (New York: D. Appleton, 1897), 2, pt. 2:305.

31. Carter, *Object Lessons*, 92.

32. Jacques W. Redway, quoted in ad for C. W. Bardeen, Syracuse, New York, in *School Bulletin* 30, no. 346 (1904): xlviii.

33. Hart and Anderson, *The World in the Stereoscope* (New York: Hart and Anderson, 1872), xi.

34. William Culp Darrah, *Stereo Views: A History of Stereographs in America and their Collection* (Gettysburg, PA: Times and News Publishing, 1962), 10.

35. William Culp Darrah, *The World of Stereographs* (Gettysburg: W. C. Darrah, 1977), 49.

36. Darrah, *The World of Stereographs*, 50.

37. Darrah, 50.

38. McMurry, *The World Visualized for the Classroom*, xvii–xviii.

39. Schiavo, "From Phantom Image to Perfect Vision," 128.

40. Underwood and Underwood, *Canvass and Delivery: The Underwood Travel System* (New York: Underwood & Underwood, 1908), 39.

41. Albert Osborne, *The Stereograph and the Stereoscope: With Special Maps and Books forming a Travel System* (New York: Underwood & Underwood, 1909), 6–7.

42. Lawrence A. Cremin, *The Transformation of the School: Progressivism in American Education, 1876–1957* (New York: Knopf, 1961), 13–14.

43. Cremin, *The Transformation of the School*, 72

44. McMurry, *The World Visualized*, vii–viii.

45. McMurry, 5.

46. McMurry, 259, 406.

47. McMurry, 360, 377, 431, 436, 447.

48. *Visual Education: Teacher's Guide to the Keystone "600 Set"* (Meadville, PA: Keystone View Company Education Department, 1920), 46, 59.

49. *Visual Education*, 438, 467, 468, 590.

50. *Visual Education*, 42.

51. *Visual Education*, 124.

52. *Visual Education*, 206.

53. *Visual Education*, 419, 505.

54. *Visual Education*, 585.

55. Carter, *Object Lessons*, 111.

56. Judith Babbitts, "Stereographs and the Construction of a Visual Culture in the United States," in *Memory Bytes: History, Technology, and Digital Culture*, ed. Lauren Rabinovitz and Abraham Geil (Durham, NC: Duke University Press, 2004), 139.

57. Crary, *Techniques of the Observer*, 132.

58. Spencer, *Principles of Psychology*, iv.

59. Schiavo, "From Phantom Image to Perfect Vision."

60. McMurry, *The World Visualized for the Classroom*, iv, xxxv.

61. Underwood and Underwood, *Canvass and Delivery*, 96.

62. Hugo Münsterberg, *Psychology and the Teacher* (New York: D. Appleton, 1911), 131.

63. Hannah Field, *Playing with the Book: Victorian Movable Picture Books and the Child Reader* (Minneapolis: University of Minnesota Press, 2019), 102.

64. Field, *Playing with the Book*, 121.

Notes

65. Babbitts, *Stereoscope and Construction of Visual Culture*, 130–132.

66. Münsterberg, *Psychology and the Teacher*, 131–132.

67. *Visual Education: Teacher's Guide to the Keystone "600 Set,"* xviii–xix.

68. McMurry, *The World Visualized for the Classroom*, xxiv; Underwood and Underwood, *Canvass and Delivery*, 48.

69. McMurry, xiv.

70. Joakim Landahl, "The Eye of Power(-Lessness): On the Emergence of the Panoptical and Synoptical Classroom," *History of Education* 42, no. 6 (2013): 803–821, 810–812.

71. Landahl, "The Eye of Power(-Lessness)," xxii; Underwood and Underwood, *Canvass and Delivery*, 23.

72. Robert Bruce, "The Hand as Optical Instrument," *School Journal* 58, no. 4 (1899): 133.

73. Underwood and Underwood, *Canvass and Delivery*, 22–23.

74. A paradox at the heart of psychology's developmental paradigm.

75. Mary Tyler Mann and Elizabeth Prentiss Peabody, *Moral Culture of Infancy and Kindergarten Guide* (Boston: T. O. H. P. Burnham; New York: O. S. Felt, 1864), 58.

76. *Visual Education: Teacher's Guide to the Keystone "600 Set,"* xvii.

77. McMurry, *The World Visualized for the Classroom*, xxxviii–xl.

78. Philip Emerson and William Charles Moore, *Geography through the Stereoscope: Student's Stereoscopic Field Guide* (New York: Underwood & Underwood, 1907), xiii–xiv.

79. "The Stereoscope in the Schoolroom," *Pennsylvania School Journal* 17, ed. Th. H. Burrowes (Lancaster, PA: Wylie & Griest, 1868), 150.

80. Cremin, *The Transformation of the School*, 20–21.

81. Philip Emerson, "Field Work in the Classroom," *Journal of Geography* 6, no. 7 (1907): 56–57.

82. Gleason, "Metaphor, Materiality, and Method," 4–19, 9.

83. "Editor's Chair," *Illinois Teacher* 13, no. 11 (1867): 378–391, 382–383.

84. Babbitts, "Stereographs and the Construction," 141.

85. Carter, *Object Lessons*, 52.

86. Carter, 78–79.

87. Underwood and Underwood, *Canvass and Delivery*, 6.

88. Carolyn Marvin, *When Old Technologies Were New* (Oxford: Oxford University Press, 1988).

89. McMurry, *The World Visualized for the Classroom*, xv.

90. John Plunkett, "Selling Stereoscopy, 1890–1915: Penny Arcades, Automatic Machines, and American Salesmen," *Early Popular Visual Culture* 6, no. 3 (2008): 239–255.

91. Gleason, "Metaphor, Materiality, and Method," 13.

92. Benjamin Herold, "Chromebooks Gaining Popularity in School Districts," *Education Week*, November 12, 2014, https://www.edweek.org/ew/articles/2014/11/12/12chromebooks.h34.html.

93. Natasha Singer, "How Google Took Over the Classroom," *New York Times*, May 13, 2017, https://nyti.ms/2raVLDR.

94. Singer, "How Google Took Over the Classroom."

95. Launa Hall, "I Gave My Students iPads—Then Wished I Could Take Them Back," *Washington Post*, December 2, 2015, https://www.washingtonpost.com/opinions/i-gave-my-students-ipads--then-wished-i-could-take-them-back/2015/12/02/a1bc8272-818f-11e5-a7ca-6ab6ec20f839_story.html.

96. See, for instance, Carla Hannaford, *Smart Moves: Why Learning Is Not All in Your Head* (Salt Lake City: Great River Books, 2005); Ron Nash, *The Active Classroom* (Thousand Oaks, CA: Corwin Press, 2013), 39.

Chapter 7: Conclusion

1. David D. Etzwiler, "Refocusing the Middle Class Debate," *Huffington Post* (blog), August 4, 2016, https://www.huffingtonpost.com/david-d-etzwiler/refocusing-the-middle-cla_b_11332240.html.

2. Andrew B. Raupp, "The Rise of the STEM Toy," *Forbes*, May 29, 2018, https://www.forbes.com/sites/forbestechcouncil/2018/05/29/the-rise-of-the-stem-toy/.

3. Elizabeth Weiss, "Can Toys Create Future Engineers?" *New Yorker*, December 12, 2013, https://www.newyorker.com/business/currency/can-toys-create-future-engineers.

4. Such as the one that began this book: T. William Erle, *Children's Toys, and Some Elementary Lessons in General Knowledge Which They Teach* (London: C. Kegan Paul, 1877).

5. "About KiwiCo.," KiwiCo., accessed September 27, 2018, https://www.kiwico.com/about-us.

Notes

6. Raupp, "The Rise of the STEM Toy."

7. Babette Allina, Karen Bartleson, Jo Boaler, Knatokie Ford, Roger Malina, Rafael Núñez, and Lucinda Presley, "Decoding STEM/STEAM: The Toy Industry Association STEM/STEAM Strategic Leadership Committee Report," Toy Industry Association, May 2018, 4.

8. For more on neoliberalism and American education, see David Hursh, "Assessing No Child Left Behind and the Rise of Neoliberal Education Policies," *American Education Research Journal* 44, no. 3 (2007): 493–518.

9. Rebecca Onion, *Innocent Experiments: Childhood and the Culture of Popular Science in the United States* (Chapel Hill: University of North Carolina Press, 2016), 4.

10. Josef Nguyen, "Make Magazine and the Social Reproduction of DIY Science and Technology," *Cultural Politics* 12, no. 2 (2016): 233–252, 237. See also Sara Tocchetti, "DIYbiologists as 'Makers' of Personal Biologies: How Make Magazine and Maker Faires Contribute in Constituting Biology as a Personal Technology," *Journal of Peer Production*, no. 2 (2012), http://peerproduction.net/issues/issue-2/peer-reviewed-papers/.

11. Onion, *Innocent Experiments*, 9.

12. Allina et al., "Decoding STEM/STEAM," 5.

13. Carol Vincent, "'The Children Have Only Got One Education and You Have to Make Sure It's a Good One': Parenting and Parent–School Relations in a Neoliberal Age," *Gender and Education* 29, no. 5 (2017): 541–557, 545–548.

14. Peter Temin, *The Vanishing Middle Class: Prejudice and Power in a Dual Economy* (Cambridge, MA: MIT Press, 2018), ix.

15. One review describes the kit and its components in more detail here: Xenia Sundell, "HABA Discover the Building Blocks Technics Optics Pack (Review)," *Thanks, Mail Carrier* (blog), September 10, 2013, http://www.thanksmailcarrier.com/2013/09/haba-discover-building-blocks-technics-optics-review.html.

16. *GoldieBlox and the Movie Machine* (2014), 3, 7, 11.

17. Elizabeth Stinson, "These Incredible Animated GIFs Are More Than 150 Years Old," *Wired*, December 11, 2013, https://www.wired.com/2013/12/these-150-year-old-gifs-are-insane/.

18. "Largest Zoetrope," Guinness World Records, December 4, 2008, http://www.guinnessworldrecords.com/world-records/largest-zoetrope.

19. John Belton, "Introduction: Digital Cinema," *Film History: An International Journal* 24, no. 2 (2012): 131–134, 131.

20. Mary Ann Doane, *The Emergence of Cinematic Time: Modernity, Contingency, the Archive* (Cambridge, MA: Harvard University Press, 2002).

21. George Griffin, "Concrete Animation" *Animation: An Interdisciplinary Journal* 2, no. 3 (2007): 259–274, 262.

22. "Mar Collishaw," accessed November 7, 2013, http://www.blainsouthern.com/artists/mat-collishaw/selected_works/26720-the-garden-of-unearthly-delights.

23. Ameena Walker, "Help Create Dazzling Light Shows at a New Midtown Art Installation," *Curbed NY*, February 14, 2018, https://ny.curbed.com/2018/2/14/17013128/midtown-public-art-installation-loop.

24. Maggie Martin, "LOOP: An Interactive Art Installation with a Fairy Tale Ending," Houston Public Media, December 11, 2018, https://www.houstonpublicmedia.org/articles/shows/houston-matters/2018/12/11/314862/loop-an-interactive-art-installation-with-a-fairy-tale-ending/; "Be IN THE 'Loop' about Fort Worth's New Art Installation," *Art&Seek*, October 4, 2018, http://artandseek.org/spotlight/be-in-the-loop-about-fort-worths-new-art-installation/.

25. The full technical specifications are available here: Jim Le Fevre, "Holy Flying Circus Title Sequence," October 20, 2011, http://phonotropia.blogspot.com/2011/10/jim-le-fevre-holy-flying-circus-title.html.

26. "EDF Energy: Thank Yous Zoetrope," Vimeo, accessed January 25, 2019, https://vimeo.com/43107919.

27. Noreen O'Leary, "Ad of the Day: Fuze Tea," June 6, 2012, accessed January 25, 2019, https://www.adweek.com/brand-marketing/ad-day-fuze-tea-140954/; "1stAveMachine Reimagines the Zoetrope for Stella Artois," Animation World Network, accessed January 25, 2019, https://www.awn.com/news/1stavemachine-reimagines-zoetrope-stella-artois.

28. Alison Griffiths, "Wonder Magic and the Fantastical Margins: Medieval Visual Culture and Cinematic Special Effects," *Journal of Visual Culture* 9 (2010): 165–166, 163.

29. Dorothee Birke and Birte Christ, "Paratext and Digitized Narrative: Mapping the Field," *Narrative* 21, no. 1 (2013): 65–87, 65.

30. FUZETEA, *FUZE TEA Zoetrope BTS—Scale*, accessed January 25, 2019, https://youtu.be/ulYajgnHa_E.

31. FUZETEA, *FUZE TEA Zoetrope BTS—People*, accessed January 25, 2019, https://youtu.be/6cFMYTKirqM.

32. Sony, *The Making of Sony "Bravia Drome"* (2009), https://youtu.be/LBKh0M0kk9E.

33. "Campaign: Sony Bravia 'Color Like No Other,'" accessed January 25, 2019, https://adage.com/article/the-work/campaign-sony-bravia-color/105625/.

34. Jonathan Gray, *Show Sold Separately: Promos, Spoilers, and Other Media Paratexts* (New York: NYU Press, 2010), 19.

35. Gray, *Show Sold Separately*, 19–20.

36. "1stAveMachine Reimagines the Zoetrope for Stella Artois."

37. Klaas-Harm de Boer, *Efteling—Coca Cola 3D Printed Zoetrope* (2017), https://vimeo.com/215802766.

38. Charles McGovern, "Consumer Culture and Mass Culture," in *A Companion to American Cultural History*, ed. Karen Halttunen (London: Wiley, 2008), 183–197, 185.

39. Andrew Salomone, "Carve a Jack-O'-Lantern Zoetrope," Make Zine, accessed January 27, 2019, https://makezine.com/projects/halloween-2016-carve-jack-o-lantern-zoetrope/.

Index

Note: Figures are in italics.

Ackermann, Rudolph, 38, 68, 106, 110, 115, *116*
Advice literature, parenting, 28, 42–43, 49, 122, 130, 142, 148
African Americans, 13, 47, 75–76, 86–88, 107, 167, 197
American Antiquarian Society
  conducting research in, 4, 20–21, 69
  materials archived by, *79*, 126, *128*, *133*, *135*, *139*, *144*, 251n54
Anthropocentrism, 76–77
Archival research, 4–5, 20–23, 31–33, 134, 145

Ball, Erica, 13
Balzer, Richard, 22, 35, 63, 97
Bellion, Wendy, 14
Benjamin, Walter, 17–18, 23, 86, 165, 243n9
Bernstein, Robin, 4, 22, 74–75, 229n31
Bill Douglas Cinema Museum
  conducting research in, 20–21, 31–32
  materials archived by, *32*, *98*, *103*
Birke, Dorothee, 219–220
Bourdieu, Pierre, 90
Boys. *See* Child; Gender
Boy's Own Paper, 31–34, *32*, 41, 74
Bradley, Milton
  color wheels and tops, *175*, 175–176
  manufacture of kindergarten supplies, 24, 40
  manufacture of zoetrope, 25, 39, 54
  Smashed-Up Locomotive puzzle, 151–153, *152*
  views on color education, 154–155, 164–166, 168–173, 178, 180
  zoetrope content, 101, 106–107, *108*
BRAVIA-Drome, Sony, 215, *215*, 217, 220–222
Brewster, David
  on debut of kaleidoscope, 25, 154–155
  on materials for kaleidoscope, 159
  on pirating of kaleidoscope, 62, 155–156
  and versions of stereoscope, *186*, 186–187, 190
Bumstead, Josiah, 65
Bush, Charles G., 159–160, *161*

Canales, Jimena, 170
Carr, Michelle Dacus, 107
Carter, Sarah Anne, 190, 205, 261n23
Cautionary tales, 107–108, *109*, 142–145, *144*, 247n67
Changeable Gentlemen (game), 68–69
Changeable Ladies (game), 68–69
Checkered Game of Life, 12, 39, 168

Child
  agency of, 74, 129, 157–158
  changing attitudes about, 9–10, 121–122, 213, 224
  as cruel, 72–75
  as innocent, 8–12, 71, 74, 77–78, 134–135
  and leisure time, 19, 42–49, 140–141, 148
  19th-century conceptualization of, 12–17, 213
  and play as racial violence, 75–77
  as spectator, 11, 16–17, 198–205
  vulnerable senses of, 91–94, 145–148, 163–170
Childhood studies, 3–4, 18
Children's Toys, and Some Elementary Lessons in General Knowledge Which They Teach, 5–10, 6, 45, 77–78, 264n4
Christ, Birte, 219–220
Chromolithography
  and emergence of color education, 147, 152–153, 164
  and the object lesson, 191
  role in children's publishing, 25, 31, 34–35, 121, 126
  and taste cultures, 122, 145
Class status, 29–30, 95, 112, 148–150
  aspirations, 7–9, 12–15, 33–35, 76, 105–106, 121–122, 209
  and economic precarity, 47, 86–87, 89–90, 213
  hierarchies, 43–44, 73–74, 81–82, 189
  and in-home education, 43–47, 49–50, 59–61, 93–96
  and spectatorship, 64, 86, 138–141, 223
  and time, 18–19, 42, 55–56, 93–94, 130–132
  and visual discernment, 67, 113–115, 124, 210
Clytus, Radiclani, 13
Color blindness, 154, 164–167, 172, 178–179

Color education
  motivations for, 153–155, 163–167
  optical toys in, 173–178, *175*
  systems of, 168–173, 179
Color wheels, 155, *175*, 175–176, 178, 180
Consumption, 9–12, 49–51, 89–90, 211. *See also* Spectatorship; Tastemaking
Cook, James, 14
Copyright infringement. *See* Piracy
Cotsen Children's Library, 4, 20–21, 57, 119
Courtship. *See* Flirtation games
Cowper, William, 48–49
Crain, Patricia, 13
Crary, Jonathan, 85, 181, 197–198
Cremin, Lawrence, 203–204
Cross, Gary, 76, 148

Daedaleum, 25, 39. *See also* Zoetrope
Danius, Sara, 105
Darrah, William, 192
Dean and Son, 119–121, 125–126, 131, 147–148
Dean's New Book of Parlor Magic, 119–121, *120*
De Toulouse-Lautrec, Henri, 149
"Digital natives," 29, 49
Doane, Mary Ann, 89
Dorris, Anna Verona, 187, *201*
Drotner, Kirsten, 33
Dulac, Nicolas, 103, 111, 129, 218
Dunbar, Erica Armstrong, 86

Edgeworth, Maria, 8, 24, 44–46, 163, 172, 211
Edgeworth, Richard Lovell, 8, 24, 44–45, 172, 211
Education, 5–9, 24, 35–42, 48–51, 54–56, 84–85, 113. *See also* Color education; Literacy; Stereoscope
  and children's social development, 72, 77–78, 87, 90–93

and children's spectatorship, 15–17, 19, 94, 99, 124, 198–205
object lessons as, 184–191
and rational recreation literature, 45–46, 51–52
reform, 33, 46–47
STEM/STEAM in, 3, 23, 29–30, 210–213, 223
theories of, 43–45, 65–66, 207
Elementary Education Acts, 47
Elsaesser, Thomas, 4
Emerson, Philip, 204–205
Erle, T. William, 5–11, *6*, 45

Fantascope, 38, 50, *116*. See also Phenakistoscope
Farman, Jason, 157
Field, Hannah, 113, 130, 199
Fiery circle, 62
Finkelstein, Barbara, 64
Fitton, William Henry, 61
Flap books, religious, 127–129, *128*
Flirtation games, 57–59, *58*, 77–81, *79*
Fröbel, Friedrich, 8, 24, 93, 172

Gaudreault, André, 103, 111, 129, 218
Gender, 76–78, 127
  in cautionary tales, 16–17, 107–108, 142–145
  and color sense, 166–167
  and erasure, 200
  and objectification, 195–196
  and STEM/STEAM toys, 212–213
George Eastman House, 4–5, 20–21
"Gertrude and Her Birds" (story), 73–74
Getton, Tom, 66
Girls. *See* Child; Gender
Gleason, Mona, 185
GoldieBlox, 209–214, *210*
Goodyear, Edith, 169, 172
Grau, Oliver, 95
Gray, Jonathan, 221–222

Grier, Kasey, 72, 96
Groth, Helen, 90, 156
Gubar, Marah, 134
Guidebooks. *See* Advice literature
Gunning, Tom, 4, 66, 238n78

Hailmann, William N., 169, 189
Hansen, Miriam Bratu, 18, 86
Herbert, Stephen, 63, 72, 106
Herschel, John, 61
Hoffmann, Heinrich, 107, *109*, 142
Holmes, Oliver Wendell, 25, *186*, 186–187
Hooper, William, 43–44
Hopkins, Louisa, 156–158
Hornbooks, 64–65, 127
Horner, William George, 25
Horton, Susan, 89
Huhtamo, Erkki, 104, 155, 157, 232n68
Humor, political. *See* Satire

Immersion, 95, 104, 118, 157
Intellectual property. *See* Piracy

James, William, 158
Jeffries, Benjamin Joy, 165–167, 172
Jenkins, Henry, 8

Kaleidoscomaniacs, 157
Kaleidoscope
  debut of, 24–25
  and discourse of multiplicity, 154–158, 162
  pirating of, 62, 155, 163
  and time, 161–163
  use in homes, 159–161, *161*
Keevak, Michael, 178
Keystone View Company
  and stereoscope industry, 191–194
  stereoscopic views, 195–196, *196*, *201*
  and Underwood & Underwood, 25, 28–29, 182–184, 192

Kindergartens
  and Friedrich Fröbel, 8, 93
  in United States, 24, 40, 168, 172, 176, 202

Landells, Ebenezer, 45, 49
Lantern shows. *See* Magic lanterns
Leisure time, 11, 26, 33, 140–141, 146–148. *See also* Playtime; Time
Literacy, 60–61, 64–66, 94, 211, 224. *See also* Reading
  and color education, 153–154, 163, 179–180
  as cultural capital, 13–14
  instruction and, 43–45, 172, 184
  and play, 27–28, 90–91, 122–123, 130, 138
  and vision, 59–60, 86
Little Showman's books, *135*, 136–138, *139*
Little Susy's Little Servants (book), 91–92, 124, 166
Locke, John, 8, 24, 43–44, 73, 188
Logan, Thad, 96
Luckey, George W. A., 158, 169, 179, 202

Macy, Robert F., 160–161, *161*
Magic Disk, 97. *See also* Phenakistoscope
Magic lanterns, 36, 101, 130, 143, 246n54
"Maker" culture, 211–213
Mann, Horace, 46, 54, 65, 193
Maxwell, James Clerk, 173–175
McLoughlin Brothers, 25, 40, 126
  cautionary tales, 142–143, *144*, 247n67
  and color perception, 146, 153
  conversation cards, 78–79, *79*
  Little Showman's series, *135*, 136–138, *139*
  Pantomime Toy Book series, 131–132, *133*
  rebus puzzles, 66

McMurry, Frank, 182–183, 192
Media, "new", 11, 29–30, 68, 105, 223–224
  cycles of, 2–3, 17–20, 23, 222
  optical toys as, 35, 49–56, 64, 121–122, 141
Media archaeology, 4
Media literacy. *See* Literacy; Spectatorship
Media studies, 9–10, 34
Meggendorfer, Lothar, 112–113, 125–126
Metamorphosis, 127–128, *128*
Mirzoeff, Nicholas, 12, 88, 93
Morus, Iwan, 106
Mother Goose in Hieroglyphics, 69–70, *70*
Motograph Moving Picture Book, 149, 211
Movable books. *See* Toy books
Munsell, Albert, 154, 168–170
Münsterberg, Hugo, 9, 114, 199
Murray, John Clark, 114
Museo del Precinema, 20–21
Museo Nazionale del Cinema
  conducting research in, 4, 20–21
  materials archived by, *108*, *110*, *112*
Museum of Precinema. *See* Museo del Precinema
Museum of the Moving Image, 83, 215

National Cinema Museum. *See* Museo Nazionale del Cinema
Naughty Girl's and Boy's Magic Transformations, 143–145, *144*
Nead, Lynda, 67–68
Neal's Penny Games, 41, *41*
Nelson, Elizabeth, 59, 80
"New" media, 11, 29–30, 68, 105, 223–224
  cycles of, 2–3, 17–20, 23, 222
  optical toys as, 35, 49–56, 64, 121–122, 141

Index

Nguyen, Josef, 212
Nichols, Herbert, 171

Optics, science of. *See* Vision science

Pantinoscope, 106–107
Pantomime Toy Books, 131–136, *133*, 141
Parenting. *See* Advice literature
Paris, John Ayrton
  and debut of thaumatrope, 25, 52–54, 61–63, 72
  and *Philosophy in Sport*, 36–37, 45–48, 80–81
Pearl, Sharrona, 68
Pearson, Susan, 74
Persistence of vision. *See also* Phenakistoscope; Thaumatrope; Zoetrope
  and children's spectatorship, 84–85, 87–89, 94–95, 104–106
  in color education, 155, 173, 177–178
  and commercial optical toys, 35–36, 55–57, 60, 82
  and film theory, 117
  as perceptual experiment, 18–19, 62–63, 83
  theory of, 1, 10–11, 227n2
Pestalozzi, Johann, 188
Phenakistoscope
  and archival research, 4
  as children's pastime, *6*, 31, 40, 53–54
  development of, 5, 25, 37–38
  operation of, 1, *2*, 83, 97–98, *98*
  other names for, 50, 97
  and time, 111
  varied content of, 113–115, *116*
  varied quality of, 103–106, *108*, *110*, 111–112, *112*
Philosophy in Sport Made Science in Earnest, 45–49, 50–54, 80–81
Piracy
  of kaleidoscope, 62, 154–156

  of phenakistoscope and zoetrope content, 52, 108, 111
  of toy book content, 25, 126, 131
Plagiarism. *See* Piracy
Plateau, Joseph, 25, 37–38, 111, 115,*116*
Play
  archival, 21–23
  as child's work, 5, 8–9, 112, 198–200, 219–223
  and color education, 173–175
  and independence, 121–125, 159, 212
  and literacy, 27–28, 90–91, 122–123, 130, 138, 142
  19th-century practices, 83, 94–97, 102–106, 145–148, 159–160, 165, 201–203
  and power relations, 55–56, 64–65, 67–69, 74–77, 93–94, 212–213, 229n32
  and productivity, 34, 42, 111–112, 177
  racial violence as, 75–77
  and resistance, 60, 129, 243n9
  and STEM/STEAM, 209–211
  21st-century practices, 214, 217–219
Playtime. *See also* Play; Time
  concerns about, 28, 134–136, 146–147
  and productivity, 42–49, 51–52
Plunkett, John, 84
Political humor. *See* Satire
Pop-up books. *See* Toy books
Prang, Louis, 154–155, 168–173, 179–180, 191
Praxinoscope
  and archival research, 4–5
  for contemporary use, 83, 225
  development of, 40–41, 102–103
  operation of, 1, *2*
Praxinoscope theater, 102–104, *103*, 129
Precinema, 17–18, 21, 224–225
Prensky, Marc, 49
Prentiss, Elizabeth, 91–92, 124, 166
Primers, reading, 60, 64–65

Psychology, 29, 85, 184–185, 191, 263n74
  and color education, 114–115, 171, 179–180
  and standardization of time, 18–19, 190
  and visual discernment, 10, 27, 106, 158
Puns, 4, 57, 60–63, 80–81, 96–97
Puzzles, *41*, 59, 68, 92. *See also* Thaumatrope
  jigsaw, 60–61, 64
  rebus, 64–70, *70*
  Smashed-Up Locomotive, 151–153, *152*, 165

Race
  as analytical lens, 22, 229n32
  and color blindness, 167, 178
  and diversity, 26–27, 33, 212–213, 220
  hierarchies of, 15, 47, 69, 86–88, 108, 126
  and silhouettes, 107–110, *110*, 124, 220
  in stereoscope views, 195–197
  stereotypes of, 75–77, 106–107, 140, 247n67
Rational recreation
  books for, 42–44, 48–49, 90, 101
  and color education, 163, 175, 179–180
  and improper content, 146–147
  and productive play, 34, 42, 177, 212, 219
Reading. *See also* Literacy
  and independence, 125
  instruction, 59–61, 65, 173, 183
  and physiognomy, 68
  and play, 63–64, 138, 145–146
  primers, 60, 64–65
  and racial violence, 75
Rebus puzzles, 64–70, *70*. *See also* Thaumatrope
Reid-Walsh, Jacqueline, 129
Religious flap books, 127–129, *128*
Reynaud, Emile, 40, 102, *103*
Ringel, Paul, 44

Ringwalt, Jessie E., 123–124, 140, 249n8, 251n55
Robertson (Etienne-Gaspard Robert), 35–36, 43–44
Robinson, David, 111
"Room-for-play" (*Spielraum*), 18, 86, 115
Rousseau, Jean-Jacques, 8, 24, 43–44, 73
Royal Institution, London, 15, 37, 43
Rusert, Britt, 88

Sampson, Scott D., 147, 253n77
Sánchez-Eppler, Karen, 26, 130
Sands, Benjamin, 128, *128*
Satire, 37, 63–64, 70–71
Screen time, 7, 11, 49, 208, 228n13, 237n68. *See also* Time
"Scriptive things," 22
Scripture, E. W., 171, 176–177
Silhouettes, 107–110, *110*, 124, 220
Slovenly Peter *(Struwwelpeter)*, 107–108, *109*, 142–143
Smashed-Up Locomotive (puzzle), 151–153, *152*, 165
Socioeconomic status. *See* Class
Sony BRAVIA-Drome, 215, *215*, 217, 220–222
Space
  of the family parlor, 15, 95–96
  of the home, 87, 93–94, 115, 118
  and industrialization, 19, 28, 160, 178–180, 206
  public, 14, 217
  restriction of, 17
Spectatorship, 6–7, 9–13, 19, 23–24, 224
  and agency, 36–37, 84–85, 98–99, 105–106, 147–149, 158
  and children's vision, 15, 89–93, 122
  and discernment, 27, 89, 94, 102, 105, 138, 210
  and race and class status, 64, 75, 86, 93, 140, 223
Spencer, Herbert, 67, 190, 198
Spielraum ("Room-for-play"), 18, 86, 115

Spinning tops, 45–46, 114, 155, 173–178, *175*
STEM/STEAM education, 3, 23, 29–30, 210–213, 223
Stereoscope
  as apparatus of control, 200–207, *201*
  debut of, 25
  and educational discourses, 181–185
  industry, 28–29, 114, 191–193
  and object lessons, 185–191, *186*
  for sensory training, 198–200
  use in classrooms, 193–198, *195*, *196*, 203–205, *204*
Strong National Museum of Play
  conducting research in, 20–21
  materials archived by, *108*, *152*, 153
Struwwelpeter (Slovenly Peter), 107–108, *109*, 142–143

Talmage, Thomas De Witt, 162
Tastemaking, 43–45, 59, 122, 148, 164, 180
Thaumatrope. *See also* Rebus puzzles
  and advertising, 62, 233n9
  and archival research, 4, 21, 57
  as children's pastime, *6*, 19–20, 31–32, 52–54, 238n78
  contemporary, 83, 225
  and courtship, *58*, 77–81
  development of, 25, 35–37, 61–63
  integration of language with picture, 59–61, 63–64, 66–67, 82
  operation of, 1, *2*, 45–46, 63, 96
  and power relations, 72–77, *75*, *76*
  varied content of, 70–72
The Boy's Own Toy-Maker, 45, 49
Time
  concerns about screens and, 7, 11, 49, 208, 228n13, 237n68
  and industrialization, 42–43, 180, 206
  and the kaleidoscope, 161–163
  leisure, 11, 26, 33, 140–141, 146–148

  and middle-class values, 18–19, 55–56, 130–132
  mothers', 124–125
  narrative, 132–134, 136–137, 149
  and the phenakistoscope, 111
  standardization of, 48–49, 136, 170–171, 178
  and the stereoscope, 201–203
  and the zoetrope, 216–221. *See also* Playtime
"Tirocinium" (poem), 48
Tissandier, Gaston, *2*, 89, 102
Titchener, Edward B., 106, 114
Tops. *See* Spinning tops
Toy books, 149–150
  and archival research, 4–5, 21, 120–121, 134
  cautionary tales in, 142–145, *143*
  and childhood as fun, 130–131
  and childhood innocence, 134
  complaints about, 145–148
  flourishing industry of, 121, 126
  mechanics of, 120–121, 127–129
  and narrative progression, 131–134, *133*
  promoting independent play, 122–125
  social stratification in, 112–113
  and spectatorship, 138–141, *139*
  variety of formats of, 125–126
  and visual absorption, *135*, 136–138
Transmedia, 141, 252n64
Tremin, Peter, 213
Tupper, Martin Farquhar, 162

Underwood & Underwood
  instructions for stereoscope use, 200–204, *204*
  and Keystone View Company, 25, 28–29, 182–184, 192
  and stereoscope industry, 191, 193–194
  stereoscopic views, 181–184, 197–198

Vandell, Kathy, 64
Victoria and Albert Museum of
    Childhood
  conducting research in, 4, 20–21
  materials archived by, *76*
Vision. *See also* Persistence of vision;
    Spectatorship; Stereoscope
  and abolitionism, 12–13, 80, 96,
    245n45
  in education, 54, 124, 153, 170–173,
    174–177, 183–184
  as metaphor, 12–15
  and middle-class orientation, 89–90,
    105, 113–115
  and "new" media, 17–20, 21–23, 56
  and power relations, 60, 67–68, 72–75,
    80–82, 105
  and the scientific ideal, 25–26, 35–36,
    86–88
  as subjective, 10–11, 28–30, 67, 91–93,
    104
  testing, 158, 165–170
Vision science, 10–11, 67–68, 84–85,
    123–124
Von Gurowski, Adam, 88
Von Stampfer, Simon, 25, 37, 111

Wendte, Charles, 145, 148
Wheatstone, Charles, 185–187, *186*, 211
Wheel of life, 39–41, *41*, 50. *See also*
    Zoetrope
Whirligig of life, 40. *See also*
    Praxinoscope
Wonder-turner, 36–37, 50. *See also*
    Thaumatrope
Word play. *See* Puns

Yumibe, Joshua, 177–178

Zelizer, Viviana A. Rotman, 33
Zoetrope, 5, *6*, 19–20
  advertising of, 40–41, *41*, 53–54
  advertising with, 214–215, 219–223
  contemporary, 83, 209–214, *210*,
    215–218, 223–225
  development of, 24–25, 35, 39,
    173–175, 178
  mechanics of, 113–114
  operation of, 1, *2*, 83–84, 177
  and spectatorship, 98–105, *100*, 117
  and time, 216–221
  varied content of, 107, 111–112
  varied quality of, 106–107, *108*